Both Sides of the Bench

Barrington Black

≋ WATERSIDE PRESS

Both Sides of the Bench
Barrington Black

ISBN 978-1-909976-31-3 (Paperback)
ISBN 978-1-910979-00-6 (Epub ebook)
ISBN 978-1-910979-01-3 (Adobe ebook)

Copyright © 2015, 2016 This work is the copyright of Barrington Black. All intellectual property and associated rights are hereby asserted and reserved by him in full compliance with UK, European and international law. No part of this book may be copied, reproduced, stored in any retrieval system or transmitted in any form or by any means, or in any language, including in hard copy or via the internet, without the prior written permission of the publishers to whom all such rights have been assigned worldwide.

Cover design © 2015 Waterside Press using an original photograph © Barrington Black. Design by www.gibgob.com

Main UK distributor Gardners Books, 1 Whittle Drive, Eastbourne, East Sussex, BN23 6QH. Tel: +44 (0)1323 521777; sales@gardners.com; www.gardners.com

North American distribution Ingram Book Company, One Ingram Blvd, La Vergne, TN 37086, USA. Tel: (+1) 615 793 5000; inquiry@ingramcontent.com

Cataloguing-In-Publication Data A catalogue record can be obtained from the British Library.

Printed by Lightning Source, Milton Keynes and other locations.

e-book *Both Sides of the Bench* is available as an ebook and also to subscribers of Myilibrary, Dawsonera, ebrary, and Ebscohost.

First published 2015, this revised 1st edition published 2016 by
Waterside Press
Sherfield Gables
Sherfield-on-Loddon
Hook, Hampshire
United Kingdom RG27 0JG

Telephone +44(0)1256 882250
E-mail enquiries@watersidepress.co.uk
Online catalogue WatersidePress.co.uk

Table of Contents

Acknowledgements *iv*
Dedication *v*
About the author *vii*

1. **Beginnings** 9
2. **Hitler, a Bee in My Father's Bonnet** 13
3. **The War Trundled On** 17
4. **Louis Black** 21
5. **School Daze** 25
6. **"Lloyd George Knew My Uncle"** 29
7. **University** 33
8. **From Rank Outsider** 49
9. **To Becoming an Officer and a Gentleman** 61
10. **Clarence Darrow or Perry Mason?** 67
11. **This Crime is Just Not Cricket** 75
12. **Murder Most Foul** 79
13. **Donald Neilson, Known as "The Black Panther"** 81
14. **The Heart Valve, the Tie Round the Neck and Alban Beresford Elcock** 97
15. **The Murder Where the Victim Was … the Judge** 119
    The trial *127*
16. **Courts Martial** 133
    A very different location *139*
17. **A Sad Day for Justice** 141
18. **Some Changes in the Law, and Mainly for the Good** .. 145
19. **Murder Within the Walls of a Prison … and Other Places** ... 159
    The Boarded Barn Murders *162*
    The death of a policeman's mother *164*
    An open-and-shut case *166*
20. **A Little Nostalgia** 169
21. **Deuteronomy Chapters 18–20** 177
22. **The Circuit Bench** 187
23. **Recycled for an Unexpected Second Innings** 197

Index *216*

Acknowledgements

My thanks to my faithful staff at Barrington Black LLB, Walker Morris & Coles, Barrington Black & Co, Barrington Black Austin & Co, my former partners Stanley Bland, Ian Percy, Frances Heath, Bob Moore, Kenneth Dickinson and Taryn Turner who then transferred to the bar and carved a fine reputation, to the long-serving staff, my secretary Liz Lord, who I employed on-and-off for nearly 30-years, Kath, Betty the cash, Joan Lloyd, Vanda, Maria, Pat, Wendy, Joan Horsborough, ex-Chief Inspector Jasper Mann, ex-PC Brian Clegg, an outstanding articled clerk Richard Manning, to the staff at Bow Street and Marylebone Magistrates' Courts, to Judge Roger Sanders and Judge David Mole and Judge Dawn Freedman, Judge Nick Madge and Judge Edward Bailey, and that most important person, the list officer Linda Benjamin, at Harrow Crown Court.

And latterly to all at Gibraltar Supreme Court, the President, Sir Paul Kennedy, Chief Justice Anthony Dudley, Mrs Justice Karen Prescott and Mr Justice Christopher Butler, Hazel Columbo, the chief executive and Andy and all the lovely lady court clerks who kept feeding me sticky buns, who made the sunset of my legal life in Gibraltar so pleasant.

Thanks also to my family to whom this book is dedicated opposite including also my ten grandchildren, Holly, Louis, Lilly, Bella, Alex, Leo, Nathalie, Hannah, Phoebe and Eli. I should perhaps explain that I have mentioned all their names because they firmly indicated that if I didn't they wouldn't buy my book, and that's despite the fact I have offered it to them at a reasonable discount. They all come to tea every Saturday afternoon. They arrive at 4.30 and leave at 6.15, and I have often said that my weekend begins at 6.30.

And last but not least an enormous expression of gratitude to Bryan and Alex Gibson for their expertise and advice in creating this publication.

I dedicate this book not only to my parents, who encouraged me to enter the law for what was a most fulfilling career, I dedicate it to Diana and the children who suffered the trauma, the upsets, the long hours I worked, to Jonathan and Harriette who followed me, and Matthew and Anna, who didn't. To Vinnie, the dog, who listened to me when others wouldn't.

List of Illustrations

Barrington Black is the one on the left — *8*
Grandmother's sister Auntie Gertie, married to Solomon Levy who played cricket for Gloucester in 1911 — *11*
My father with two friends, Alexandria 1944 — *17*
Grandmother's brother, Uncle Louis, the family icon — *21*
Circa 1918: Uncle Louis on a tank with Lloyd George, for whom he wrote speeches — *29*
President of Leeds University Union 1952 — *33*
Leeds University Rag Revue poster 1952 — *37*
In front of me is The Princess Royal with Margot Fonteyn — *48*
I was told off for telling the colonel how smart he looked — *60*
Diana receiving her scroll from the Lord Mayor of London after 38 years as a JP — *73*
My Jensen Interceptor at Oxford Crown Court during Neilson's trial — not an explosion, just boiling over — *81*
Hair today, but gone tomorrow — *169*
Supreme Court Justice Gibraltar — *196*

About the author

Barrington Black was for many years one of the UK's best-known criminal defence lawyers and founder of a solicitor's firm in Leeds now commemorated in the name of a practice known as "Black's". He was later a Metropolitan Stipendiary Magistrate (now district judge) following which he became a Circuit Judge serving at various Crown Court centres across London. His final legal role was as one of four Supreme Court Justices in Gibraltar. As a lawyer he appeared in many high profile cases. His incisive letters have frequently been published in newspapers such as *The Times, Guardian* and *Jewish Chronicle* whilst he contributed for many years as a legal expert to Richard Whitely's topical *Calendar* programme on Yorkshire Television as well as appearing on BBC's *Look North* and on radio.

A long-time resident of Harrogate and a local councillor and Parliamentary candidate before moving South to take up his judicial appointment, married to Diana and the father of four children (two of whom are also lawyers) and ten grandchildren, he now lives in North-London.

Barrington Black is the one on the left

Chapter 1

Beginnings

Let's get it straight right at the start. I was never an idealist. I would not be able to sleep at night if I thought that I had given the impression that I went into law to separate right from wrong, to rescue those treated unjustly, to bring justice to the deprived, to free the oppressed and defend those wrongly accused. It was something far more basic than that. I became a lawyer simply to earn a living, and to spend my days doing something which I enjoyed. The fact that it meant I was in fact helping others was a satisfying addition to that process. But it very nearly didn't happen. I might well have spent my life filling, drilling and conserving teeth, and I would have hated it.

My childhood memories are sparse, mostly because my childhood was a long time ago. Had I then realised that I would be writing this book I would have made some notes, but even I have never been able to read my own writing, and then it was even worse. Life in Leeds was reasonably comfortable; my mother was an attractive woman and my father tall and good-looking, though the effect was spoilt by his habit of wearing a Burberry-style trench coat with a bowler hat, something which, even though I was only two, I thought was not quite right. He never talked about his business which was something to do with selling radios, or as they were then called, wirelesses. He ran a small Hillman car, and we had a maid who came from a mining village, dressed in a black skirt with a white pinafore and a little white hat. I suggested to my mother that this was rather pretentious, but she replied, "Don't use long words when you don't know what they mean," and she was right.

This was a good time to be a child, for children were not expected to read newspapers or listen to the preparations for the world turmoil being discussed on the wireless. The traffic was not hectic, and you could park your car without being attacked by yellow-clad vultures. On the trams, buses and trains people sat quietly and kept themselves to themselves, no-one shouted into mobile phones and when they did speak it was in a language one understood, or at least I tried to understand. A particularly popular phrase, not, I hasten to add, used at home, was "Eee bah gum". We didn't do Latin at nursery school, but I had a sneaking feeling it had something to do with the fact that many people could just not get it into their heads that our main city was no longer called *Eboracum*, but simply York.

The Yorkshire accent did pose some pitfalls, especially for a man from Leeds whose dog died, and he wanted a memorable replica. He took photos of it to the local goldsmith and asked for a golden statue to be made, the goldsmith asked, "Do you want it 18 carat?" and the Yorkshireman replied, "Nay Lad, don't be daft, I want it chewin' a bone."

People could, in the main be trusted, mugging had not been invented, there were a few instances of highway robbery, but there was little serious crime.

You could leave your doors wide open, and in the evening the whole family would huddle around a roaring fire. Though I often thought that if we hadn't left the doors wide open, we wouldn't have needed to huddle round the roaring fire.

We holidayed each year in Blackpool, staying always at the same small hotel called *Bella Vista* run by a Mrs Battersby, one of hundreds of similar establishments, each with a silver tiered cake dish on a table in the window.

I was perplexed by a sign in the window which read "No Vacancies", which I was convinced was the French for "No Holidaymakers", and I firmly believed that we had been admitted under false pretences.

Holidays were a time for dressing up rather than dressing down, particularly as each day would have as its highlight the walk on the North Pier. People would sit in long rows of deckchairs watching the promenade of escapees from the industrial West Riding, for that was our week. There were other weeks known as the Glasgow Week, the Manchester Week and so on. The ladies would parade in the latest fashions, in probably more fox furs than there were foxes in the countryside, and the men, invariably hatted, all wearing three-piece suits, although when the temperature was high, as sometimes happened, a waistcoat button or two would be undone, and bright red braces revealed.

Despite the temperature, which on a sweltering hot day might touch 60 degrees, my grandfathers, on both sides, wore stiff white collars made from a shiny material which had been washed with a sponge each morning. Some 40-years later I was to rediscover and myself own such collars, in winged form, to wear with court dress.

However, that was where the similarity between my grandfathers ended.

On my father's side, my grandparents had been born in England, and four of my grandfather's five brothers had served in the Royal Flying Corps during the 1914 war. More later of my grandmother's brothers, the dentists, but I can mention her brother-in-law who played cricket for Gloucester in 1911. Solomon Levy was born in Stroud in 1886, and was a batsman and bowler, mentioned in *Wisden*, a tall angular man who married my great-aunt Gertrude.

Grandmother's sister Auntie Gertie, married to Solomon Levy who played cricket for Gloucester in 1911

On my mother's side, a different story. My grandparents came to England at the turn of the century from Kovne in Lithuania, where my grandfather dealt in timber and was a talented horseman. He would fascinate me with tales of galloping through the forest in the depths of winter, with wolves and heaven knows what other wild animals urging the horse on even faster. In England he became a coal merchant, and owned several horses, all of which to add to the confusion were called Tommy, so we never knew which one he was talking about. He would hire a collection of daily labourers and dispatch them with a horse and cart to fill up and bag the coal in the yard, returning to the office and then being dispatched to various houses, bakeries and factories in the city.

He ran the business, barely making a note, but relying on a remarkable memory of addresses, customers and amounts delivered. His customers trusted him, though occasionally one of the ladies would come to the office and say she had counted the empty bags after the man had delivered, and they did not tally.

He loved the horses which were stabled a short walk from where he lived, and if one was unwell he would think nothing of spending the night at the stable, wiping the horse down and ensuring that it was properly fed, watered and comforted; and if necessary he would call the vet.

Even though their English was limited and their major form of communication in a Germanic-orientated central European linguistic mixture, it was these grandparents who played such an influential part in my formative years.

Chapter 2

Hitler, a Bee in My Father's Bonnet

My father had a bee in his bonnet about Hitler from as long ago as I can remember. And of course he was right. I cannot think of any other political matter being discussed around our dinner table, and that's not just because it was really more of a supper table.

I was very young at the time, but I heard the name Hitler mentioned so many times and in such terms that made me frightened. What is extraordinary is the premonition, because in 1937 the full blast of the horrors of the Nazi regime was still unknown.

Threats, political rallies, marching feet, attacks on the Jews, the full picture could certainly not have been so widely promulgated in those pre-television days. But my father was certainly affected by it all and was convinced it would all blow up.

However, young as I was, I certainly picked up the message that my father had joined the army, had been given a smart uniform to wear, and brought home a pistol which fitted into a leather holster on his belt and which he kept locked in his wardrobe, and that he went away for days on end "to learn how to fight Hitler".

He had joined the Territorial Army, and was in the Military Police. His belief was that there would be war; he was fit, that he would be enlisted, and that he might as well get on with it. At least this way he would have some choice in the branch in which he would serve and he might as well start climbing the promotion ladder. He would go off to something called "Parade" taking his pistol, smelling of fresh polish from the wardrobe, and then come home some time later, the pistol this time having an acrid burnt bitter smell.

Not to be outdone, my mother enlisted for something called Civil Defence, and although not given a uniform she had a box with a special gas-mask and an arm-band with the initials C-D on it. She too would go out for lengthy "training" leaving me in the hands of the redoubtable Carrie, our maid.

On 3 September 1939 war was declared and my father was called up that very same day. It was a strange parting. There were no tears, just feeling "there is something to be done", and no real explanation of what that "something" would entail.

Many hours had been spent in the previous weeks sitting round the kitchen table with the somewhat crackling wireless being moved from station to station by the big dial on the front. Shouting foreign voices were interspersed with speeches I couldn't quite understand, but the word "fight" was used with frequency.

Over the next few days my mother was often out of the house, and came back speaking of a place called the "depot" and "headquarters".

One day Carrie announced that she would have to go home as her brother had joined the army and she was needed on the farm, and I was told that the house would be closed and I would go and stay with Aunty Rose in London. Aunty Rose, who was my paternal grandmother's sister, had no children of her own, and was inevitably spoken about in the same breath as my grandmother's other sister, Aunty Gertrude.

I was duly packed off to London. As I boarded the train, I could see that on the next platform there was another train disgorging scores of children who had been evacuated to Leeds *from* London. I wondered why I was being sent in the opposite direction, towards the danger zone.

By the time I arrived at Aunty Rose's house, 114, Norval Road, South Kenton (amazing, isn't it, I can't remember where I left my reading glasses 20 minutes ago, and that address still trips off my tongue 73-years later), I discovered that she had also taken in two girls, Annaliese and Laura, who had arrived through the *Kindertransport* from Germany. Perhaps I am being unfair, and without doubt they had gone through far more than I had, but I took an instant dislike to them both.

They oozed politeness and thanks in front of Aunty Rose and Uncle Dick, her husband, but behind their backs showed little gratitude, made rude comments and complained how they came from an upper-class background and had been hurled into a very middle-class situation. The word "class" was a new one to me; I thought it only related to something at school.

Aunty Rose and Uncle Dick were a delightful, smiley couple and they showed me the solid steel dining table under which I would shelter if the bombs came down. But it wasn't the bombs I needed protection from, it was Annaliese and Laura.

We persevered and I was enrolled into a pleasant local school, but then the bombs started dropping gradually nearer and the nights in the shelter more frequent, so there was a family conference.

This time I was invited to be evacuated to Aunty Florrie and Uncle Maurice, who was my paternal grandmother's brother, a dentist in Pentre, a small village in a valley near Cardiff. But there was a problem, sheep. Bombs I could take, Annaliese and Laura I could just about take, but the roaming wild sheep of Pentre bugged me totally. They were everywhere, in the roads, on the pavements, in the gardens, almost in the houses, sheep, sheep, sheep, and the ones with curling horns also, fierce, curling horns. I dreamt of them, I could hear them everywhere, all the time, bleating out a noise which sounded like "Tekiah, Terumah, Gedolah". Even to this moment when I hear that noise I just can't eat a thing all day.

And so, once again, with my gas-mask in a square cardboard box tied with string and a label with my home address I was deposited on a train for the seven-hour journey back to Leeds.

My father was now with the British Expeditionary Force in France, and our home had been sold because my mother did not have the time to run it. Her responsibilities had grown and she was supervising a considerable area around Leeds. Her base was at the home of her parents, and it was there that I landed.

They were pious people, far more observant than anyone I had previously come across, my grandmother probably more than my grandfather. A prayer book was kept permanently on the table, together with a copy of the *Old Testament* and the various commentaries on it. After supper each day she would patiently and slowly read a passage from it, digesting every word and regaling my dozing grandfather with some moral it contained. They ensured that I was enrolled for religious tuition, and every day except Friday I would make my way to that teacher from school from 4.30 till 6 o'clock and on Sunday morning from ten till 12.30.

Supper each evening was a silent gathering, silent that is with the exception of the radio and the six o'clock news with the latest news of the war. In addition to my father, my mother's brother Mick was in France as a sapper in the Royal Engineers, so that interest was understandably intense.

In May 1940 the British Forces were forced out of France and escaped through Dunkirk. News came through that Mick had landed safely back in England, but there was no news of my father. Days and then weeks went by, and still no news. We feared the worst.

Then, five weeks after the final boats left Dunkirk beaches, out of the blue came a message, "I'm back."

My father's task in the Military Police had been to help and direct all the British Forces down to the beach area from just outside Dunkirk. This he had been doing with three others all on military motorcycles, which were then disguised by changing the paintwork, though they had still kept to their military uniforms to avoid being classed as spies.

He later told us that on the day after the last boat left they were well inland, hiding in an abandoned French barn, listening to their radio when they heard it announced from London, "The British Expeditionary Force has been safely evacuated from France." "Then what the bloody hell are we?" asked one of them, "Boy Scouts?"

For five weeks after Dunkirk the four of them roamed around northern France towards the Brest peninsula, and finally escaped in a small French fishing boat which miraculously brought them back to England.

Chapter 3

The War Trundled On

My father with two friends, Alexandria 1944

The Germans heard that I was back in Leeds and made one or two half-hearted attempts to drop bombs on me, and although I heard them, and spent several uncomfortable nights in the cellar air-raid shelter, they missed me by several miles.

They did, however, drop an unexploded bomb in the garden of the house which some 30-years later we would inhabit in Harrogate; this is true because our startled gardener found it, and the street, sorry, lane, for after all, this was Harrogate, was temporarily evacuated.

Many years later I discovered the reason for that bomb. That evening Leeds had been the target for the Luftwaffe, but one plane in the squadron had been ordered to fly to the North of Leeds and bomb Eccup Reservoir, situated at a high point and containing much of the water for the city. The instructions, a copy of which I later obtained, ordered the plane to then continue North to Harrogate, and bomb the Majestic Hotel which was used by the RAF as an air plotting base. Our home in Harrogate had been in a direct line between Eccup and the Majestic. The bomb at Eccup did no damage, the one on the Majestic did destroy an unoccupied wing of the building, and as was discovered some 20-years later, the one in our garden had not exploded at all.

The air-raid siren was quite scary, a warbling scream to indicate alarm and a long straight scream to sound the all clear; in between the whistles, the crack of anti-aircraft fire and the thump of the actual bombs. I think the noise of the engines of the pilotless planes, the German V1, were even more frightening, though it wasn't the noise of its engine, it was when the engine cut out and you knew the missile was ready to drop straight down. And when all this happened even if she was not on duty at the time, my mother had to put on her steel helmet, grab her gas-mask and rush out on to duty, directing the ambulances, the fire-engines and all the other paraphernalia of the home war front.

There was no TV to keep track of the war, so we sat and watched the radio. Someone in the room asked why we were watching the radio and I thought of saying, "Because television hasn't been invented yet," but hesitated, and just as well, because moving pictures had been invented, and its first demonstration had, in fact been done by a man called Le Prince in what became the BBC studio in Woodhouse Lane in Leeds. I know because I once read the blue plaque which said so, and I believe everything I read on plaques.

My father had been involved in the Africa campaign, initially in the desert, and then in Cairo and Alexandria where for part of the time he came in close contact with the world leaders, Churchill, Stalin and Roosevelt, who figured in photographs he later showed us, and I recall he was particularly smitten by Madame Chiang Kai Shek, the wife of the Chinese war leader who was also at the Cairo Conference.

The scariest moment he had at that time of the war was when Uncle Mick, who had taken a little unofficial leave from the 8th Army, turned up at my father's police headquarters, looking more than somewhat bedraggled at that bastion of bullshit. My father decided the safest thing to do was pretend he had been arrested, and have him put in the detention area while he arranged for him to be cleaned-up and whisked out of the compound soonest.

It became a race against time. The war in Europe ended in May 1945, and although some demobilisation started then, Japan still had to be finally dealt with. It was hoped that as my father had joined the war so early he would have been returned to civilian life with appropriate promptness.

There was a particular reason for that, namely my Bar Mitzvah. That unique transformation from boyhood to manhood is a hoop which every Jewish boy has to jump through on his 13th birthday. Mine was in August, and so several months before that date, the brother of my maternal grandmother, who doubled the task of Hebrew teacher and tobacconist, took me under his wing. My teacher had two sons of differing talent: while Jerry played the piano in Geraldo's orchestra, Monty became a doctor and was eventually consort to the Lord Mayor of Preston, when his wife held that office in the 1970s.

The teacher, cajoled, bribed, urged and implored me to chant that short extract from the *Torah*, which is the expectation of every candidate to the status. The minister of the synagogue to which my family had belonged, and of which my great-grandfather had been the founding president, was a young Welshman, looking very much the stage curate, called the Reverend Aaron Cohen. He was delightful, a fiery orator, and always with an amusing story to end his sermons. I lost touch with him when I was 13-years and some weeks, and the next time I came across him was when I became a circuit judge and sitting in a London court met a fellow judge, His Honour Judge Aaron Owen, and indeed it was the very same young "curate". I recognised him by the fact that he told the same stories he had told 40-years earlier, and had been telling them regularly in the interim.

I should mention that my great-grandfather, Abraham Black, whom I recall seeing just on a few occasions, was known as Avrom der Bord, which was a reference to the large black bushy beard he sported. I thought he was called that because he was uninterested and fed up with all things around him.

The days ticked away, and we awaited news of my father's return. At this stage he was somewhere in Germany, we knew not where. Would he get back for the big day? My mother had to organize the lunch which would follow. It would all be quite low-key, in fact at that time due to rationing and wartime restrictions there was a limit of about one shilling and sixpence to be spent per meal.

It was about three days before the event, and no sign of my father. An executive decision had to be taken, and it was. That was to delay the Bar Mitzvah by two weeks. To all the family and guests this meant merely an alteration to their diary. For me it was a devastating decision. For each week of the year there is a different reading of the law, and if mine was to be postponed two weeks, then a whole new portion must be learned, and this I did, to my total astonishment but not without blood, sweat and not a few tears on the part of the teacher.

We started the service, my father had still not arrived, and he was known to be in England. Remember that even though the main war was over there was a significant ban on information about military movements. Various relatives and friends were called up to the dais to read the portions leading up to mine, and just at the moment that I was about to be called up, there was a noise at the back of the synagogue, the door opened, and in walked my father, still in full uniform. Our hopes and prayers had been answered.

The meal may only have cost one shilling and sixpence per head, but it was the best meal of my young life.

Chapter 4

Louis Black

Grandmother's brother, Uncle Louis, the family icon

The first known Louis Black in our family was the brother of my maternal grandmother, Minnie Brash, whose maiden name was coincidentally Black. The second was my father, and the third my eldest grandson.

I recall as a child, thumbing through some papers in a drawer at her home, and coming across an official-looking envelope. I must have been about eight-years-old at the time, and what I read gave me a terrible shock. It would have been around 1940, and my father, having been in the Territorials, had gone into the army on the very day that war broke out. By this time I had already been evacuated to London, and had also spent a similar period in

South Wales, but now I was back in Yorkshire and staying at my grandparents' home.

So what gave me this shock? I slowly read the letter, which was short and typewritten. It was not clear to whom precisely it was addressed, but the contents were stark and to the point. "I regret to have to inform you that Louis Black has been killed in action."

There was no mention of his rank or his regiment, and with several decades of hindsight I now realise that this in itself was strange, but had it been more precise, then my fears would have been allayed. Clearly I immediately thought this related to my father.

I rushed into the room where my grandmother was sitting; she was, as usual for that time of day, reading her copy of the *Old Testament*, an ancient book with a dark brown cover. My face was a picture of misery and covered in tears. "Grandma, what is this? Why has no-one told me, when did this happen?" I broke down and could say no more. This scrap of paper had changed my life.

My grandmother took the paper from my hand, she smiled. I remember thinking how could she smile at a thing like this, what has got into her? She laid down her book and pulled me towards her. "Don't worry, don't worry," she said, "it's not your father, it happened a long time ago, and he was my brother."

The years went by, and from time to time I reflected on that day. However it was not until the evening of 4 August, a few weeks ago, that the incident came back into my mind. We were watching the commemoration service for the start of the First World War. The old films, the memories, the reflections about the millions who had died. My mind went back to the first Louis Black.

I felt guilty that I knew so little about the first Louis Black, and particularly now, when the possession of an iPad can bring so much back so easily. It took no more than a few minutes to reveal that my assumption of a soldier having died in the Flanders mud was quite wrong, because the war records website told a very different story. The first Louis Black was described as having being born in Russia, though this must, at the time, have included Lithuania, the border of which changed hands almost weekly. He must have been a small child, if not a baby, when brought to England, landing no doubt at Hull, which must have doubled at that time for the Golden Medina, and found the end of the line was Leeds Central Station. The address which his papers gave was the exact same one where my grandmother and grandfather were living, and where I found the letter that had shocked me.

He had volunteered in 1914, when 21-years-old. I could not determine whether he first enlisted in that regiment, but by 1917 he was serving in the 38th Battalion of the Royal Fusiliers. This regiment was in fact the Jewish Brigade, and among those who served in it were David Ben-Gurion and Jacob Epstein, and also many tailors from the East End, so many that it was dubbed the *Schneiders'* regiment.

The regiment had served at Gallipoli, but was then directed under General Allenby to continue what was to be the successful fight against the Ottoman empire, an important one being the Battle of Megiddo, just South of Haifa, which set in trail an unbroken series of victories, eventually including Damascus and Beirut, and the relief of Jerusalem, victories in the light of which Turkey sought an armistice.

By 20 September 1918, as they advanced, the left flank of the line had been astride the rail and roads converging upon Nabulus, and the right flank, against considerable resistance from the Turkish army, faced North along the Jerusalem/Nablus Road, and the cavalry, for this was a cavalry regiment, after occupying Nazareth, and then amalgamating with an Australian and New Zealand regiment, closed all avenues of escape across the Jordan, and severe losses were inflicted against the Turks.

There were, of course, allied casualties, and sadly, during the Battle of Megiddo, on 17 October, just less than three weeks before the armistice, the first Louis Black, then aged 25, was killed in action. He lies in the Jewish portion of the Chatby Military Cemetery in Alexandria, his grave, like the other 20, marked with a Star of David. Nearby there was a more ornate memorial for Captain Montefiore, previously of the East Kent Regiment.

There is a strange coincidence. My father, the second Louis Black, after surviving Dunkirk, served with the 8th Army in North Africa, for a time based in Alexandria. One of his tasks was the supervision of military transport movements during that campaign, and he did this, as I have now discovered, though presumably without him realising it, from a unit based less than half-a-mile from that cemetery.

I feel very ashamed. That young soldier, a relative of mine, has probably lain in his grave for nearly a 100-years without a visit from family or friend, particularly as I had spent time in Egypt about 25-years ago, gazing at the relics of their ancient civilisation. But as a result of a false assumption had not the wit to discover and pay tribute to someone who had given his life at such a young age.

My elder son Matthew bought one of the ceramic poppies which surrounded the Tower of London to mark the centenary of the start of the 1914 war. He dedicated it to the first Louis Black.

Chapter 5

School Daze

I was never invited to join the Bullingdon Club; perhaps because my school didn't have one, after all it wasn't quite the type. Though perhaps not as famous as some, it owed its origins to the benevolence of Earl Cowper. It could also be said that the sons (and daughters) of the noble houses of Mexborough and Saville were, over the years, enrolled as pupils. There was also some evidence that the sons of one of those houses, called Louis and Francis, also left their mark in the area, and there was a small town with a chapel in the distance.

However, I could never forgive my parents for sending me to a school (I was a day boy) where in the dark-green painted ironwork above the entrance and for all to see, were the words "Mixed Infants". So there was I, neither a boy nor a girl (though it was said that had I been the girl my mother anticipated, my name would have been Barbara) but a "mixed infant", really? I am sure this was an act on her part of good intent, only to be equalled in later years when I was perhaps the only child to be evacuated from the then safe Leeds to London.

School days came and went, but one of my earliest recollections was that immediately after lunch, cooked badly and served ridiculously early, small camp beds were trundled out into the school hall and we were expected to sleep for about an hour. In the next bed to me was an unprepossessing small girl who was later to become ennobled and appointed a whip in the House of Lords. This did at least give me the opportunity in later years to brag that I had slept with a member of the government.

There was also an extremely annoying self-righteous male child who got up everybody's nose, who wore strange coloured clothes, called Gerald Kaufman, and I often wondered what became of him.

I was eventually given a scholarship to Roundhay School, a redbrick grammar school, or in other words a state-maintained secondary school, which provided an education for pupils "selected by the eleven plus examination, teacher's reports, or other means". It was just a little pretentious; in that the school song, chanted at every opportunity, was "Forty Years On", which by coincidence was also the school song of Harrow. Who knows, maybe it was thought that if as well as whistling that song you also wore a pure black tie as a sign of mourning for Queen Victoria, you had an open sesame to the good things of life.

Many of the teachers had recently been demobilised from the army, and were finding civilian life rather demeaning, but they ran the Army Cadet Force with a great deal of enthusiasm, and I looked forward to Thursday, which was cadet day, to which I set off feeling quite smart because my father had examined my uniform like a sergeant major, very carefully making sure that not a button went unpolished, a boot unshined or a belt unblancoed.

I was as enthusiastic about the cadets as I was unenthusiastic about the game of rugby, which tormented my Monday afternoons. I think it was after that first arrival on the pitch to see a rugby scrum that I became convinced that they were talking about me.

Mr Farrow was the headmaster, a patrician gentleman with a large black master's gown; he had a slim young leggy secretary with whom he conferred long into the afternoon, no doubt going over her Latin nouns. The school seemed to be run by the deputy headmaster, G G Hall, one of whose tasks was to deal with boys who had arrived late each morning. They queued outside his room at break time to proffer excuses and receive punishment. He was known to be an ardent Conservative and I recall the morning after a General Election result in which the Tories had been defeated telling him I was late because I had been "so upset by the election result". It didn't work; I received double the normal punishment.

During my period in the sixth form the realisation that the exams which were approaching needed a greater devotion to work led me to the Leeds Reference Library which was in the city centre, above the art gallery and next to the town hall. Boys and girls from other schools would use the library. Leeds Grammar School, Leeds Modern School and Leeds Girls High School students would come in the evening and during school holidays; it was a quiet, comfortable place to be. The large mahogany tables and comfortable armchairs were in great demand and you had to get there early to bag one. In fact they were so comfortable that they were an attraction to some of the not so young.

Most afternoons, just a little while after the pubs closed, a smell of alcohol would waft through the library as a somewhat unkempt gentleman with a florid face and ragged overcoat would pick-up a book, any book, and sit in one of the armchairs; within moments he was fast asleep. Most sleepers were gently awakened by the librarian, and persuaded to leave. But not this one.

He was a local treasure, but the extent of his treasury was only to be realised in later years. He was Jacob Kramer, an artist whose works later would command considerable sums.

Another frequent user of the "Ref" was a boy who went to Leeds Modern, quiet, pleasant and friendly, but somewhat shy. He was Alan Bennett. Many years later when sitting as a metropolitan stipendiary magistrate at Bow Street, when driving home I would occasionally stop at the Inverness Street market to buy some fruit and vegetables. Walking round a corner on one occasion I came face to face with him pushing his bike along. I knew he lived across the road in Gloucester Crescent because that previous evening I had been listening to an excerpt from "The Lady in the Van", a story he had written about a character who made her home in an abandoned van outside his house.

I said the first thing that came into my mind, which was "Did the lady really live in that van?" He immediately responded in those instantly recognisable and slowly modulated Yorkshire tones, "Oh yes, she did...and I know who you are, you're Barrington Black, you were a lawyer... didn't you become a judge or something?" I always knew Alan Bennett was amazing on detail, but why me, I mused. In fact, it went a little further, as he actually mentions me in his book *Untold Stories* (p. 225). He also sent me a response to a note I sent him following a BBC4 programme he did about the Yorkshire Symphony Orchestra, saying he remembered me.

Doing my homework at the "Ref" played a seminal part in the structure of my life. Medicine, or at least dentistry, loomed in the target of ambition, perhaps to emulate the success of each of my grandmother's three brothers who became dentists, and my grandfather's brother Dr David Black, a GP, who became Lord Mayor of Bradford in 1957. It was for this reason that I had opted for the science sixth form at school.

One morning walking down the Headrow in Leeds towards the "Ref" I noticed the Union Jack unfurled and fluttering in the wind above the town hall. I asked the man in uniform at the door of the art gallery if there was any significance in the flag, and he explained to me that the Assizes were sitting in that building, and that because the judge represented the queen, the flag flew in his and her honour.

"Can anyone go in and watch?" I asked, and he pointed to a door which he told me led to the students' gallery. All thoughts of grappling with a physics problem disappeared as I climbed the stairs to a small area which provided a ringside view of the proceedings. My mind was blown within minutes, and all because of Ogden Swift, who was the defence barrister in this case of rape and he was everything that John Mortimer must have had in mind when he created Horace Rumpole. A florid, loud-voiced, grandiloquent being, dressed in a black jacket, from the top pocket of which a red silk handkerchief flopped out, a black waistcoat, striped trousers, all covered occasionally by a black gown, falling well down off the shoulders and sleeves of its wearer, a gown stained and torn and ragged at the edges which yelled out that it had been used daily in the courts since the time when precedents were first thought of. Ogden Swift shouted, the witness wept, and the judge took a white plastic nasal inhaler and sniffed it through one nostril while closing the other nostril with a hand which also managed to hold a large fountain pen.

It took minutes for my mind to be blown, but only moments for me to reassemble it, and as I did so I could hear a voice from within which simply said, "This is for me." Within days I had transferred from the science sixth form to the arts sixth form, and spent many hours at the "Ref" looking up books on how to qualify and be admitted as a barrister. The qualification needs did not seem to present too much of a problem, but the financial requirements and speed of potential returns did.

CHAPTER 6

"Lloyd George Knew My Uncle"

Circa 1918: Uncle Louis on a tank with Lloyd George, for whom he wrote speeches

There was one thing about the happy, carefree, student days to come, which caused the hairs on the back of my neck to stand on edge. I knew it was inevitable that my friends, once I arrived at university, in the rugby club, after the game, as we sat singing around the union bar, would probably break into "Lloyd George knew my father" and it would go on, repetitively, forever. After all the words were so simple that even the most intellectually challenged could, would and did churn them out.

And when they did, I was convinced they were getting at me. Did they know my secret? Had they found yet another thing, apart from my total hatred of rugby and all it stood for, that set me apart from them? Maybe not. For after all it wasn't my father who knew Lloyd George, it was my uncle, or to be more precise, my great-uncle.

Uncle Louis Simmonds was an icon in the family. He was one of three brothers of my paternal grandmother, all of whom practised dentistry. However, Uncle Louis was different, he was qualified. He had been to university and dental school, Uncle Jack and Uncle Maurice hadn't, but that didn't deter them from practising, and indeed being very good dentists. All three went from their native Yorkshire, Leeds in fact, to two Welsh valleys not far from Cardiff.

Tonypandy and Pentre were the strange words my grandmother would mention with a look of sublime affection in her eyes when they were mentioned, for those were the mining villages in which they opened surgeries.

Don't be dismayed by their lack of formal qualification. It was not necessary to have qualifications until 1921 and practice rather than theory was their road to enabling the burly miners to bite into their lunch sandwiches, and they both flourished. They certainly looked the part wearing three-piece suits with white stiff collars, even when on a camping holiday

But if my grandmother looked sublime in their company, then when Uncle Louis visited there was an outbreak of total adulation. Within a short space of time Uncle Louis had become a jaw surgeon with a splendid house in Park Parade, the Harley Street of Cardiff, looked after by a uniformed lady called Elvira, skiing holidays, a horse to ride, a shiny Lanchester motorcar, and of course the Lloyd George connection.

I have no idea how that introduction was formulated, but no doubt through the local Welsh political channels. He might, of course have been a patient, whose mellifluous tones owed much to the craftsmanship of Uncle Louis, for Lloyd George was a great speechmaker, and Uncle Louis wrote some of them for him. I must confess this information is totally anecdotal, but my grandmother rarely got things wrong, and my impression of Uncle Louis was that he had no need to brag. Uncle Maurice and Uncle Jack also kept a close eye on his activities and reported loyally to my grandmother.

We do however have one piece of evidence, and that is a photograph of Lloyd George clearly making a speech. He is standing on top of an army tank, of the Dreadnought type, and there behind him, rather like Zelig, is Uncle Louis.

And so it came to pass, that although we all had much respect for the other uncles, it was Uncle Louis who firmly gained the icon status. I can still hear the words ringing in my ears, "You will have to grow up and be like Uncle Louis." And so from an early-age it had been decided for me that I was going to be a dentist. But little did the family know of that life-changing visit which I had paid to the Leeds Assizes.

CHAPTER 7

University

President of Leeds University Union 1952

Having August as my birthday meant that I left school at the age of 16, and entered university at just 17, having gathered together the requisite number of Higher School Certificates.

The transfer from the science to the arts sixth form had brought about a more positive attitude to schoolwork. I chose German as a second language, despite the textbooks then being in Gothic print, and encouraged by familiarity with the quasi-German language which my maternal grandparents spoke, although I was frequently told by my tutor that "*schmendrik*" and "*nebach*" were not really Hoch Deutsch. I also developed a genuine interest in economics which seemed more related to reality than algebra or physics.

Apart from the influence of Ogden Swift, there was another attraction; it was less difficult to gain admission to the law faculty than to the medical or dental school.

In 1949 Leeds University had 2,999 students and me. Although termed a red-brick, the white tower of its Parkinson Building was a lofty landmark as was the Brotherton Library. Apart from a distinguished medical school, which was part of the Leeds General Infirmary, it was famous for the textiles, leather and engineering departments, each spawned by the university's proximity and roots in the industrial West Riding.

Tucked away in the Parkinson Building was the law faculty, presided over by the delightful Professor Hughes. Professor Hughes was no disciplinarian; he had been "The Prof" since time immemorial, and even in 1949 referred to the 1925 Law of Property Act as the recent Act. There was the Dean, Mr Hagan, Dr Davies, the senior lecturer, and two or three other lecturers. The fine thing about the law faculty at Leeds University at that time was that no-one, but no-one, had ever been known to fail their degree.

It was said that after the final examinations, The Prof would gather all the papers together, and take them to his room. He would then throw them all in the air, and those which landed passed, and if they landed on a particularly favourite rug in his study, they were granted the status of a first-class degree.

Halfway through my final year, there dropped a bombshell. Professor Hughes, who was not a young man, was to retire, and to retire straight away. The immediate question was would his successor be so refreshing in his approach to exam results. His successor was to be Professor Philip James, the author of *An Introduction to English Law*.

Philip James was a laconic and distinguished-looking man. In deportment clearly more at home at Trinity College, Cambridge than the rough and ready red-brick, and although seemingly bred in the backwaters of academic law, his speciality was criminal law, and that was the subject of the leading book he had written on the subject. He had married late in life, in fact shortly before arriving in Leeds, and his new wife was a tall, slim, attractive Scandinavian. As we would say in Yorkshire, "The boy done well."

One of the things to which one became accustomed at the dining table of Trinity is the frequency with which the claret jug is passed around, and one need have little care of the aftermath because in such a college the rooms of the senior academics are but a short and pleasant stroll away. In Leeds the topography was somewhat different. The vice-chancellor occupied a stately official residence in one of the leafy terraces, Headingly Lane, and Professor James had secured an elegant apartment a few miles further North near Bramhope. When, within the first fortnight of his appointment to the chair of law he was invited to dinner by the vice-chancellor it was not an easy stroll. He and his wife would have to ease themselves into his small but ancient yet cherished MG sports car at the end of the evening as well as the beginning, notwithstanding the generous amount of good red claret which had been poured into the cut glass which matched his accent.

It was past midnight, and the two sleepy officers parked in their patrol car in the lay-by on the Otley Road were initially more interested in the highly-polished red MG sports car which roared past them, though the streaming long blond hair of the person in the passenger seat may well have generated some interest. They followed, they stopped, and they sniffed. Like Professor James, It didn't take them too long to recognise good red claret.

Whilst his wife was driven home by the police officers, Professor James was taken down to the bridewell beneath the courts at the Leeds Town Hall, and the police surgeon Dr Alastair Stuart Ritchie Sinton was awakened from his slumbers to come down and perform the various tests which were then part of the examination process. "Close your eyes and touch your nose." "Walk along this straight line." "Let me look into your eyes with this blinding little torch," until finally Dr Sinton, despite being a friend of his, had little alternative other than to pronounce Professor James as being unfit to drive.

Professor James's choice of counsel was interesting. He selected a friend, and moreover he chose a friend who had little, if any, knowledge of criminal law. It was Robert Megarry, a solicitor turned barrister who specialised in property cases, whose own academic career got off to an inauspicious start and later admitted having fallen into law "out of sheer inertia" and was on at least one occasion congratulated on "his economy of effort". With one less mark he would have failed his exams.

Megarry proved his mentors wrong. He became a QC and later a High Court judge in the Chancery Division, but when he came to Leeds Quarter Sessions to defend his friend Philip James he was a simple chancery barrister who was also pursuing an academic career lecturing at Cambridge and at the bar school.

Number Two Court at Leeds Town Hall, where the Quarter Sessions were held, had rarely been so packed. Public gallery, students' gallery, press box, probation officers' box and every conceivable ledge and seat, apart from those occupied by the judge and counsel, were filled with dark green, maroon and white coloured blazers, ties and scarves. The dean, Mr Hagan, Dr Davies and both other lecturers who made up the law department must have been facing empty desks in their lecture halls because all the students in the faculty, except possibly for a couple of swots, were packed into the courtroom.

Professor James stepped into the dock, an appreciative smile on his lips as he saw the crowd of supporters, as he deliberately tried not to recognise any one of them. They responded with a silent murmur.

The case depended upon the evidence of Dr Sinton especially, who had a pronounced lisp and a further quirk of speech, which caused him to communicate in a rather croaky drawl. This resulted in Dr Sinton describing the defendant as what sounded like "having repeatedly spurred his sleech."

Robert Megarry coaxed him into pronouncing it in that manner on more than one occasion, raising an eyebrow every time it happened, and looking meaningfully towards the jury.

After a short retirement the jury acquitted Professor James, the court erupted, the students scattered and the professor's reputation was saved, if not totally enhanced.

This was not to be Megarry's only appearance in a criminal court, for it was only two years later that he found himself in the dock at the Old Bailey when he himself was prosecuted for tax evasion. Megarry answered to these charges that they were a result of laxity on his part and mistakes and misunderstandings by his wife. The judge decided he had no case to answer.

This calumny, be it major or minor, did not prevent him being awarded silk some two years later, appointed a High Court judge in the Chancery Division, and then vice-chancellor, the title given to the head of that division.

I became involved in the Rag Revue. This was performed during rag week at the Empire Theatre in Leeds. This was not just a one-off show, but in this 1,800-seat theatre we performed twice nightly for six days, and sold out almost every seat. The quality was high, and in due course over three years, including a period after I came back to Leeds from National Service when I was again asked to produce the show.

Leeds University Rag Revue poster 1952

I recall that we were conducting auditions. Along came a singer who was also a student at the Leeds Art School. He said he would impersonate Al Jolson, and he did, and he was extremely good. There was a problem, however. He just stood there in front of a microphone, and didn't seem to know what to do with his hands. We had to give him something to create movement, and so we had the idea of his coming on to a stage empty except for one chair. The stage would be darkened but there would be a spotlight on the chair.

The curtain opened, the spotlight went on, the music started, the singer would come on to stage wearing a Burberry-style belted raincoat, and he also had a dark brown trilby… think Humphrey Bogart, and you will get the idea. As he came on, singing, he would look at the chair, walk round it, and then slowly take off the raincoat, loosening the belt and buttons and after taking it off fold it with care, place it on the chair, be dissatisfied with how he had laid it down, pick it up and put it down again, still singing all the time, then take off the trilby, look at it, dust a few specks of dust off with his sleeve, and place it on top of the coat… carry on singing and then put the items back on himself. All this was to give him something to do with his hands. And it worked. On the first night he stopped the show, as he did at every subsequent performance. Thus was born the career of Frankie Abelson, or as he was soon to be known, Frankie Vaughan.

University was an eye-opener. It may have only been a 40 minutes' tram ride away from home, but there was a sense of liberty for one who apart from a few months' war disservice as an evacuee to an aerial combat area had continually been under a parent's or grandparent's watchful eye.

It was 1949, I was still young, in fact just turned 17, and there were nevertheless quite a fair proportion of students who had been in the services, and in many cases in battle. Even those who had not spoken of the nights they had spent at the university, not studying, but fire watching. The Parkinson Tower at Leeds University, placed on top of a hill, gave an uninterrupted view of Leeds and its surroundings.

One of the most interesting discoveries was that the union had a vacation work department, which acted as what we would call nowadays a job centre to enable students to earn a crust particularly during the long summer vacation, but more importantly during the Christmas vacation, for it was then that there was a demand for student labour. I was a keen candidate for this opportunity because I knew my parents could not really afford to provide me with more than the bare essentials.

Accordingly I signed up for anything going, and at one time was doing three jobs. In the early-morning I was a postman, sorting and delivering parcels for the GPO. In the afternoon my employer was the railway company, based at Leeds city station, where I also hauled boxes filled with the parcels which were to give much pleasure over Christmas to others, and my evenings were taken up at Leeds General Infirmary, where the new National Health Service, for we were in 1949, gave cause to that hospital to renew and revise the forms and documents pertaining to patient admissions, and we did this amid clouds of smoke, sitting at long tables surrounded by mounds of green forms and cardboard dockets. In those days we were not the only ones to smoke in the hospitals. The patients did, the visitors did and I don't recall a doctor who didn't.

Even though at university there were more mature people around me, I found myself nudged into prominence, not, I hope, by being pushy, but by my choice of extramural interests. The students' union had an active and popular debating society and the debating chamber would be packed every Friday lunchtime.

One of my new friends from my year in the law faculty was a larger-than-life character called Gilbert Gray. He came from Scarborough, had chosen to do his National Service before university and was therefore three or four years my senior. This was not only because of having been in the army for two years, but also because he had initially embarked upon a theological course before transferring to law.

He had presence, a silver tongue and a fine command of language. He was to become a firm friend, and our careers became intertwined over a period of 50-years. As a result of those attributes he participated frequently in debates, and persuaded me to do likewise.

I remember the very first debate in which I took part as a principal. The motion was "That this house believes a Rose by any Other Name would smell as sweet". We were on opposing sides, and although I cannot recall the minutiae of the argument I do remember that he ended his peroration with a flounce in my direction, and a quotation from Macbeth. "The devil get thee gone, Black, thou cream faced Loon".

Gilly, as he was known, was seconded by a student called Leo Small, and summoning inspiration I remember responding on the lines of, "Let us show forgiveness and understanding for amongst All things bright and Beautiful, are all creatures Gray and Small, and the Lord God Made them all." I found myself debating quite frequently. Gilly was elected president of the union, and at the completion of a successful year, suggested I might be his successor, and so I stood for office. There were three other candidates, and during my final year, I was elected. This meant staying on for an extra year after graduation, but I combined this with my first year of articles to a very tolerant solicitor in Leeds called Malcolm Featherman.

Being president of the then 3,000-strong student union presented enough problems, heaven knows how more onerous must it be today with 33,000 students. If my maths were more reliable I would hazard a guess at eleven times. Apart from the normal administrative duties of running the union buildings, representing the union throughout the year at about 15 different university dinners and balls, there were other ceremonial duties and one rather fearful one. The most memorable ceremonial duty must have been representing the university at the coronation of Queen Elizabeth. Such a privilege was worth the exertion of rising at five a.m. to be there just after six a.m.

Another duty was being the official mace-bearer at university ceremonies such as honorary degree awards. I would have to attend upon the chancellor, the Princess Royal and wife of Lord Harewood, in her room in the Leeds Town Hall where the ceremonies were held. We would stand at a window overlooking the city art gallery where the academics and recipients would have robed and were processing round the building to the hall where the ceremony was to be held. We would while the time away, here were just the two of us playing a little game in which we made up honours for the various and sometimes highly-coloured robes with furs and strange hats such as for an elderly man wearing red, yellow and green, which he got "for designing traffic lights". Or a red one with a dark green hood, which he received for "inventing a method for ripening tomatoes". The only recipient of an honorary degree who even vaguely interested me was Margot Fonteyn.

The one fearful task, only comparable with Prime Minister's Question Time, which went with the office of president, was to have to chair the AGM of the union. For this event the 900-seat Riley Smith Hall was packed to capacity. It was always on a Friday at two p.m., lectures were cancelled, and for the hour or so before two p.m. there was clear evidence that the members of the rugby club and students from the engineering faculty, often the same people, had been making full use of the bar facilities.

It was usual for the accounts to be submitted and passed at the meeting, and it was traditional for one particular item to be in the spotlight. That related to the cricket ground. Rugby club members had little time for the namby-pamby game of cricket, yes, even in the heart of Yorkshire and literally seconds away from that holy ground called Headingly. The item in question was shown on the accounts as the expenditure on grass seed. It was a question, the answer to which was the level by which one's success as a president was measured. The question was simply: "How much money has gone to seed this year?" I think I answered to their satisfaction because at the end of the meeting I was still in office. One further requirement of the president was to represent the university at the two conferences each year of the National Union of Students.

Before long, I found myself elected vice-president of the NUS, then a breeding ground for politicians, and in some cases members of government, the extreme example being Jack Straw, a president of NUS who later became foreign secretary.

As an organization it was slightly to the left of middle of the road. Those influences within the NUS who came from the London School of Economics and Regent Street Polytechnic, which were both hotbeds of the left wing, sought to drive it to the left, the majority, however, were more middle of the road, and as my own sympathies at that time were more liberal, I could sit astride a fairly wide fence. I have to admit that when among the left wing I am the sort of person that they would bring out the right wing in me, and vice versa.

This was a time when the International Union of Students, IUS, was governed from behind the Iron Curtain. The most influential person was called Alexander Shaliapin, and he was chair of an organization called the World Federation of Democratic Youth. There were those who urged the NUS to steer clear of the IUS, and this included government influences who did not wish to see British Students tarred with the Communist brush. Of course the effect of this upon me was to make me more curious: let's at least have a look at them, talk to them, was my view. Just as there were those seeking to keep clear of the IUS, there were those who wished to get closer for other reasons.

I had little difficulty in seeing the sense in finding out more. Of course at that time it was not possible to visit as an individual tourist, the only people allowed in were groups or delegations, whom the Communist regime hoped to influence and impress. The IUS was the type of organization into which the regime pumped financial support to encourage potential leaders from outside to be shown their progressive system.

In August 1952 I was invited at fairly short notice to a large conference in Bucharest and they also invited my immediate predecessor, Gilbert Gray. He was about to be called to the bar, but for the purpose of this adventure he postponed the ceremony of the call. Nevertheless, he proudly wore each day the black jacket, striped trousers and bowler hat as a mark of his status. Even though, strange as it may sound in the present era, students actually wore suits complete with shirt, collar and tie, Gilbert in his ensemble cut a particularly elegant figure.

There was no direct flight between the UK and Romania so we were given train tickets on the old Orient Express, which ran from Paris to Istanbul and took a period of four or five days, with a break in Vienna to change stations and trains. Austria was divided between the East and West, and Vienna in those Harry Lime days was a multi-controlled city, the different powers occupying what had been the luxury hotels as their headquarters in a city patrolled by jeeps each containing a British, American, French and Russian soldier.

My first taste of opera, an appetite for which was to be lifelong, was to attend the post-war opening night of the Vienna Statsopera for a production of *Die Zauberflote*. The invitation came from a university friend who had lived in Vienna, and had returned there to claim back the family clothing business which had been confiscated by the Nazis. The theatre had escaped damage but it had taken some years to refurbish, and the opening was a glittering occasion largely attended by American senior officers and the rest being people who looked like the cast of *The Third Man*.

The following morning, in order to proceed to Bucharest we needed to change over from the *Westbahnhof* to the *Ostbahnhof*, and it was here that there arose a degree of confusion. Having travelled in a normal third-class carriage so far, when we arrived at the *Ostbahnhof* our eyes lit up with envy at the second carriage on a train with two quite different types of carriage. The ordinary ones with wooden seats were packed to suffocation, not only with people but also with both domestic and non-domestic animals, though come to think of it, even the people looked as though they could be divided into domestic and non-domestic. The objects of our envy, the second type of carriage, were smart, newly painted and lushly upholstered, though here again that description could also be applied to their occupants. Further distinctive features of these carriages were the flags and slogans, the colour firmly red and the hammer and sickle prominently displayed. As we walked along the platform our fascination in the occupants was only matched by their apparent fascination with us, particularly Gilly's bowler hat, which by their lewd demonstrations indicated a belief that by its shape it could be inverted and used for some purpose other than headgear. Notwithstanding all this, those compartments certainly appeared more comfortable than those we had previously occupied, and we were baffled but delighted to be invited by the guard to enter one of those carriages and make ourselves comfortable. We soon learned that the occupants too were travelling to Bucharest, but to a different conference from the one to which we were bound, a conference clearly even more deeply designed for political purposes than ours.

These were the days of "peace petitions", numerous sheaves of paper endorsed with scores of signatures seeking peace, with the small print hiding the conditions for peace. Small groups would make their way shyly towards us, many speaking English. "Hello comrade," one would say, "are you fighting for peace?" "Yes," we would reply, asking them in return, "And are you fighting for peace?" When they said, "Yes," we would lean forward and enquire, "So who are you fighting?" Both our fellow travellers and the train guard had laboured under the mistaken belief that we were bound for the same conference.

The first train had brought us through France, Switzerland and now we had another two hours through Austria before reaching the Austro-Hungarian border, well within the Iron Curtain at the town of Hegyeshalom. The train drew to a steamy halt, and soldiers all armed with rifles surrounded it. They stood about ten metres apart, slim, grim-looking men, their fingers on the trigger and their eyes firmly on the train while other uniformed men made their way through it asking for passports, tickets and any other documents we might be carrying. Luggage had to be opened and was inspected with minute care, a pair of shoes which I had wrapped in newspaper had the wrapping taken away and confiscated. Gilly made some remark about them probably never having before come across the *News of the World* and the fun they would have translating it. I muttered about it being a pointless exercise since, as I understood, they had already imprisoned all their merchant bankers, which caused Gilly to laugh out aloud, and I immediately wished that I had held my tongue because one of them jabbed Gilly with his rifle in his generous stomach area, nudged him to move and he was marched off the train and I saw him being taken along the rail track. This put me in a total sweat. What on earth had I started by making that crass remark? Where was the consulate? How could I contact it? For this was the age before the mobile phone, in fact several ages.

No-one else seemed to be the slightest concerned, and certainly not our fellow travellers who averted their eyes and would not become engaged in my dilemma. Gilly returned about ten minutes later, still with his armed new best friend, and told me they had just marched him once round the train and then back again. After about two hours the train puffed slowly off, accompanied by the various animal noises we could hear coming from the lower class, but it was not they, in fact it was their animals.

We reached Budapest without further incident, and even there it seemed that our "special" carriages had been isolated from the rest of the train, and no-one moved either in or out of them. Our only contact with anyone was with vendors on the platform who were selling unappetising food from metal containers or wicker baskets. We then moved through Hungary at a similar slow pace to that through Austria, catching sight from time to time of a brown river which we gathered was the Blue Danube, another illusion shattered.

Then the border between Hungary and Romania loomed ahead, but when the train slowed down at this small gathering of buildings an amazing scene met our eyes. The place was bedecked with flags and banners fluttering in the wind, there were about four or five hundred people waving smaller flags and an eight-man brass band. At the point where the train stopped, and directly opposite our carriage there was podium on which stood men, some in uniform but whether uniformed or not, all were bemedalled.

Our fellow travellers were as excited as the welcoming party. The train was a high one, well above the ground level of the platform, but this did not stop the throng jumping up and trying to grab our hands.

I could make out two words common to most of the placards being thrust in front of us, which were "Welcome" and "Peace". But judging by the number of armed police and soldiers, it seemed that if we did not cherish and even reciprocate our "welcome" there would certainly be no "peace".

Within moments trays of glasses and bottles of drinks arrived, but were not drunk. Protocol clearly required that messages were to be delivered first. I couldn't imagine that people were hesitant because they wanted to hear the message before approving it by drinking to it; they were just fearful of doing the wrong thing, which was drinking in advance of the speech.

In the carriage next to ours on the left was the Russian delegation. In those days Russian women were not the tall slim blondes of today, but the small dumpy babushkas of yesteryear. The men were just as sinister as the current crop of oligarchs.

Their head man grabbed a microphone which was passed up in one hand, and held his glass high in the other. "Comrades," he shouted (I thought thank goodness the chosen common language is English). "Comrades, we bring greetings of peace and freedom from our people to your people, we bring greetings from Comrade Stalin." He barely got that word out before the entire crowd responded in *Seig Heil* style, "Stalin, Stalin, Stalin." It went on for some moments.

The microphone was eventually passed back to one of the welcoming party who gave the next speech, which took up the simple and repetitive theme, "Comrades, we bring greetings of peace and freedom from Georghe Gheorghiu-Dej." He was the Prime Minister of Romania, and his very name provoked a great cheer as the crowd repeated in full voice, and with much hand-clapping in time, to the rhythmic name of Georghe Gheorghiu-Dej, Georghe Gheorghiu-Dej, Georghe Gheorghiu-Dej". Almost as enthusiastic as for the Russians.

Soon the East Germans were on track with their very own Wilhelm Pieck, and so it was, "Wilhelm Pieck, Wilhelm, Pieck, Wilhelm Pieck," whose name rang around the railway track.

Gilly and I had been quietly watching, and to some extent dreading the inevitable movement of the attention of the crowd in our direction. But it came, and I think that as much as he was the picture of gravitas, it was his dress which fuelled their curiosity, and the microphone by-passed me and ended in his hand. He rose to the occasion, doffing his bowler in their direction, and this itself provoked a roar, and there came a moment of inspiration.

"Comrades, we bring greetings of peace and freedom from our people to your people, we bring greetings from Sir Gordon Richards (for years a champion jockey), who sends good wishes from the English turf to the Romanian sods."

And they clapped and cheered, as though as well rehearsed as they had been for the others, "Gordon Richards, Gordon Richards, Gordon Richards," they chanted. Gilly passed the microphone to me, and with his hand over it he whispered, "Now do better than that," and so I tried. "Yes, comrades, from Gordon Richards, a man in our country with a very great following, who leads in many fields." I often thought that if we had been charged over the *News of the World* incident, we could possibly have had Gordon Richards taken into consideration.

The conference itself lasted about ten days, and was a load of political ballyhoo, about how progressive and helpful the Eastern bloc governments were towards education, and how destructive, menacing and hell-bent upon war the West was. We tried to put our spoke in occasionally, but were heavily outnumbered.

One man who did figure frequently in our mural and extramural discussions was a rather mature student from Russia who happened to be chairman of the League of Democratic Youth and for some reason he was always anxious to know about those students in England who were particularly left-wing and what influence they genuinely had. Gilly and I were never good at remembering names, so we couldn't help him, which was perhaps just as well, because I did remember his name and two years later I read that Alexander Shaliapin had been appointed head of the KGB.

There was one further trip behind the Curtain, this time in my capacity as vice-president of NUS, and that was to Budapest. This time I was able to fly there, but had to change aircraft in Prague. The replacement plane was part of the fleet of Malev, a now defunct and bankrupt airline, and even then the future of the airline manifested itself in the technical deficiencies of that aircraft. It was a grounded aircraft. There was, however, the promise that it would fly the next day, and I was given a 24-hour visa to go into Prague and a reservation was offered to me at the Alcron Hotel. From this offer I did not demur, having heard of its reputation. It turned out to be as slick and buzzy as any western capital city hotel with a lobby which was a hive of activity, some of which was directed towards a rather weary woman, clearly English and with two small children. It seemed that everybody wanted to talk to them, and I was told she was a Mrs Maclean. Had I obtained an English newspaper that morning I would have realised the significance. She was the wife of Maclean of the infamous spy duo, Burgess and Maclean.

It did not take me long to realise that I had been allocated a *shammos* who followed behind at far too close a range to even imagine that he had not been detected. Charles Bridge and Square were magic on that winter's day, and I can still smell the roasting chestnuts being sold by scores of street vendors, though the only custom those vendors gained from me was for a warm fur hat to cover my ears from the harsh easterly wind. The hat was something which must have made the task of my shadow a little more difficult, because identical hats were worn by absolutely everyone on those streets.

I wandered around, with my discreet *shammos*, enjoying the delights of that beautiful city, had a good meal and slept in a comfortable bed. Arriving the following morning at the airport I was told that the aircraft was still unserviceable, and splendid, I thought, another pleasant day in Prague. But that was not to be. I was told that my visa had been valid for only 24 hours and the regulations did not permit any extension, and that as I had arrived without a visa I would now have to go into restricted custody.

The custodial area was on the far side of the airport, a brownish grey building with a high wall and armed guards on the large gates. There were none of the courtesies and smiles with which I had been greeted at the Alcron; the room certainly did not have the same amenities, and the food could be categorised as nearer to adequate than appetizing. Nowhere to sit after the dining room other than my small bedroom, and certainly no facility to encourage discussion or even meet up with any of the other occupants, of whom there were but a few. Happily though, Malev must have received the necessary spare part overnight, and on the following morning I was able to fly to Budapest. There followed a crowded few days occupied with meeting students in a variety of establishments from those quite young to the exceedingly mature.

I was booked into a hotel in Budapest which was a glorious old-fashioned place situated on an island in the middle of the Danube, the only other occupants of which were the Hungarian national football team, who were anxious to talk to me as they were due to shortly visit England to play an important match at Wembley. Their captain was called Puskas, and there were other players with names like Hidukarty; they took me to a match in Budapest when they played Sweden, the only time I have ever travelled to a match in the players' coach, and sat in the directors' box. When they came to England my friends were most impressed when I described them as old friends and showed them pictures of us taken together on that short bus ride.

I was to return over 50-years later to Budapest when I stayed at that very same hotel on Margarite's Island. I went to have some dental work done when the Hungarians became experts on implants, and far less expensive than London. I even tried to get a discount when they remembered my famous footballer friends.

Leeds may have been a redbrick university, but it taught me much and I cherished the experiences and memories of student life and travel.

In front of me is The Princess Royal with Margot Fonteyn

Chapter 8

From Rank Outsider

Great, I was now a solicitor. However, there was one more hurdle to jump, a little matter of two years' National Service.

The war had ended some eleven years earlier, but there had been quite a number of smaller wars, that is, if you can properly describe the decimation of Korea, the long-drawn-out explosive situation in Vietnam, the division of Cyprus, the damage in Aden, the battles in the Middle-East and the insurgence in Kenya by words other than war. The resulting problems for the British government of involvement, excursions and the need to provide defence in any of these areas were to find the military personnel to do it.

There had been an immediate demobilisation in 1945, immediate in that those engaged in the war knew they would be entitled to return to Civvie Street, and so they were, although in some cases it took several months. This left a gaping hole in the number of servicemen available, and so the call-up when one reached the age of 18 continued in a modified form until 1961. It varied over the course of the years in period from 18 months to sometimes just over two years, but two years was the norm.

If one was accepted by a university, then deferment was granted, but not so for a training or technical college. If one required further time to complete professional qualifications, then it was granted. Therefore doctors, dentists, accountants, solicitors, who needed to do training and obtain qualification by examination following their degree, were allowed to do so, but the requirement of National Service did not disappear, and still loomed large.

My feelings towards it were mixed. I was naturally anxious to practise the profession for which I had spent so many years seeking qualification. Three years at university to obtain a degree, three years' articles, and six months at a law crammers preparing for the final Law Society examination, and then a lengthy period awaiting exam results. Facing the challenge of practice and earning money was uppermost, but the army did have a sneaking attraction.

I cannot claim to come from a military family, though one of my earlier memories was that photograph of four of my grandfather's brothers who were in the 1914–18 war, all lined up and wearing the uniform of the Royal Flying Corps, the predecessors of the RAF.

When my father had joined the Territorial Army in 1936 when Hitler's influence in Europe was revealing itself, he justifiably anticipated that there would be hostilities. I was pretty young at the time but was in awe of his appearance in full blue-and-red uniform, with a real pistol and a bullet pouch in his belt. The small brass insignia on his shoulder signified CMP, and I bragged to my junior school friends that this stood for the Canadian Mounted Police, which taking into account the blue uniform and red peaked cap they readily believed.

In fact CMP stood for Corps of Military Police, which was the arm to which my father, who was a tall man, had been recommended. As well as being tall he was always very smart. Shoes highly polished, trousers perfectly creased, starched white shirt collar and cuffs, an immaculate man. I don't think he felt terribly extended by his daily business, and the army, particularly when he was going off on exercises, seemed to rejuvenate him.

He loved his time in the army, and would regale me with stories, and show me photographs of war in the desert. Probably his proudest moment was when he came to my passing-out parade at Mons Officer Cadet School, and my most worried moment was when I saw him chatting to my commanding officer.

In addition to the influence of my father, I had also enjoyed that period at school when I was in the Army Cadet Force. Thursday at Roundhay School was when you turned up in an itchy khaki uniform, wore it to lessons in the morning, and for Corps in the afternoon. The French master, Mr Peacock, and the history master, Mr Gordon, turned up as captain and major respectively because that had been their rank in the real army during the war.

We marched around the schoolyard, held rifles from which the bolts had been removed, and from time to time went into the school cellars where a firing range of sorts had been set up. The captains of rugby and cricket respectively assumed their rightful places as sergeant major and sergeant and did the requisite bawling at everybody. I think I was the only cadet who never got into trouble on parade because my father had always insisted on giving me a minute inspection before I went to school on Thursday morning, and had also taken great pains to instil into me the not insignificant difference of standing at attention, at ease and easy, and also how to salute properly.

So, the sneaking attraction of army life was there. I had never been away from home, having attended school and university in Leeds. And there was also the fact that after all, I did have the qualification of being a solicitor.

I had heard about the initiation into army life and did not relish the thought of barrack-room living with a crowd of 18-year-olds six or seven years younger than myself, and probably rougher, and no doubt at all, tougher. I wondered about the food, having enjoyed my mother's cooking for all of my life, and of course there was the ambition to commence work in my chosen profession as soon as possible.

One possibility did cross my mind, and that was to enlist on a regular commission in the Army Legal Corps, this would enable me to enter the army with an initial degree of comfort, and at the same time practise some law. The problem here was that the length of a short service commission would be at least three years, and possibly longer. No, let's get in as soon as possible, endeavour to get a National Service commission, and then get on with earning a living.

There was just one other stage to get through before I could accept the Queen's shilling, and that was a medical examination. I had heard of chaps taking all sorts of medications, herbs and potions which might affect their readings, but not for me. I attended, coughed, supplied and did all that was necessary before the doctor put a funnel-shaped torch into my ears.

I decided to help the doctor. "You will probably see that I have a perforated eardrum, I have had it since being very tiny and it means I can't swim." "Oh don't worry about that," smiled the medic, "You're going into the army, not the navy, congratulations. A1."

A brown envelope announcing that it came directly from Her Majesty arrived about two weeks later. I was quite pleased to get the project moving. The euphoria of having a professional qualification after six years of study would take a long time to disappear and at that time, whatever the envelope contained my reaction would have been, well, another stage before earning money, so let's get on with it.

The envelope contained a rail warrant, an invitation to use it to get to Aldershot, a short list of essential toiletries and the statement that whatever I came dressed in would almost immediately be parcelled up and sent back to my mother.

And so it was. There were quite a few miserable young men on that train from Waterloo, and at Aldershot the first thing one saw was a large notice that army recruits should assemble in the car park. On the platform two or three corporals and lance-corporals glared in the direction of the young men, and with the not over-cordial greeting, "You, over there," they pointed towards a line of army trucks which had their rear-hinge boards lowered.

To my surprise they did not pick on me for that brusque invitation, and I was about to walk through the car park, thinking I had escaped the first selection stage, and that having seen and assessed me, perhaps they had decided they didn't need me after all. I then realised that they had allowed me to pass because I looked older than the rest, that the period of six years' deferment to pass exams meant that I was of rather more mature appearance than the 18-year-olds, and not least probably because I was wearing a tie. I had almost reached the gate when caution dictated that I should at least make some enquiry. I flashed my brown envelope in front of the kindest-looking of the soldiers, and with barely a glance at me he pointed to one of the trucks and said, "Up there." At least two of the agile 18-year-olds had a streak of kindness in them and they held out an arm to assist me to climb on to the back of the truck.

The next few hours shall ever remain a blur in my memory. Little did I know it at the time of arrival but Blenheim Barracks would play a large part in my National Service, but that first day or so was sheer hell.

I was thrown into a group of 30 assorted 18-year-olds. I would later discover there were maybe two or three others who had been deferred and were nearer my age, but in the main they were 18. They came from all over the country with a variety of accents, some more intelligible than others. Many wept openly at the screaming, shouting and yelling of the group of non-commissioned officers with just a single stripe of authority on their sleeve.

They came from varied backgrounds, some despite their age were married and had young children, many were tattooed, some bragged of having been in young offenders' establishments, but even the toughest were chastened by the bullying. There is no other word for it of the NCOs, some of whom were only two or three years older than the recruits, but who nevertheless wore the medal ribbons of campaigns which I recognised, such as Palestine and Korea.

We were lined-up for everything: to hand over our civilian clothes which would later be posted home, to receive a bundle of uniforms, equipment, blankets, mattress, boots. "Sign here for this," "Sign here for that," and "Then carry them back to your barrack room, and assemble them by your iron bedstead," and so on.

The barracks were long wooden sheds called "spiders" for some strange reason. I examined the bathroom and toilet facilities, which seemed totally inadequate, and we were hustled, hustled because we could not yet march, to a large room where some inedible food was sitting in large tepid containers. I asked a soldier in white where the vegetarian food was, and he smiled as he said, "Wherever you can find it, but you can tell it's vegetarian because it doesn't move like the rest, it just sits still," he guffawed to his white-clad friends.

As we were rushed around, across the vast parade ground I could see a building that looked as though it had been created with some grace, ivy-clad, with flower beds in front of it; the windows had red curtains and I could see normal table lamps with shades and there were silver candelabra: this was the officers' mess. It became my immediate and ultimate target. Now there, I thought, there, I could live.

Blenheim Barracks, Farnborough, was the intake battalion for the Royal Army Service Corps, or the RASC. I had been asked on the application form if there was any arm or regiment with which I had connections, and although my father had been in the Military Police I had put down "Guards or Cavalry", because I understood they were the important regiments. In fact I had always admired the rather tasteful striped ties worn by guardsmen, and had assumed riding a horse would be less exhausting than marching.

I think, however, that that week the guards and cavalry must have been full, because it was to the RASC that I was directed. I think the reason was simply that they were the corps to which they sent solicitors. The thinking was simple. As indicated by their name, they serviced the army.

They provided transport, which used to be horse transport, hence the nickname donkey wallopers, but in more modern times they provide the drivers and the clerks, and to be a clerk it was anticipated you might have to write, and if you had qualified as a solicitor there was a not unreasonable presumption that you could write, and if you didn't become an officer then they could use you as a clerk.

For six weeks we were confined to barracks, being instructed in the basic soldierly duties, how to march, how to hold a rifle, how to clean a rifle, how to polish boots, how to take the little bubbles out of the leather in a pair of rough boots with the aid of a spoon and a candle and some black polish, and make them glisten. How to administer Blanco to our webbing, and distinguish between the brass bits which needed to be polished and the canvas bits which needed Blanco. How to make a squared-off bed in the style dictated by the army which ensured you had to start at the beginning every evening, and reassemble it every morning.

As a student like most in those days I had smoked cigarettes, and as I was now having to exert myself physically to a degree unknown I decided that perhaps giving-up cigarettes would be a good idea, quite apart from the expense on a wage of 28 shillings a week, less a deduction for the barrack room damages which I knew I would never knowingly cause.

Life was a challenge, a challenge not to trail behind the 18-year-olds when running cross-country with a full pack on or scaling walls. The decision to cut out cigarettes came after a few days during which, following the six a.m. bugle call 30 pairs of hands would come from under the bed-clothes, reach out for a cigarette and light up, and there would be barrage of coughing. I said to myself, the army has to do you at least one good thing, and that's stop smoking.

I discovered two or three like minds among my fellow trainees. One I recall was Michael Freedland who later became a BBC and *Times* journalist. There was a newly qualified chartered accountant, and a terribly nice chap with a double-barrelled name whose father was something in politics and who, when we were allowed to leave barracks, drove us up to London at the weekend for a splendid meal at his lovely home in Eton Square. Neither he nor I could understand why he never got into one of the smarter regiments; maybe there was some family reason for blackballing him.

I next came across Michael Freedland about ten years ago, when I was rummaging through the new titles at a book fair, and opening his book saw a paragraph on his National Service in which he wrote, "I remember there was a solicitor from Yorkshire who cheered us up, I think he later became a judge."

I bought a copy of the book and took it over to the table where he was signing. I opened the book at the cover, passed it to him, saying my name as I did so, "Barrington Black, page 185." He looked up... his face was a picture. He reminded me that I had once shown him a letter from my mother in which she had mused, "I do hope they have given you a nice room, and if not ask to see someone in charge."

At some stage during the six weeks I was told that on the basis of my time in the Cadet Force at school, and subsequent qualification my name would be placed on a unit list of potential officer cadets, and I became a sheep whose selection from the flock was denoted by a slim white ribbon in my epaulette, which was also an indication of invitation for verbal abuse from the lower-rank NCOs. The sergeants had the good sense to realise that here was someone who might eventually be in command over them, so they were less abusive, but the nicest of all were the officers.

My company commander Captain Mike White invited me to baby-sit, and as this meant an evening of solitary (except for the well-behaved baby) comfort in an armchair in front of the TV, I readily agreed. One evening in conversation it came out that I could type pretty quickly, a talent I'd picked up as a student and articled clerk, and the following day I was invited in to see the colonel. The colonel said he knew I was interested in a commission (I controlled myself by not saying the thing that first came to mind, which would have been, "Not really, why can't I have a weekly wage like everybody else?").

I said, "Yes Sir, and would like to take the usual step of going before the War Office Selection Board (WOSBIE)." The colonel suggested that I shouldn't rush things, and that if I held back and took a job in his office, dealing with his letters and admin matters, he would give me a couple of stripes, making me a corporal. This would mean being transposed immediately out of the barrack room into a little room of my own, though not exactly the gentlemen's chambers my mother had imagined, use of the

NCOs' mess to eat in, and a trebling of my pay, which, he added with a wink, "would continue through Officer Cadet School if you later still want to be an officer."

The prospect of getting out of the barrack room just two months after joining was attractive. I could work office hours, be working with civilised people in a warm office, wear shoes instead of boots and not spend my time bulling and marching, not have to do guard duties, and not be deployed for nights on end, as was then happening, beating out forest fires which were prevalent around the Surrey countryside.

So I became Corporal Black, the Colonel's PA, and with my printed card showing "Solicitor" pinned in my door. This provoked a few frowns from senior officers but no-one made me take it down. In fact the occasional senior officer came in to see me, always starting the conversation, "I have a friend who has this problem…"

My position caused me some amusement, because one of my duties was to accept phone calls coming into Battalion HQ. I have been told that I have quite a smooth telephone voice, and I had the habit of answering the phone, "Black speaking." Numerous majors and captains, scores of lieutenants and hundreds of regimental and company sergeants-major would embark upon and indeed continue their telephone conversation with me, by addressing me as "Sir", and I did little to disabuse them of their belief. It all came to an end when, after ten minutes conversation during which a major had been calling me "Sir", and when he said, "No doubt I'll see you in the mess at lunch-time," I foolishly blurted out, "In my dreams."

As I was the hub of everything that was happening in the battalion, everyone, but everyone, treated me with kid gloves. If they wanted to know anything about their postings, their promotion prospects, I was the person who knew, so no-one crossed me.

Word also got out that when at university I had produced and directed the Rag Revue at the local Empire Theatre, and so when time came to produce the Christmas show *Snow White and the Seven Dwarfs,* I was volunteered by the colonel to do this. The nearby RASC barracks called Buller Barracks had a superb stage with full theatrical equipment, and there it was produced. The RSM and various CSMs took the named lead parts, and it gave me a great opportunity to write lyrics which took the mickie out of everyone on camp. I wrote one to the tune of a current radio programme called *Much Binding in the Marsh*. It went:

> "At much Bulling in the Camp, some of us are here on National Service
> At much Bulling in the Camp, we often fail to understand the purpose
> Of dragging us away from home for some two years or more, just to run
> Odd errands, or to polish up the floor
> And where would Dixon-Savage be, in an atomic war?
> Why, at Much Bulling in the Camp."

Dixon-Savage was the provost-sergeant, and much a figure of fun with his waxed moustache, looking the very cartoon version of a sergeant-major. It was a knock-out success and confirmed my position in battalion headquarters as the regimental wit, or that was what I thought people said.

There came a stage when the colonel said that he knew I had once expressed an interest in a transfer to legal services, and he had been told of a vacancy at the War Office in London for someone with my qualifications, would I be interested? I certainly was, and a few phone calls later I was told to pack my belongings including uniform in my old kit bag, because one didn't wear uniform at the War Office. In fact you wore a civilian suit, and were allocated to live in civilian lodgings somewhere in central London. I duly made my farewells to all at Buller Barracks, and arrived at the War House, as it is called. They were expecting me, and showed me to my room and introduced me to some convivial-looking colleagues.

I was given a slip of paper with an address and told to take my belongings and then come back when I had unpacked. I found the address; it looked comfortable indeed, and the landlady seemed most accommodating.

I had barely started to unpack when the phone rang: would I come back to the War Office straightaway, because an unfortunate mistake had been made. I arrived to find an apologetic junior intelligence officer waiting to see me. It seemed that they had checked, albeit somewhat late in the day, my security.

My personal vetting, as security for a War Office job is known, had revealed that I had travelled behind the Iron Curtain on more than one occasion, I had been to Russia, Czechoslovakia, Hungary, Eastern Austria,

Romania, all unheard-of places for one to visit in the normal course of events in the early-1950s, but it showed that I had been there. I admitted that I had, most certainly not as a Communist sympathiser, but in my capacity first as president of the Union of Leeds University, and then as vice-president of the National Union of Students I had, together with other student leaders, been invited by the International Union of Students as an observer to various student functions held in those countries. The intelligence officer was apologetic. There was nothing he could do, the blanket restriction on security applied to anyone who had visited countries behind the Curtain. I was to return to my unit in Aldershot. I was rather put out to say the least, but as a good soldier, did as I was told.

My job was still available to me at Buller Barracks, and I returned the following morning, but I was of course furious that my security level had been questioned. I cynically asked if I could now apply to go to WOSBIE and a commission. To my surprise the security restriction which I had logged-up did not prevent this. So, ironically, although I could not be a minor cog in the wheels at the War Office, I might still hold a commission in Her Majesty's army. But first I had to get through the formal requirements.

The WOSBIE procedures were based in a lovely country house in the Home Counties. You were treated well, with excellent food and a comfortable bed, and some rigorous exercises, both physical and mental, and well-constructed enquiries were made of you. It was a common rumour that they watched your every move, even down to the correct use of knife and fork at mealtime. You had the well-known exercise of commanding a group in the task of getting a barrel over a river with a minimum of tools and ropes, or in my case the task of getting me over a river without looking like the minimum tool. You had to give a lecture, not much trouble there, and survive an interview—don't overdo it there. At the end they gave you an envelope which contains a slip saying either you have passed for selection as an officer, you have failed, or you have not passed, but please come back in three months' time. Mine simply said that I had passed.

I was then sent to Mons Officer Cadet School. You wear a smoother uniform, certainly get better food, still live in a barrack room and are known as "Mr". You wear a black beret with a white circular disk behind the badge and broad white epaulettes on your shoulders. You wear brown leather gloves. You purchase (if you don't already have one) a hat, either a peaked country-style hat, or a brown trilby. You purchase a riding mac, and if in town you wear the hat so that if a soldier sees you, recognises you and salutes you, you can raise your hat or at least touch the brim to him. When in uniform you carry a bamboo cane.

The RSM greets you with the firm but well-tried message: "Gentlemen, you will call me Sir and I will call you Sir, the difference is that you will mean it."

The standards are high, and if your parade ground appearance is untidy or your deportment slovenly you will be pulled-up and if necessary punished with extra drills. Equally so for the cleanliness of your barrack room.

I managed all the lectures and all the practical exercises when you go out overnight through the countryside and take turns in commanding a group of trucks carrying a company of soldiers who are ambushed or otherwise attacked by another company. What I did not manage was one of the physical exercises involving crossing a river on a rope. I just could not do it and fell into the river which thankfully was shallow. However, I was relegated, which meant being put back four weeks.

The fact that there was another camp show to be produced and which was due during the time of my relegation may have had something to do with my remaining for those extra weeks.

Eventually I passed the course, but was still not an officer. One had to return to Buller, this time to the Officer Cadet Section in order to learn aspects particular to the RASC before being let loose as an officer. I quite enjoyed this period, which involved instruction in driving and maintaining heavy goods vehicles and running them down to the coast for the day, though once again, this time at Buller, I was relegated due to a certain physical tardiness, something to do with having to successfully run ten miles with a full pack on my back.

Eventually the day came for my passing-out parade. My parents came down to Aldershot and I think it was one of my father's proudest moments. There was something thrilling about marching to a full military band, and wearing one's best officer blues for the first time.

We did the ceremonial marching, and then at the end they call out the senior under officer, who steps forward and is given the sword of honour, and the junior under officer is called for the baton of honour. Fine athletic figures, each of them from the right school and the right background, for that's how it was in those days. There was then a pause, and the RSM roared, "Second Lieutenant Black, one step forward, march." I was shocked, but did as he ordered: "Second Lieutenant Black, right turn, quick march, halt," he ordered in succession. As he did, the regimental band played a slow march and the company sergeant major marched towards me carrying a velvet cushion. He halted and I saw that on the cushion was a large cardboard disc with a bright ribbon, inscribed "The Buller Long Service Medal". Another sergeant marched forward and placed it round my neck. I had apparently spent more time than anyone known at Blenheim, Buller Barracks, as a National Service recruit before eventually becoming an officer. I was marched back to my place, and we all marched off to the music.

The first thing one then does is run to the door of the barracks where there is pinned up the postings for the new officers, Germany, Cyprus, Kenya, Aden. Mine read: "2nd Lieutenant Barrington Black to Blenheim Barracks, Aldershot."

I was told off for telling the colonel how smart he looked

CHAPTER 9

To Becoming an Officer and a Gentleman

The removal from the ranks to actually being a fully-commissioned officer is like how I imagine a transfer by celestial influence from Hell to Heaven must be like. On Friday the RSM reigned supreme over me, the very man who had introduced the "Sir" title as being "something you will mean," and there we were, on the following Monday, when anything, but anything that moved and had less than one pip on their shoulder automatically called me Sir whether they meant it or not, and anything I would call Sir would have at least a metal crown on its shoulder.

I recalled my mother's enquiry about having been given "a nice room". As a recruit, a barrack room shared with 30 others could never have been described as a nice room, though if I'd had it to myself I might have made something of it by descending into my favourite occupation of moving the furniture around a bit. But the officers' mess, even at Blenheim Barracks, Aldershot, was like the Garden of Eden, or for a nearer comparison, a gentlemen's club in St James's. Now I had a room of my own, the bathroom with a vast old-fashioned bath was just down the corridor, and the room itself was furnished with the basics, a bed, leather easy chair, coffee tables, bedside tables, bed lights even — and above all privacy.

Privacy that is, until there was a knock on the door, and my batman, Bob (they were all called Bob) came in to introduce himself. Batman I should explain was not a character with a grey vest black underpants and a blue cape, but a retired non-commissioned officer, who lived in Aldershot and couldn't get the army out of his blood, so was paid by the services to come in each morning, bring me a cup of tea, lay out my uniform freshly pressed, my boots highly polished, and a fresh bucket of coal for the open fire which he proceeded to lay before I got out of bed. It was all that I fondly believed marriage would be like, but that mistaken vision revealed itself a few years later.

The mess had been built many years ago, and furnished with gentlemen's furniture, leather armchairs, a long highly polished dining table, and walls filled with portraits of military men with moustaches and feathers and shiny knee boots and horses and dogs.

The mess housed about 25 officers, breakfast was from seven a.m. to eight a.m., and you served yourself from silver salvers and platters on the sideboard; hot toast was brought by the mess servants, and coffee and tea poured out of silver pots. There were two golden rules. You didn't speak to anybody over breakfast. You picked up one of a pile of newspapers, placed it firmly in front of you, and read, ate and sipped. The second was that you filled the table up as you came in, no selection of place, just one after the other, irrespective of rank. Quite different from other meals when the red tabs were at one end of the table, and the junior subalterns at the other end. You wore whatever uniform your particular duties involved for the day, normally battledress without a belt; or if you held office for the day, your number two kit. Blues were reserved for special evening meals.

Lunch was at about one, and dinner promptly at 7.30, but when you finished the day's duties, usually at about half-past-four, you came in for tea, toast and Marmite. With the colonel's permission you could entertain a guest to dinner, but not a woman. They were restricted to being entertained in the ladies' room, a rather severe drawing-room where you could feed them on tea and cakes, or in the case of some, champagne.

Blenheim was an intake battalion which I had been through when I was called-up, with about 200 recruits every fortnight. As subaltern I was in charge of about 50 of them.

The reason I had been sent there was simple, and really all my fault. When I had gone through that initial mill it came out that at university I had produced the rag revue, and so I was made responsible for the camp show. My name had remained on the mind of the commanding officer, so a special requisition had accompanied me that when commissioned I should be returned intact to Blenheim, and it was so.

Advantages? Yes, not too far from London, close to Guildford where I knew my way about and still had some contacts, it avoided me being sent to somewhere like Kenya or equally uncomfortable parts of the world, but it also precluded me from selection to serve at one of our embassies in more pleasant world locations, as some of my friends did. There was one other special advantage. Among the 200 recruits each fortnight were several who before being called up had fallen foul of the law, and were due to appear in court. What better way to have them dealt than to send 2nd Lieutenant Black, who was also a solicitor, to make a plea for them to be allowed back to the unit, "so that the Army could make a man of them"?

I had a great run of successes following this line, and it also helped me experience being on my feet in the magistrates' courts. This developed, notwithstanding my rank, to being asked to do some Courts Martial as defending officer, and here with contested matters I really did sharpen my nails.

Part of my duty was to ensure that each intake was settling in well, and I would go over to my company on some evenings to check there were no problems, and in particular that there was no bullying by the corporals and drill sergeants. I also kept a sympathetic eye on the more mature recruits who, as in my own case had been deferred to take professional exams, and were struggling at the age of 24 to keep up with the 18-year-olds.

One evening I found a miserable soldier who fitted that description, and told him that it would be tough for a while, maybe the first eight to ten weeks, but after that if he aimed at a commission, things would get better. He said he would try. I next met him about 25-years later, as a fellow judge at one of the London courts. He had obtained his commission, decided to stay in the army, been seconded to the Army Legal Service, of which he eventually became the head, and had retired with the rank of Major-General.

About three months before being due for demobilisation I began to think about the future. In fact I had been thinking about it for some time but urgency was now creeping in and I started to read the legal columns of *The Times* to see what was happening out there. One day I came across an advert put in by a solicitor whose name was familiar. He had dealt with politicians and with the unions, and although this sphere was not strictly that which interested me, namely crime, he definitely had a certain get-up-and-go which I admired. He was called Victor Mishcon, so I wrote to him, and he invited me to come up to London to see him, which I did.

For someone reputed to have such notable clients the offices were smaller than I imagined, and the number of people working seemed on the low side, with only about three staff. His personal work, he told me, was almost entirely connected with looking after the unions, and this had attracted other work and he needed someone young and enthusiastic to join him. We seemed to hit it off, and he said that he would write to me over the following few days with a proposition.

As I drove back to Aldershot I reflected on the prospect. To live in London rather than Leeds certainly sounded tempting, and an equal attraction was to join someone who already had a nucleus of clients, and powerful clients too. On the other hand, I thought of my parents. I was an only child and the centre of their world. They had supported all my activities and ambitions and I knew they were counting the days to my return to Leeds. They expected me to fulfil my earlier hopes of setting up practice in Leeds and making a name for myself there, which they might vicariously enjoy from close quarters. I hadn't told them about Victor Mishcon, but I phoned him when I arrived back and explained the situation. He was a little disgruntled that I had come to see him, spent time with him, given him the impression I was keen to join him, and then when it became a possibility had responded with a rejection. Mishcon de Rea became one of the most prestigious firms in the City, ah well…

And so I went home, the uniform was hung up, well not quite, because together with the discharge papers was notification that I had been promoted up a notch to the dizzy height of full lieutenant. This meant I was on the reserve list. I remembered what had happened to my father, recalled what had happened at Suez, and prayed for peace.

I took my parents for a short holiday, and on return went to see Jack Levi who was the doyen of advocates, not only in Leeds, but also in the whole of West Yorkshire. A small tubby man, looking not unlike Billy Cotton, a bandleader of the age. Not very smooth, but a great lawyer with a terrific reputation, though this did bound back on him, as it does with most great criminal solicitors. "If you have so and so, then it means you are guilty," they would say. But have him, they did, and many were found not guilty. Gentleman Jack, as he was known, could charm the blue rinse off many of the ladies who chaired the bench in those days, and I heard that he was keen to meet me. Suffice it to say that he did, but the offer he made was not generous to say the least, so I made an excuse and left.

Fate plays strange tricks, because as I left his office in Park Square I walked towards the Headrow, turned right along East Parade and there on the corner of East Parade and South Parade, at ground level, and with large glass windows visible to all passing, both on buses, cars and walking, were two rooms in Pearl Chambers, a short stone's throw from the criminal courts in the town Hall, and a notice was at that very moment being put up indicating they were to let. The agent was Hollis and Webb, and I was just passing, to my right, their offices. I went in, and without seeking any further details of the rooms said, "Can I take them please, but just let me have a peep inside." The obliging agent did so, and they were perfect for my purpose. I paid a deposit there and then, and rushed home to tell my enthusiastic parents the good news. They were overjoyed.

Chapter 10

Clarence Darrow or Perry Mason?

The name on the brass plate firmly fixed to the stone wall next to the door of Pearl Chambers, East Parade, Leeds, 1, and also painted large upon the ground-floor windows ensured that any passer-by and those on the bus route could clearly see that "Barrington Black LLB Solicitor" was installed here. Two rooms, one my consulting room, with a leather-covered desk, one armchair behind it, and two less comfortable chairs in front. My degree and admission certificate, framed and nailed to the wall. The other room was an outer office with a desk for the receptionist/secretary, whom maybe one day I would employ, but originally manned for a few hours each day by my mother, and a few chairs and magazines upon which the multitude would sit and read.

On that first day my desk looked empty, so I brought out all the briefs, neatly tied in pink tape, from the Courts Martial which I had done while in the army.

They sat there side-by-side, and to the uninitiated, or those who could not read upside-down writing, they might have looked impressive, but I was just a little concerned that some potential client might wonder with all that array, how I had the time to deal with their case. Happily I did not have long to wait for the first client to step through my doors. My years of involvement with the university meant that my name had appeared regularly in the pages of the *Yorkshire Post* and *Yorkshire Evening Post*, each of which, together with the *Yorkshire Evening News* had quite a large circulation in the West Riding. There were also a number of friendly solicitors practising in the area who were quite happy to refer work to me with which they did not have the time to deal, and knowing that at that stage I would not refuse anything.

I also volunteered my name for the legal aid list kept by the magistrates of those willing to accept cases for which legal aid would be granted, and although at that time they paid very little, there was a gradual progression of fee rates, and provided one had enough work, that is more than just one or two cases in the courts, then it became worthwhile. In those days there was a far more sensible approach to remuneration for legal aid cases; it was reasonable and provided the practitioner organized his time well, it could be quite profitable.

People more used to dealing in commercial work would often ask how you can make a living from legal aid. The answer was simply by doing enough of it, not being greedy, and being reassured that if one billed promptly then the authorities made payments equally promptly, so there were none of the cashflow problems which often blight the commercial practitioner.

There were three or four solicitors who dealt with most of the crime in Leeds and its environs, and there were a considerable number of courts sitting. Some courts sat each day, as in Bradford and Wakefield, and on different days of the week in other smaller towns. The prisoners, that is those kept in custody, for cases in all of these towns were remanded to Armley Prison in Leeds, which was only 15 minutes from my office, and it stood to reason that if I had a few satisfied clients in that prison, then my name might well be passed around to other inmates. Satisfied meant several things, not least of which was giving attention to them and their cases, and in particular visiting them in prison, which for me was easily accomplished, and so my days were made up of being in court in the mornings, visiting them in prison in the early-afternoon and seeing clients in my office in the late-afternoon.

Leeds Town Hall was a blackened Victorian edifice with a dome and pillars and simulated stone lions keeping a watchful eye upon those who climbed its 23 steps to gain entry to the portals, where, in addition to the Victoria Hall and its magnificent organ, were three courts of Assize, criminal, civil and matrimonial, and eight magistrates' courts, or as they were originally known, police courts. The bridewell below housed the cells and interview rooms, known now by the more friendly title of custody suites. All the prisoners shared a common cell area, and when the door from the police counter opened to let a solicitor into the interview room to see a client who had called upon him, many faces gathered at the cell gate to see if he had come for them. It was not unusual therefore, that the client who had asked for me was asked for the name of his solicitor on his return, and when I crossed the road back to my office, I had a call from the police saying, "There's another one or two or even more, who are asking for you."

The reason this happened was simple. I always arrived early at my office, and the police knew that, and that if called, I would come over straight away, thus avoiding the scrum from 9.00 to 9.30 onwards, when other solicitors arrived at work.

There was another important aspect, which I realised early in my career. The remand court, being the one in which all prisoners initially appeared after their arrest, and at subsequent adjournment hearings before their case was actually heard, was Court No. 8. This court had a large dock with direct access from the cells below. Prisoners were brought in six or eight at a time, and when the first was called, stood to the bar. The others were seated at a slightly lower level, but could hear every word spoken in court, that is, provided one spoke in a sufficiently loud voice, and I made sure I did this. Some advocates made the mistake of mumbling, or at least addressing the court in conversational tones, but not me. I made sure the whole court could hear me, and that included the bench, but also my client, my client's relations and all the other waiting customers.

The old title of police courts was still there when I first began, and the most important man to any young or even not so young advocate was Sergeant Gibbs. He wore the now old-fashioned police uniform buttoned up to the neck, and had a voice and presence, and indeed attitude akin to the company sergeant major. He had neither the bite nor bark, nor even the gravitas of the regimental sergeant major, but he was central to one's programming because he was the caller, who called on the cases, and decided on the order in which they, and therefore you, would be called to appear in court. If he liked you, and you didn't mess about, he called you shortly after you came into court; if he didn't, you could sit there all morning awaiting a simple five-minute adjournment application. For this important favour I learned that the simple exchange of a bottle of whisky at Christmas worked wonders for the rest of the year.

Another indication of police influence, though this was still to last for many years, was the fact that a police inspector conducted the prosecution.

Happily my relationship with these officers was quite good. The main one was Chief Inspector Thomas Gallagher, and there were two or three others. They trusted me, and I trusted them; we didn't waste time, we didn't pull tricks on each other, we gave each other such information as was just and proper to ensure the cases were properly presented without anything up our respective sleeves, and the only bonding unit was measured in a perfectly open invitation to the office Christmas parties, an event to which eventually everybody came, everybody that is, except the defendants. And of course, except the magistrates, that would never have done.

My first stipendiary magistrate was Ralph Cleworth QC; a very pleasant man who most people believed had made a mistake in applying for silk. He spent more hours than he would have wished playing chess in the *Gambit Café* in Park Row, and it was a relief that he was invited to become the stipendiary magistrate. It was not uncommon in the various London metropolitan stipendiary magistrates' courts for the magistrate to be a QC, for such an appointment was deemed prestigious, enabled generous lunch breaks to be taken, and not usually a strenuous afternoon list of cases. He became a compassionate, yet firm "stipe", and I found him courteous (I extend this to all the Leeds stipendiaries, who were a pleasure to address). One evening Mr Cleworth and his wife were mugged when returning to their home and after that any violent robber received short shrift from this mild-looking man. He was followed by John Randolph, a former RAF pilot, who did not suffer fools gladly, and last by David Loy. I must be grateful to him, for I have little doubt that he would have been sounded by the Lord Chancellor as to whether I was stipe material before I was appointed a metropolitan stipendiary magistrate, in the first but cautious step on my judicial ladder in 1984.

Lay magistrates drawn from a wide spectrum of society, however, manned the majority of courts, and I spent 26-years before them. In general terms I had nothing but respect for the way they performed their duty.

It was clear that the choice was largely political. One could discern the grandees of the Tory Party, Bernard Lyons, the chairman of UDS, Major Peter Dobson, always dubbed the major, Mr Roscoe, known as the emperor, Miss Stead, the heiress to a leather fortune, and Alderman Cowling. I recall making a plea for bail, and Alderman Cowling asked, "And why exactly does your client want bail, Mr Black? "To which I responded, "To be with his siblings, his loved ones, and those who see the good in him." "Ah!" the magistrate replied. "That he will be, Mr Black, that he will be, because bail is refused."

At the other end was a collection of union representatives, with some indeterminate Liberals and the wives of some of the hospital consultants adding a touch of elegance. The wives that is, not the Liberals. The Tories would grunt and sigh, but they would listen and one could influence them with a strong plea. The Labour people were set in their ways; many had made up their minds before I opened my mouth and they were stubborn. But there was one man who would always listen and that was Arnold Ziff, a shoe and property magnate, whom I suspected from time-to-time would open his wallet and quietly send a handout to some poor wretch about whom I had given a heart-rending explanation for his misdeeds. I once stumbled into court after a ski accident, using a walking stick and bent in two. "Oh," said Ziff, "Been lifting some reporting restrictions, Mr Black?"

The police court atmosphere remained for many years in some of the courts outside Leeds. I appeared in Morley to ask for an adjournment because one of my witnesses was not available. I suggested a two-week adjournment to 3 March. "Oh," said the lady magistrate wearing the hat, who was in the chair, as she turned to ask the inspector, "Will that be all right for our witnesses?"

In my office the receptionist/secretary desk became two separate desks for a receptionist and a secretary, and then I needed to employ someone to visit the people in prison, or take statements from those on bail who came into the office, and whose problems I had initially diagnosed.

Towards the end of the first year I was approached by a Bradford firm called Walker Morris & Coles, who wanted to represent themselves in Leeds. They were a commercial firm with builder clients, which led to a considerable amount of property conveyancing in the Leeds area. At this time I needed more space, and they had in mind a large suite in a modern block in Park Row. They were prepared to give me a partnership in their Bradford practice, which would have a branch in Leeds where I would have my criminal department. Thus I would be a partner in a large firm yet still doing my own thing and in more comfortable surroundings and with greater secretarial support. The partners were convivial souls, and so it was done. That partnership lasted some ten years, during which both their commercial practice and my personal practice grew, and it was while I was with them, in 1962, that Diana and I got married.

I lived in Leeds, and Diana lived in Harrogate. When we got married we compromised, and lived in Harrogate. We had met in Leeds, both serving on a small charity committee. Diana was working in Leeds as PA to a well-known political figure and we lunched in the *Cubana*, a gastro coffee bar in Park Square. It was called "gastro" after some of the discomforts many of its customers suffered. Diana attracted me because she has a lovely deep voice, and a great sense of humour, by which I mean she laughed at all my jokes. On a Saturday evening we would go over to York to the Society Club, going haywire over a bottle of Mateus Rosé. I hated the wine, but my mother loved the table lamps. Her elder brother Michael accompanied us. Diana also had an elder sister, Sasha, married to Derek, described to me as a geriatric consultant, and he certainly seemed to know the tricks of his trade because at the time of writing he is 93 and still playing tennis twice a week.

After our marriage, which was a great opportunity for me to meet her mother, who somehow or other managed to hide whenever I visited Diana's home during our courtship, we lived for six months in a small wooden house belonging to a client in Linton. This was the winter of 1962, the coldest on record. Getting married during the previous summer was the best thing I could have done because in Linton our water pipes were frozen solid and in any event you couldn't buy a hot water bottle for love nor money.

Diana has been a great support to me in my career, though she was appointed to the bench long before I was, and at a much younger age. At the age of 32 she was appointed a magistrate on the Harrogate bench, and when some 18-years later I was appointed a metropolitan stipendiary magistrate she said, "Right, what do you want to know about the job?" She was soon appointed a chairman of the bench, and when we eventually moved to London did not have difficulty in transferring to the extremely prestigious City of London bench, retiring in 2009 after 38-years' service, and enjoying a retirement dinner given by the lord mayor at the Mansion House.

She doubled this with an astonishing career as a tour guide, astonishing because it started when she, the granddaughter of a line of rabbis whose lineage could be traced back to the 15th-century, began this work at York Minster. As a Harrogate justice, she had sat on appeals in the Crown Court in York, which is in the ancient castle. Sitting on the bench in No. 2 court, looking directly out of the window the first thing she saw was Clifford's Mount, where in 1190 following an anti-Semitic outburst, 150 Jews perished. This encouraged her interest to know more about York, hence the Minster job, and thereafter a full-blown qualified Yorkshire tour guide. When we moved to London, she became a London tour guide, specialising in gardens, legal London and Jewish London. She juggled this with the bench, pandering to my wishes, four children, Harriette, Matthew, Jonathan and Anna, eventually ten grandchildren, two Labradors, a border terrier and a cross-border collie.

Diana receiving her scroll from the Lord Mayor of London after 38 years as a JP

CHAPTER 11

This Crime is Just Not Cricket

This case happily did not involve the ultimate crime of murder, but it nevertheless attracted a considerable amount of publicity.

There could only be one thing which would arouse the curiosity and ire of the British public to a degree which would equate with murder, and that was the interruption of a game of cricket, particularly when the interruption came at a crucial point on the last day of a test match.

In March 1974 an armed payroll robbery took place at the offices of the London Electricity Board. In the course of that robbery a police constable was shot and injured. The police had received information that this was going to happen, and George Davis and his associates had become targets and had been shadowed by the police for some time. On the anticipated date of the robbery a number of undercover officers were deployed, both with cameras and also those in a position to give eyewitness evidence of the happening. There was also some anticipation of those who would be involved. In fact there was so much information that the detection, depending upon identification evidence, became convoluted and the roles of the participants confused. The arrests depended on two things, the identification evidence and blood samples found in the area, but there was a problem. Davis had been identified by no fewer than five police officers, but his blood did not match with that found at the scene. Nor did it match any of the bloods of his three co-accused.

There had been complaints of a suppression of evidence and an abuse of process. But despite all the protestations in 1976 Davis was convicted and sentenced to 20-years' imprisonment, for robbery and wounding with intent to resist arrest. His friends and family and particularly his wife Rose began an intense campaign over what they considered to be a miscarriage of justice. All over the walls and bridges of the East End of London and beyond there appeared the words, "George Davis is innocent OK." One of Davis's loyal friends, Peter Chappell, was firmly convinced that he had seen him elsewhere at the time of the crime, and was sure that Davis was convicted purely because of his associates. Chappell drove his lorry up the steps and into the front doors of half the country's national newspapers; other supporters chained themselves across Fleet Street. He emphasised his point by driving his vehicle at the gates of Buckingham Palace. There was a march on Downing Street, and the main London river bridges had the slogan "George Davis is Innocent" painted on them. The campaigners fused the lights on the Trafalgar Square Christmas tree and the infamous slogan replaced the fairy at the top; they threw bricks at the window of the Serious Crimes Office.

Then one year almost to the day after Davis's conviction the Court of Appeal cleared the other three, but the appeal of Davis was rejected, although his sentence was reduced to 17-years.

There were calls to change the law where a conviction could take place based upon one act of identification, and a commission to this point was established, chaired by Lord Devlin. This was a time when the police were disclosed as being bribable, and over 300 officers were dismissed.

Despite all these protestations, the only national incident was the climbing of Big Ben. Otherwise it was a local matter, engaging the interest of the East End. Something was needed to make it a national issue. What was there that national interest could be diverted from in August 1975 when all interest was devoted to the last day of the test match at Headingly, When all eyes would be on that very test pitch? And so it was that as the fans arrived at Headingly in Leeds expecting a thrilling finish to the third day of the Ashes, what met their eyes was a strange message daubed on the walls in whitewash: "Sorry it had to be done, but free George Davis."

For those who attended and hoped to see England demolish the last few batsmen, within minutes the name George Davis was to become the name on everybody's lips. Chunks of earth had been dug from the pitch, and oil spread across it. The match was abandoned, and England, who had hoped to win, were devastated. Tony Gregg, the captain, said, "This pitch has been played on for 100-years, it's not funny." The title of the leader in *The Times* simply said: "Anarchy". The *Daily Telegraph* said: "Any support for George

Davis has been offset by this act."

Within a short space of time the perpetrators were caught, and were charged with conspiracy to cause criminal damage. Their London solicitors were soon on the phone to me to represent them. This was one of the few cases where the perpetrators were insistent on pleading guilty from the outset. Coachloads came to support them at every stage of their trial at the Leeds Quarter Sessions, and in 1976 the main culprit, Peter Chappell, received 18 months, to the unanimous approval of the Yorkshire cricket loving public. It was ironic that two days after this sentence was imposed, the home secretary Roy Jenkins, who had initiated an inquiry about Davis, concluded that he may well have not been present at the crime and persuaded the Queen to exercise her prerogative of mercy, and he was released. And Peter Chappell remained in custody.

But that was not the only irony. Shortly after he was released George Davis was caught red-handed doing the Cyprus Bank in North London.

The graffiti inscriptions "George Davis is innocent", still there for all to see on the walls of the East End, was soon amended to read "George Davis is in a cell" or "George Davis is in again". He received 15-years for this robbery, reduced to eleven on appeal, which he served. There is a poignant end to the story. In May 2011, the Court of Appeal declared the 1976 conviction unsafe.

Chapter 12

Murder Most Foul

There are those who believe that the moment of true drama in any murder inquiry does not come until the end of the trial, when with baited breath the entire court awaits the delivery of either one or two short words, "guilty" or "not guilty". Of course there has been an element of drama in the searching questions put by counsel, which may result in the telling admission or equally telling hesitation by a quivering witness, made evident, one hopes, to the jury, the press hanging on to every word and the judge who has heard it all before, a smile trying to break out on to his face, but giving way to merely a raised eyebrow, as in quiet satisfaction he notes that the defendant has assisted him by tying his own noose around his neck.

The detective will differ; for him the most dramatic part is when, after lengthy interviews the very first crack reveals itself in the version given by the defendant, that first inconsistency, that first look of fear which creeps into guilt-ridden eyes.

For my part the drama began with the phone call. I never knew when it would come, where it would come from or whether it would come at all. But when it did come it brought a fresh flow of adrenalin. It meant I would soon be dealing with a life-changing situation for somebody, a drama which could change his or her life permanently. If it did not affect them, then it would affect their loved ones, and it most certainly must have already affected someone else. I had to be permanently available, and time was always a factor. There was no time in the mind of someone in police custody; they needed help and advice straight away. This was before the days of the duty solicitor, the lawyer kept in the cupboard of every police station in the land.

The Police and Criminal Evidence Act which gives an accused person the right to see a solicitor had yet to be introduced, although there had been a halfway house to that act, which gave a person arrested the right to have a phone call made to a solicitor or friend (the two were not necessarily synonymous) informing that person that the accused was safely tucked up in a cell.

When that call came, and it did with frequency, and not always during sociable hours, it meant one of two things, either, and this was the more frequent one, a relative or friend was alarmed, as their loved one had just been taken away and they felt he needed protection. They wanted to know where he (occasionally she) was, what he was in for and when he would be released. The police were not always happy to give this information, and a straight reply was often difficult to obtain. The difficulty manifested itself in various ways, either a straight "Don't know" from the police, or a fencing match with them while they endeavoured to find out who was so concerned about the welfare of the arrested party.

Clearly the police wished to distinguish between the genuine worry and concern of the next of kin and the worry born of the self-preservation of a potential co-accused, or even the anxiety of a family member concerned, not to put too fine a point upon it, to hide the loot.

Or there were other phone calls which did not come from relatives or friends. These were the calls which I preferred; they were more straightforward, more specific and more likely to mean that I would be on the case. They would come from a senior detective, because it was usually a senior detective who was in charge of a murder investigation. They were often officers known to me since they had been junior officers, and there was always a glow of pride in their voice as they told me their news. The words were usually, "Good evening Mr Black." I always insisted on that degree of formality, both from them and to them, as I did with clients, though I knew that some solicitors lapsed into first-name terms to and from both policemen and prisoners. "We've someone who's been asking for you… he has just been charged with murder," There was pride in their voice because the implication was that they had solved the crime. There was not much more to be done. Perhaps a few forensic details, the taking of the procedural statements, but the hard work had been done. They had their man, they could go home and sleep, or perhaps down to the pub for a few drinks. Their work was finished, but mine was just beginning.

CHAPTER 13

Donald Neilson, Known as "The Black Panther"

My Jensen Interceptor at Oxford Crown Court during Neilson's trial—not an explosion, just boiling over

Donald Neilson, referred to by the police, press and almost everybody else as "The Black Panther," was no ordinary client. Quite apart from the chilling and bloodcurdling nature of the accusations against him he stood out in one other respect from the run-of-the-mill client who sought my services as a defence solicitor to deal with the unwelcome attentions of the police. Perhaps run-of-the-mill is an ill choice of words and I will correct myself, because no two cases were ever alike. There is always the exception, and Donald Neilson was certainly different in one particularly noticeable way. Whenever I came into the room or cell in which he was lodged, he would immediately jump up, stand at attention with his arms straight down, extended thumb pointing down his trouser seams. He and I had one thing in common: for him National Service had been the highlight of his life, and for me, one of the highlights. Donald Neilson was a man made for uniform, for discipline, for preparation, even if necessary for killing. He had served in Kenya, Cyprus and Aden and seeing Neilson standing there at attention brought back memories of that time when a single pip on my shoulder generated authority.

Neilson was not to know of this, but it was one of the aspects of his calculating preparation that brought me to his cell on that dark December day in 1975. It had been late-afternoon, that part of the day when my desk would be somewhat untidy, not unreasonably so, just strewn with files bound with red tape, out of which the paperwork spilled. Each file represented a case to be heard the following day in different courts of varying degrees of seriousness, which had reached different stages. Some involved a first appearance at which a bail application might need to be made, relatives seen and either legal aid sought or financial arrangements negotiated. Some were at that midway stage about to be transferred to a higher court for which I had to appoint the appropriate barrister.

I would also be checking when those in custody had last been seen so that I might if necessary arrange a visit to the cells before they appeared in the dock. I made sure that reports from the probation service had been received and digested, that witnesses had been warned and had confirmed their attendance, and reminded myself of the essential parts of each case. This was not entirely a last-minute exercise, because I employed two retired police officers who generally visited those in custody on remand, and clerks and trainees had already been through the papers in each case, bringing them up to date before they arrived on my desk. There would still be those who were arrested overnight to add to my list, which might easily amount to about 30 cases each day.

I stopped for a cup of tea, and at this moment my phone rang. "There's a reporter on the phone for you, I think he said from the *Daily Mirror*." This was rather unusual, not that a reporter was calling, but that it was someone from the *Mirror*. I knew the legal correspondent of *The Times*, and the various court reporters from the *Yorkshire Post* would often call for clarification of something said that morning. The BBC and in particular the local Yorkshire TV station often called me in for a studio appearance on some legal topic of the day, but the *Daily Mirror* was not one of my regulars. Could they still be interested in the Headingly test match wicket case which I had recently completed? I took the call.

"Someone in the Midlands has been asking for you." I didn't know what he meant initially. I should confess that whenever a murder took place in the Leeds or West Yorkshire region I ensured that the phone at home was used to a minimum, and that calls were kept short, just in case, as frequently happened, a police station or distraught relative of someone recently arrested was seeking my service, as they often did. But the Midlands? It took a mini-moment to sink in. Maybe if he had said "Dudley" I would have realised immediately. The morning news bulletins had been full of the arrest of undoubtedly the most wanted man in the country. The caller had been in that court in Dudley, a small town in the Midlands where the man for whom four police forces had been searching for weeks, Donald Neilson, the Black Panther, charged with the kidnap and murder of Leslie Whittle, and who was also to be charged with four further murders and an attempted murder of a security guard, a court which had in fact only been sitting for a few minutes before the man in the dock had asked for me.

With not inconsiderable alacrity the journalist had dashed out of court, found a phone and found my number.

"Yes, he has asked for you to defend him … please remember I was the one who told you and maybe we can talk again."

"Of course we can talk, but what I may be allowed to say is another thing," I replied.

He laughed, rang off and the phone rang again. This time it was the clerk to the justices, and sure enough when Neilson had appeared in the dock, the first thing he said was that he wanted me to represent him, and could he have legal aid for that purpose.

Anyone who is charged with a serious crime is entitled to legal aid, and on such a serious charge without the need for form filling, but by direct application to the bench, and although a request for the lawyer of one's choice is not always automatically available, in this case it was clear that no obstruction would be put in the way.

I soon learned that I was not just a name chosen from a list of those willing to take legal aid cases, though I was indeed on that list, and legal aid formed a formidable proportion of the cases which I did.

But Donald Neilson did not choose my name from any list. I was later to discover that his home, although his crimes were committed over a wide span of the Midlands and North of England, was a humble terrace house in Bradford, and there were some quite interesting things in his attic. Apart from an armoury of weapons, a selection of disguise materials, maps and outdoor living equipment, he had a file of newspaper cuttings, which contained a number of press cuttings of cases in which I had appeared over the 17-years I had already been in practice as a defence solicitor prior to his arrest in 1975. In short, he had earmarked me in advance as being his lawyer of choice should he be arrested. This in itself was a strange thing, because most criminals do not think they will be arrested, they convince themselves that they are committing the perfect crime. There was also to be revealed one other strange coincidence, in that one of the sub-post offices which he robbed and where he murdered the postmaster was only about a mile from the house in which I lived at the time in Harrogate.

It was as well that I had earlier made sure that all my files for the following day were in order, for they were distributed to my partners and assistants and counsel hastily briefed for some of them, as I drove the old car across country to meet my newest client. There was a problem straightaway. The police said that because of his violent disposition I could not be in a room with him and no-one else. There would have to be at the very least three burly officers to protect me. I responded that there was no way I could agree to this. I was entitled, as was he, for our meeting to be completely private and confidential. It took quite some time and several phone calls for this to be resolved, but I did succeed at last. It came back to mind some 15-years later when I saw *The Silence of the Lambs*. But Donald, at least to me, was nowhere near as menacing as Hannibal Lector.

When I walked into the room to see him, he immediately stood up to attention, and addressed me as "Sir" as he did throughout our subsequent relationship; he behaved thus whenever either counsel or I came into the room or spoke to him. The discipline of army life was deeply ingrained into Donald Neilson. I was a little taken aback, because those whom I had recently represented were not easily disposed to follow such basic niceties.

In fact the last time this happened was when I had defended men at Courts Martial during army service. He presented a slim, woebegone figure, dressed in the white paper overall given to a prisoner whose clothes had been taken away for forensic examination. His eyes were blackened, there were bruises all around his face, but he made no mention of them. He accepted that he had been arrested and that there had been some violence used in the course of his arrest. He was slight and hesitant until it seemed I had gained his confidence.

When one meets a client for the first time, particularly one charged with murder, it is vital to gain their confidence and hear their story before time has facilitated thought and embellishment.

Let me deal at an early-stage with the hoary old questions which have been put to me time-and-time again: "How can you defend somebody whom you know quite well has killed?" "How can you start to persuade a court that such a man is not guilty of a heinous offence of which there is abundant evidence?"

The simple answer is that when you act for people in that position you are not there to decide for yourself, that is the task of a jury, and yours is to advise the jury about the law and the evidence, and assess how it can be tested. The prosecution will need to prove the case to a jury so that a jury is satisfied. Indeed I would go so far as to say they would in most cases prefer to prove it piece-by-piece before a jury so that each individual item of evidence is weighed and tested. The defendant is entitled to have the evidence so analysed and questioned to the utmost extent which the law of the time demands.

For instance, there had recently been a reinterpretation in the law, not a statutory change, but one arising from case law, and it is the precedent of case law which determines decisions, as they interpret the statutes. The case of *R v Hyam* necessitated a fresh approach to a charge of murder, namely that if a defendant knew that what he or she was doing would probably result in grievous bodily harm even though he or she had not intended it, they would be guilty. The prosecution had to show, therefore, that Neilson exposed the girl to the risk of grievous bodily harm and that his act was deliberate and unlawful. Neilson was insistent throughout that he did not intend that she should be hung, and that he had taken every sort of precaution to avoid that. Uncomfortable, yes. Kidnapping, yes, demands for money, yes. But he emphasised time-and-time again that harming the girl was not part of his agenda. Although she was in a vulnerable situation, held below the ground, tethered by a chain to a ladder, with very little room to move, he had nevertheless made sure that the chain around her neck was padded and that it wouldn't hurt her. He also insisted that having her injured or dead would not help the exercise, the objective of which was to obtain money.

He had studied in great depth and details a case which had involved two brothers who had endeavoured to kidnap the wife of a newspaper magnate, and had demanded a large sum of money. The lady was never seen again, and it was believed that animals had devoured her. Neilson had contempt for these two men. He said they did not plan it correctly; they did not do it properly. And here we come to the nub of everything he did. Everything was planned in the minutest detail. In his flat, his lair as the police, in Bradford, called it all the plans, maps and paraphernalia of someone who works in great detail on what he hoped to accomplish were found.

The farms and post office which he would visit would be observed with care, and he would know everything that went on there. He would pay several visits, ticking off in his mind whether they had dogs, whether there was a gate which clanged, his route there, and always, to allay the possibility of recognition, the different route which he took back. He would splash along streams in order to avoid being detected and followed by dogs and to stop them picking up his scent. It was the remarkable planning throughout which set this man apart from others.

As a client Donald Neilson was exemplary. He told me his version of what happened, and what he thought of the prosecution evidence. He had answers, some perhaps beyond the normal stretch of credibility, but nevertheless they were answers the context of which could properly be put to witnesses. He had an opinion on each of the prosecution witnesses, and why they had said or done certain things. He was open to me in the full history of his childhood, his background, his work record and best of all his army life. To everything he had an answer. The only offences to which he was prepared to plead guilty were the offences of kidnap and demanding money with menaces, namely a ransom, but he said actual killing had not been part of his plans.

There was a massive amount of evidence against him, and for the first trial at Oxford Crown Court for the kidnap and murder of Leslie Whittle, the jury were only out for an hour-and-a-half, and they convicted him. His repeated evidence that he did not intend to harm her, let alone kill her, fell on stony ground.

There had been a considerable amount of publicity about the case. It had been on the front pages for two full weeks and it was followed by the second trial. The case had been transferred from the Midlands down to Oxford Crown Court because of fears of local prejudice in the area where the kidnapped girl had lived, but even in Oxford one could not expect to choose a jury who had never heard of Donald Neilson, nor for that matter could one expect to find such people in any of the four corners of the land. Such is the genuine independence and common-sense of an English jury, however, that despite the flood of publicity to which they must have been subjected they nevertheless listened with care, and took their time over deliberating upon the various counts on the second indictment, and after a retirement which lasted over six hours they found him not guilty on certain of those counts, but guilty on others. The lawyers, both for the Crown and defence, admired the jury for their reasoning and their conclusions.

The two hearings at Oxford lasted six weeks in the oppressively hot summer of 1976, and Oxford Crown Court was not air-conditioned. We started on normal court hours, that is from 10.30 am till 4.45 pm, but it was so hot that we had to break every half hour. Gradually we altered our day so that we were sitting at 9 am and finishing at 2.30 pm without a break for lunch.

The case called for much work and research, both in books and in practice. Counsel and I visited the site of the murder; we climbed down and through the labyrinth of water pipes and ducts below the park. Indeed, we did all that we could and that I believe was expected of us in the circumstances. At a tribute dinner at the banqueting rooms in Whitehall some years later for Gilbert Gray QC, the barrister whom I had instructed, his speech to the jury at Oxford Crown Court was described as one of the greatest jury speeches in English criminal history.

Mr Justice Mars-Jones conducted the trial, in an exemplary manner; he was fairness personified, and the one matter with which we had cause for concern in his summing-up and which formed the basis of the appeal, was rejected by the Court of Appeal. The judge's marshal was a young man, smartly attired, as was the custom at the time in stiff collar, black jacket and striped trousers. His job was to carry the judge's papers and books, place them on the desk and generally act as a go-fer. He performed his tasks efficiently, for he was Adam Mars-Jones, the son of the judge and a graduate of Trinity Hall, Cambridge.

Neilson could not have been described as being frightened of the police being called in. He knew it was inevitable that they would come at some time and for that reason he planned various forms of escape. In fact he had the utmost contempt for the way in which the police mishandled the whole episode. He believed that people would follow his instructions. He did not think that the police would become involved at that stage because he thought they would care about the safety of the girl. He thought that they would allow her brother to do what he had asked him to do, and that if there were to be a chase it would be at a later stage. He had plans ready to put into operation. He had different routes. There was not just the one entry and exit from the Bathpool Park system, there were many of them, and he knew about them and he knew how he would travel. However, when the police suddenly converged upon him in various police cars, the fact that they did not know about the involvement of other police cars from other forces made for total confusion, which also affected him and caused him to go down the iron-runged ladder at such a pace and with the tragic conclusion.

It is difficult to know what the jury made of this; the implication drawn by the prosecution was that she was so frightened by his appearance that she jumped off the ledge by the ladder, seeing the urgency, fear and horror on his face. Neilson did not believe she jumped off the ledge, he believed it was a ghastly accident, that she fell off the ledge the wrong way, so that the chain was stretched to a maximum; had it been the other way, and the chain not so stretched, her feet would have landed on the ground, not affecting the noose around her neck.

The question of whether he really believed or considered that she might be caused harm was something that the jury had to consider. This was his case as put to his defence team. It may seem strange that a man who was meticulous in his planning could say that if anything goes wrong it isn't his fault, but what should be borne in mind is that when a man commits a crime it is with the overreaching belief that he will not be caught. Most people commit a crime in anticipation that they have the solution; they will get away with it, otherwise what would be the point of following it through? On the other hand, there are those who are careful in their assessment of every possible situation. It may be that Neilson had his precise defence planned, but this was very unlikely, as he could hardly have anticipated the exact manner in which things went wrong, and how he would be arrested. It may well be said he had killed already on three occasions, and on a further occasion he had injured somebody so badly that they died. Did he think he had nothing further to lose?

The jury found that he had murdered Leslie Whittle. Their decision was to no small extent brought about by the brilliant conduct of the prosecution case by Philip Cox QC, DSC. He was the newly-appointed leader of the Midland and Oxford Circuit, and so was the first choice to lead the prosecution. A distinguished lawyer, he had at the age of 21 been awarded the Distinguished Service Cross. The secret of this achievement was not known to many at the time of the Neilson case, for Cox was a man of considerable modesty, which was only discovered recently when the importance of his bravery caused those at the Imperial War Museum to urge him to speak about it. His bravery was summarised in his obituary in *The Times* late in December 2014, when it was revealed that after an outstanding period of scholarship at Cambridge he was groomed to be one of the first naval radar operators of the war. In 1943 he was rowed between the destroyer *Escapade* and the corvette *Narcissus* in raging Atlantic seas to repair vital damaged equipment. He climbed a slippery ladder, dismantled the radar, unwound the tape of the valve to remedy the fault and then reassembled the machine so that it could continue its work of detecting U-boats. He might well have remained a scientist, but was so horrified by the destruction of the war that he turned away from science and began study for the Bar.

His tactics revealed the very best in the traditions of British forensic skills. He acted with courtesy throughout, never bullying—and there is a fine distinction between bullying and being persistent. This was before Jeremy Paxman's famous interview of Lord Howard, when he asked the same question 12 times; however, 22-years before, Philip Cox QC asked the same question 13 times. It related to a vital matter of identification. Neilson had been called the Black Panther because he always wore a black balaclava while committing crime. He had insisted that all the time he was in the presence of his victim he had worn the balaclava, and there was therefore little point in the prosecution's suggestion that he killed the girl because he feared that having been recognised by her he might consequently be identified. After these 13 questions on this very point, Neilson fell into the trap set skilfully by Cox and said she had "fallen accidentally after seeing the look on my face." How could this be so, if he was wearing a balaclava? If she had seen the look on his face, then she might have been able to identify him. And thus did Neilson contradict himself on whether he had a motive for killing the girl.

What actually happened underground is something that we only have his version for, because he was the only one who survived. And I can only relay that which is public knowledge, that which he said in court, for to do otherwise would breach the relationship between solicitor and client relationship which exists even after his death. He felt that tethering her round the neck would cause her least harm. To tether her, say round her wrist, would enable her to bite herself free and cause herself harm in her anxiety to escape. At the trial he said he tried to give her comfort, and one might realistically ask what comfort could there be 60 feet below the ground in a dank and dark environment, although the area was not as small as one would imagine.

His version was that he provided her with a mattress, food and hot soup as and when she needed it. He maintained that if he was not going to allow her to survive why would he have taken all that trouble. The prosecution countered that he wanted to keep her alive for the time being so that if it was necessary to send back messages via a tape-recording she was there to do it, and that would provide evidence for those who were to bring him the money.

The presence of the police and the helicopter noise overhead made him realise it was all over, and he believed that the police now knew where she was and they were going to save her. He presumed that they were going to pull her out, and his intention was just to get away as fast as he could.

He believed everybody was clever, but no-one as clever, cautious and capable of pre-planning things as he was. He had little respect for the police, because he had managed to escape their clutches on so many occasions previously.

Kidnap was a rare offence at the time, so the police were dealing with a situation to which they were not accustomed. Moreover they were not assisted by the numerous cock-ups which occurred on the ransom trail. The media knew about so much, and journalists were at the telephone boxes at the Swan Shopping Centre, particulars had been given on the radio and television about the trail, a phone call was made to a telephone box by Neilson, as he said he would, yet the surveillance on the phone box had been called-off two hours earlier. At least one of the officers had messed things up, and Ronald Whittle, Leslie's brother, had not been able to find the tape in the phone box. This was a setback for Neilson, who thought his instructions would be followed implicitly, and he made no allowances for such human cock-ups. After all he was a meticulous person on detail, he always had been, and he believed others would follow his details. I have pointed out that he was a strict disciplinarian, and that was something which he expected of others, he just took it for granted that they would follow all his instructions.

One asks whether he took into account human frailties, the police calling-off the search, the interference by the media and people not picking-up messages when they should have done. My belief is that these were not factors which Neilson would have taken into account. He thought the money would be handed over and he would be on his way back to his lair in Bradford.

This is an "if only case" if ever there was one, if only his instructions had been properly followed over those crucial hours and days. He persisted in saying throughout his trial, if only they had done as he had said, then Leslie Whittle would still be alive. How much the surrounding circumstances showed that this would be in any way credible was a matter upon which the jury reflected.

He told the court of seeing in the *Daily Express* an item about the dispute over a will relating to a member of Leslie Whittle's family. His plan therefore was to go for any member of that family, kidnap anybody. They were clearly a close-knit family, and if one of them were kidnapped, the others would rally to pay the release money. It was entirely an accident of fortune that caused him to take Leslie. It could have been the mother or the brother, he said in court.

One might ask why he turned to crime in the first place. He felt the time had come to make a quick buck, following his catalogue of failure over the years. He had been a taxi driver, he had manufactured garden furniture and so on, but each of the succession of four or five different enterprises failed, so he resorted to crime. It should be remembered that before the crimes which resulted in the deaths of others, over a period of two years and without anyone coming to any physical harm, Neilson had perpetrated around 400 burglaries, in most of which using the same method of operation, that is, a brace-and-bit to open doors and windows. One cannot tell why he turned to using weapons. We just do not know, and never will, if he carried weapons with him on those numerous burglaries.

He never accepted the fact that he was a coward. He was a man who was never going to be caught and he never accepted the theory put to him that he was the sort of man who would shoot first and ask questions later. We know he went out dressed in black, hooded, with a sawn-off shot-gun with two live cartridges down the barrel, a bandolier, a handgun, knives and a garotte, but his evidence was that he dressed and carried items in this fashion because of his one fear, namely dogs. The gun, the knife and the garrotte were in case vicious guard dogs attacked him, and this was the answer he gave in court.

One must also look back at his army career. His army service was the happiest in his life. He was serving in Kenya at the time of the Mau Mau uprising, as well as other places. He used to embark on military exercises with his wife and daughter, dressed in combat uniform, in an ex-army jeep which he had acquired. He kept a hoard of photographs showing the family on these expeditions, with the others also dressed in military fashion. The army stayed in his blood, the method of dress, the use of camouflage, the bravado, but at the same time was rather sorry for himself because his various enterprises had not met with success. If any of them had succeeded and had earned him a living and provided him with a means of supporting his wife and child, would he have been satisfied? And more important, would he have avoided the necessity, as he felt it, to turn to a life of crime.

To what extent can one lay responsibility for his defects in personality, his anxiety, and his lack of self-esteem, at the fact that he started life with the unusual name of Nappy. The extent of all the barbs at school and among other childhood friends must have seemed never-ending. He was a man with some intelligence, and one can only surmise what might have happened had that been directed in a more proper way,

My only insight into the circumstances in which Neilson lived in Bradford during the period prior to his arrest and presumably during those years when he was engaged in criminal activities relied upon the photographs provided as evidence in court, and also whatever information had been gleaned by the press.

It was a perfectly ordinary terrace house, the kind that could be seen in many parts of the country, particularly in the northern counties. The house seemed well kept and tidy — after all he was a handyman — with nothing spectacular or ostentatious. But there in the loft was an amazing collection of knives, guns, maps, clothing and camping gear used in the course of his travels and engagements.

I gleaned little about his family life. The prosecution presented the background of military family activities, the dressing-up in combat uniforms, the use of the jeep, the camping equipment kept in it. There were no secrets about his inclinations in this direction and it seemed from the photographs that his wife and daughter fully cooperated and engaged in these activities. Initially his wife was extremely supportive and protective of him, at least as far as she could be. He was sensible enough to keep her away from what was happening to him after his arrest. Quite clearly there was an enormous interest in her and other members of the family. There was an insatiable curiosity among the press and the public about whether she knew what was going on, and how could she possibly not have had some idea, particularly with his comings and goings. Did she not put two-and-two together in the timings of his absences and the killings which were taking place around the country? Yet there was not a scintilla of evidence to suggest that she had the slightest idea of his involvement. However, there were of course those who persisted in believing that she must have known what was going on. No proceedings were brought to tie her in with the prime activities of her husband, though at the conclusion of his case there were charges against her relating to the disposal of postal orders, the proceedings of his burglaries, and she did accept her guilt in that respect. A defence of duress was considered, but that was deemed unsustainable.

According to the court evidence Neilson told his wife he had various jobs to do, that he needed to work away from home, and I don't for one moment suspect that he went home dressed in the black hood which was part of his working gear, which no doubt would have provoked curiosity.

What was curious was that here was an insignificant, little in the sense of stature, man, a failure in life, who found solace in his two years' National Service, but who became notorious, Britain's most wanted man, a ruthless killer.

I can only sum up my opinion of Donald Neilson the person, so far as what he did and what he is, by accepting the decision of the jury and the judge in imposing the sentence which he considered appropriate, and I can understand their attitude and approach. However at the time my task was to act as his solicitor. My task was not to evaluate him as a man; it was to evaluate the evidence, which was presented against him, to provide him with advice on the law and how the evidence could be tested, and it was not my task and never would be to have any opinion about the individual. From the individual we endeavour to keep somewhat detached.

But one has an opinion of anyone convicted by a jury of serious matters, just as one has regard for the victim. Neilson was a calculating individual who did not calculate that he would be caught. He was caught and at the time we did what we could on his behalf, and he spent many years in prison, as was the intention of the judge. Whenever one is presented with an uphill struggle one would be failing in one's duty if one did not point out the difficulties and problems. People ask was it a lost cause? I say that is for the jury to say, and they did talk for an hour-and-a-half on the first trial, for six-and-a-half hours at the end of the second trial, and by their verdict signified that they could not be sure about three of the charges. This was the English jury at its best.

The sentence was deferred till the conclusion of the postmaster trials, which lasted 12 days. This second trial involved the shooting of four sub-postmasters and a security guard. The jury completed their deliberations, returned to court and announced verdicts of guilty of the murder of three postmasters, but not guilty of the attempted murder of a fourth and of a police officer. There was one further shooting, with which the Crown elected not to proceed.

On 21 July, which was just short of Neilson's 40th birthday, he was sentenced to five life sentences, four sentences of ten years and one of 21 -years, Mr Justice Mars-Jones specifying that "Life shall mean life."

As is customary we went down the stairs of the dock to see our client. Neilson had the same disciplined look he had worn throughout. After his conviction he thanked us for our efforts on his behalf. We did put in an appeal, but when someone is sentenced on the basis that "Life shall mean life, and you shall not be released other than through infirmity or old age," there is nothing to lose by putting in an appeal. Gilbert Gray shook his hand, saying, "Ah well, Donald, remember life begins at forty," and for the first time, a smile came to Neilson's face.

Neilson just got on with his sentence. He was of course concerned about his wife and daughter, particularly his wife who was dealt with by the court on charges involving the disposal of some of the documents obtained from the post offices, but he was adamant that she knew absolutely nothing of his major wrong-doing.

Life did indeed mean exactly that, for Neilson died in prison 36-years later in 2011.

CHAPTER 14

The Heart Valve, the Tie Round the Neck and Alban Beresford Elcock

It was just before the committal of Donald Neilson, one Thursday afternoon in March 1976. I was wading through the afternoon list of appointments when my receptionist rang through to say that there were two somewhat distraught women who wanted to see me urgently. It seemed that the police had taken in the husband of one of them as he left the night shift at work that morning, and was being interviewed about a murder. If they are distraught they will need tea, if they are extremely distraught I will need tea, so I asked for them to be shown in together with three cups of that universal calming brew.

Margaret Elcock had to be helped in by her sister. I discover later that her name was not truly Elcock, but she had assumed the surname of Alban Beresford Elcock with whom she had lived until that morning, and was to live with again, for I managed to secure him bail after he had been charged with the murder in question, and whom indeed she would marry later. This was but the first step in a trial that was to be heard at the Leeds Assizes some nine months later and the circumstances of which remained an enigma throughout my career.

The trial had an all-star cast. Prosecuting for the DPP was Peter Taylor QC, leader of the North-eastern Circuit, who had played rugby for his county, and who could have reached the same pinnacle of success as a concert pianist as he did in the law, for he was to become the Lord Chief Justice. He led Geoffrey Rivlin, later to become a silk, then a senior circuit judge and while sitting as resident judge at Southwark, the Recorder of Westminster.

For the defence, I instructed Gilbert Gray QC, as I did in many of my murder cases, and who had become and was to continue for many years as one of the best-known and best loved criminal silks in the country, and one of the most sought-out after-dinner speakers. He never became a full-time judge because he loved being an advocate so much, although he sat frequently as a recorder, that is a part-time judge, at the Old Bailey, and he died still in harness at the age of 84. Gilbert was great with a jury; he would enthral them with his gift of language and wry humour. But at one thing he did not shine, and that was preparation, and I would never brief him on a complicated fraud that required hours of studying mountains of documents. His style was to march into the cell half-an-hour before the trial was due to start, throw the brief on the table and say to the client, "Now then Joe, you just tell me about this case from your point of view, and how you see it. Let's pretend that for the moment I know nothing about it." There was no pretence, he probably didn't, but would pick it up from then onwards as though he'd lived with it for weeks.

In the trial, Gilbert led Norman Jones, also a regular counsel whom I instructed, a truly safe pair of hands with a delightful Devonshire burr to his voice, and who would become silk, judge and eventually the Recorder of Leeds. The judge was Mr Justice Boreham.

Alban Beresford Elcock, who had come to grey, industrial Leeds from a sunny Caribbean island, had been arrested a few hours earlier as he left the firm Doncaster's Monk Bridge Forge, where he had been employed for some time as a trimmer. I telephoned Millgarth Police Station, the main one in Leeds, and there spoke to Chief Superintendent Dennis Hoban. Hoban was a policeman of the old school. His rise up the promotion ladder had been rapid, and it seemed as though he had been a senior officer forever. He was the head of Leeds CID, and together with his assistant, Jim Hobson, who later succeeded him, formed the team of Hoban and Hobson who solved every murder committed in Leeds for almost a decade. He died suddenly at the pinnacle of his career and to the deep sorrow of friend and foe alike. His funeral was attended by almost as many old lags as fellow police officers.

I say "solved", meaning that the prime suspect was at least put before a jury, and the rest was up to them. Hoban was thorough, painstaking and never ruffled. To his men, he was their ideal and if a crook had his collar felt by Hoban it was fair deal that followed. There were hardly any allegations of defendants ever having been "verballed" by him, that is the inclusion of verbal admissions purporting to have come from the interviewee, which are later denied. Hoban certainly had his share of good luck. It was said that if he walked down the street burglars would climb down ladders one-by-one into his open arms, and if it was dark, shine torches onto their own striped jerseys and bags on which the word "swag" was clearly written.

On one occasion Hoban played the part of one of the receivers who had acquired a lorry-load of extremely valuable fur coats. Hoban met them at what he discovered to be the arranged appointment, and quietly guided them to the drop, when he supervised their unloading of the loot. It was only when the lorry was entirely cleared and neatly stacked that he revealed his true identity and informed them that they had most conveniently stored the gear in the rear room at Chapeltown Police Station.

Dennis Hoban agreed that he had Alban Beresford Elcock with him, but as he had not yet asked for a solicitor I could not come and see him. This was the time before the Police and Criminal Evidence Act. He promised to give me a call as soon as it was possible for me to see the man I had been instructed to represent. He did, however, volunteer that Elcock was being held in connection with the discovery of the body of Mary Jean McCourt. I don't for one moment believe that Hoban was trying to mislead me, but to describe the discovery as that of a body was rather over-gilding his lily. A dog had found a bone, and they had found a heart valve.

The police enquiry into the death of Mary Jean McCourt had been precipitated by the happenings on a small plot of derelict land some five weeks earlier.

There is beauty, dignity and elegance in the architecture of parts of Central Leeds. Those who constructed in Victorian times had the money to build structures to reflect the power they enjoyed. However, there was another side to Leeds manifested in the sprawling mass of urban domestic development. Rows of terraced back-to-back houses with outside courtyards containing shared toilets, and a dog had to search quite a long time if he needed to find a tree or patch of grass. Artisan dwellings built for the purpose of housing the multitudes, and no more. History repeated itself during the post-war years when high-rise monstrosities without leisure areas or facilities bred boredom and frustration, a sad reflection on a city with large parks on the northern outskirts and surrounded by beautiful countryside. The workers in the forges and clothing factories saw little of this.

The terrace houses had a life of 50 or 60-years after which they were deemed beyond repair and the council pulled them down. There may well have been plans to replace them, but for the time being they were levelled. The vacant areas of land proved to be a magnet for the travellers.

Ellerby Avenue had been one such terrace, built, lived in, worn out and demolished. The rubble-strewn land had attracted such a group of travellers, but their presence had been too much for those proud citizens in the area who remained, and while waiting for their own homes to be requisitioned were discomforted by the mess and rubbish caused by the presence of the travellers, who regrettably did not travel, but remained. The local authority was consulted, and after the enforced removal of the travellers' caravans, shallow ditches were dug around the perimeter to prevent the return of other equally unwelcome settlers, and for a while peace returned to Ellerby Avenue. The demolition of the houses took place in November 1975, and the ditches were dug in January 1976. For many months that area remained just a pile of rubble containing the bricks, the slates, the wooden fittings and planks, together with the thousands of pieces of discarded dross which were all that remained of the years in which those houses were homes, and where people were born, lived and died. And now, rubble, where any piece of rubbish could be discarded, buried, hidden and would remain, unless the wind blew it away, or the rats, birds and vermin ate their fill.

Kevin Spink was a bright ten-year-old schoolboy who went to St Peter's Middle School. He had two brothers who called him William after the fictional character Just William, because the kind of adventures Kevin got up to bore no small resemblance to the adventures of Richmal Crompton's famous character. As he left school for the weekend on 6 February 1976 Kevin had that look on his face which is a mixture of serenity and expectation known the world over to liberated schoolboys, with his school cap worn jauntily at an angle and school blazer casually slung over his shoulders. Kevin, otherwise known as William, otherwise known as Batman felt a little lonely because Robin, due to some earlier misdemeanour, had been kept in to tidy up. But Batman could manage quite well without Robin. So Kevin climbed a mound of rubble and arms akimbo flew down. He didn't actually fly, in fact it was more of a jump, but the jump went wrong and he stumbled and fell.

As he tried to pick himself up his hand touched something smooth and hard. He blinked, and with a feeling of horror he realised they were a pair of legs, crossed over, but he couldn't see the feet. He looked around quickly to see if there was anything else, but there was nothing other than rubble. The full shock and horror of what he had touched suddenly struck him and he scrambled to his feet and ran and ran and ran.

When he arrived home his brothers Alan and Christopher had started their tea, and as he rushed through the door Kevin blurted out what he had seen. The brothers scarcely looked up from their plates, and they certainly didn't turn an eyebrow, for they were used to his vivid imagination, and they thought this was yet another little adventure play acted on the stage of his mind. He went on-and-on about it, but after a while realised it was of no avail. And there was no way they would believe him.

On the following afternoon, which was Saturday, Kevin returned to the topic, and as they had nothing else to do Alan said, "All right, let's go and have a look and you can show it to me." They crossed to the area and Kevin pointed, but Alan was not too sure, saying, "It might be a dummy," but as he looked closer he began to think that Kevin was right after all. He was a little older than Kevin, and he certainly wasn't going to panic. When they arrived home and told their mother she too suggested it might be a dummy, and it was only on the following day, the Sunday, that their elder sister Susan came for supper. Susan knew all about civic responsibility and felt the matter should be looked into, so they found a torch and formed a small procession winding its way to Ellerby Avenue. In Susan's mind there was no doubt. They were human legs, and the police must be informed without further delay.

Things didn't normally happen with any great speed in Ellerby Avenue, after all, there was little that could happen, that is until this particular Sunday evening. It didn't take long for two, then four, then half-a-dozen police officers to arrive in a variety of vehicles. Emergency lighting was put up, and more cars were parked in Ellerby Avenue than for the whole of the past decade. The search through that night and into the following morning revealed other parts of a badly decomposed body found in the immediate vicinity of the legs. Heads pored over plans of the area, as it had previously been, in order to locate the precise house that used to stand on that spot.

A tie or cravat seemingly tied round a piece of body believed to be the neck was a prize exhibit, and measurements were taken to try to establish whether the cravat had been tightened to less than the circumference of the neck. The most important find, however, was a small piece of metal later found to be a heart valve, which could be identified with more precision than most other exhibits, and with the certainty that it had been placed by a cardiac surgeon into the heart of one Mary McCourt. Other items found were two rings, a watch, dentures and pieces of clothing. There seemed to be little doubt that the body was that of Mary McCourt. The two real questions were how she died—was it by pulling the ligature of the tie or cravat around her neck—and who did it. The state of the evidence on these two questions was entirely circumstantial, but did point in the direction of Alban Beresford Elcock.

An examination of Mary McCourt's life was vivid to say the least. She was born in 1939, and since the age of 16 had been the source of much anxiety to her parents, though it is true to say they became accustomed to her lifestyle because there was little they could do to change it. The judge described her as self-indulgent, promiscuous, indolent, someone who never worked, lived on social security, produced children and then abdicated responsibility for them. She spent whatever money she had on drink and clothes, and devoted her time to either being married to or living with a succession of at least five or six different men, the last of whom was called Peter McCourt, whom she alleged had been violent to her, though in that respect it did not seem that he was the only one. She needed a serious operation, but that did not prevent her continuing the lifestyle to which she had readily become accustomed, and then one day in one of those tawdry, smoke-filled, public houses in the centre of Leeds, she met the defendant, Alban Beresford Elcock.

She took him home, and he stayed, and they lived together for a while, at Mary's house, 5 Throstle Square, in Middleton, one of the many areas of Leeds packed with small houses let by the council. Their discussions and arguments were tempered by talk of marriage and one day in a fit of enthusiasm, or probably still affected by the alcohol of that same lunch-time, and with a few pounds in his pocket, they bought a wedding dress. Never would the choice of a white wedding dress have been deemed less appropriate.

It was clear that the defendant also had at least one other girlfriend and knowledge of this did not improve relations with Mary McCourt. The defendant was not a total gentleman. When they broke up, and that was a frequent occurrence, he could be vindictive, and on one occasion took all the furniture, leaving her only with one spoon with which to stir her tea.

One witness, Carl Clement Cox, called by the prosecution, told of a conversation with Elcock in which he said he had been having arguments with Mary and that he would kill her. The witness thought this was said as a joke.

The defendant moved out of 5 Throstle Square, it was not long before another man moved in, but this did not prevent the defendant picking her up from the hospital where she was taken over her heart problems.

Mary's mother described her as nasty and violent, particularly after a few drinks, but there was one thing that the Crown did concede, and it was that throughout her life she associated with men of bad character, dishonest men and men who were not only capable of, but manifested, violence. But not Elcock: he was clearly the exception because he was a man with no previous convictions, and therefore in the eyes of the law a man of good character.

It was a difficult but necessary task to endeavour to trace Mary's movements over the previous years. In the summer of 1974 it was clear that she left Leeds for a time, but then returned. It was possible to pinpoint 25 September 1974, when she was seen wearing a wig in the company of the defendant but after that there was no trace until the discovery of the decomposed body. A few days after 25 September the defendant was seen without her. He was asked where Mary was, and replied that he didn't know, that perhaps she had gone off with another man, and, "You had better forget about her."

Over the following few days her daughter visited the house where she had last been living and saw empty cases, and formed the view that her mother had left, but not of her own wishes, because all her underwear was still there. She saw Elcock a few days later and asked about the whereabouts of her mother. "Where is Mary, Sandy?" He said, "I don't know," he hadn't seen her for a few days, he told her. "We went out together, we had a quarrel, and she got out of the car and walked away. Don't worry, she'll be back, and when she comes back I will have her back. I and Mary are made for each other."

He later amplified that conversation, using an unusual phrase, "She had said she wasn't good enough for him." Mary's daughter reported, "I think that's the last thing my mother would say, that she wasn't good enough for any man."

Nothing more was heard of her until the body was found on 8 February 1975, roughly where 10–12 Ellerby Avenue used to be. Evidence was obtained when each of the houses on those terraces had been boarded up, stripped of any reusable material and then knocked down in such a way that any of the brickwork dropped down to fill up what had been the cellars. There was no evidence to support any suggestion of a thorough inspection of the premises being carried out at the time the building was stripped. Everything pointed to the fact that the body must have been in the cellar of the house in question before 1 October 1974, the date when the house was brought down. The evidence also pointed to the fact that the body in that cellar was Mary McCourt, the one found as a result of the discovery by Kevin Spink. The body did not tie in with anyone living at either 10 or 12 Ellerby Avenue, so there was no suggestion other than that the body had been buried there either just before, at the time of, or even at some time after the destruction of the house. So the question remained was this the body of a murdered woman, or someone who had died from natural causes or an accident?

At first sight it looked as though the body had been clothed in tights, a bra and vest and a thin cotton garment with a faint pink pattern. There were fragments of what appeared to be nylon tights and what looked like a mini-skirt. The upper part was surrounded with a large piece of thick white material, maybe a flannelette sheet, and the body looked as though it had been lying on a thin sheet of black plastic or polythene.

Initially various bone fractures were deemed to have been caused by the digger, but then the body gave the appearance of having been first wrapped in a sheet and then in black polythene, all of which pointed to a secret and sinister disposal of it. The search of the rubble was intensified and a lump of tissue was discovered. It proved to be the greater part of the neck, and around the neck at the level of the voice box there was a patterned silk-type cravat with knots at both ends. It was secured by a half hitch at the front which produced deep grooves in the remaining tissues on the left side of the neck.

The pathologist was Dr Michael Green, a competent and likeable person, whom I had known when I produced the rag revue at the Leeds Empire when a student. He would later become professor of pathology, and during his retirement a flying doctor in Australia. At the time in question he was an extremely experienced forensic pathologist and had given evidence in many important cases. Dr Green had carefully removed the cravat, and as he did so noticed that the skin beneath it was markedly better preserved than the skin both above and below it. He measured the internal circumference of the ligature at ten inches. Moreover, when the tie was removed one could see under it the hyoid bone, which is rather like a wishbone just above the voice box. It was fractured in two places, and there was dark staining as if by blood on those fracture sites. He later stated in evidence that those fractures were sustained in life, and this was confirmed by the fact that the stains were only at the fracture sites. He described the fracture as the type seen after a blow at the nape of the neck. Various portions of the skull were unearthed on the site, and eventually virtually the entire skull could be assembled, and although there were some post-death fractures, others suggested strongly and ominously that a blunt instrument had inflicted them. Dr Green concluded that he could not entirely exclude the possibility of post-mortem injury; however, those suspicions which he held about something nasty having happened pre-mortem were supported by the discovery that both feet had been held together by nylon tights, with pieces of tights material tied in a loop and with knots also lying nearby.

Dr Green stated that the presence of the tight ligature around the neck, with the underlying fractures to the hyoid bone and that at the back of the skull, in other words, strangulation and blunt injuries to the head and neck, were strong presumptive evidence of homicide. At the trial he expressed the view that the body could have been there between six months and two years, and if it had been wrapped in polythene that might well have delayed petrification.

He concluded that the body of the woman was of someone aged approximately 35 and of a height of five feet two inches, which coincided precisely with the description of Mary McCourt given by her mother. One further discovery clinched this belief. A metal heart valve was found inside one of the pieces of flesh. In the mid-1970s heart surgery, though one of the wonders of the age was neither as sophisticated nor as widespread as it is today. Records showed that a Mary Dickinson had undergone such an operation, and Dickinson was the name Mary used when she lived for a period with a man called John Dickinson. The jigsaw was almost complete.

The prosecution would endeavour to show that the tie had been used as a ligature, that it had been tightly pulled to a neck circumference less than that of the deceased, and as it was pulled, the bone was broken. The defence put forward the theory that it was more than possible that the tie had been worn by the woman as a cravat, and had been caught up subsequently, either not deliberately if before death or perhaps after death by a mechanical digger in the course of demolishing the buildings.

The tie, as the prosecution called it, or the cravat as was preferred by the defence, for clearly the importance as to whom it belonged was at the core of the day spent demonstrating its versatility upon the shop-window dummy model standing somewhat incongruously on counsel's bench. Various theories as to how a tie could be worn as a cravat, and in a judicially careful manner many of these theories were rubbished by Mr Justice Boreham.

In the course of an open and frank interview with Detective-Superintendent Hoban after Elcock's arrest, he had not attempted to deny that the tie was his, explaining that it had probably been taken by Mary, hidden in Throstle Square, and whoever had killed her had used it to make it look like as though he was responsible.

The judge on the case was Mr Justice Boreham. He was a frequent visitor to the circuit in the North-east, particularly the Leeds Assizes. He spent much time in his summing-up in dealing with the tie: "Speculation is dangerous, you can weave all sorts of fancy theories in a case like this, beware and look at the evidence." He reminded the jury that the defence proposition was that death had been an accident but that, if that had been the case, the person disposing of the body "must have been a pretty cool customer."

The jury was told of the aspects of the case which were undisputed. Mary was seen on 14 September 1974, but not thereafter by any of her family or friends. On that day she had been seen wearing a red skirt, blouse and jacket. On 8 February 1976 she appeared as a corpse, in separated pieces. She was found in a mountain of rubble in an area which included Ellerby Avenue, part of Leeds Corporation's policy of pulling down back-to-back terraced houses which had seen better days and needed to be demolished to make way for better housing. They had been pulled down in September 1974, and that work continued until the end of October of that year. Between that time and early-February 1976 the piles of rubble just sat there, but in February 1976 there was a reawakening in the housing department, and machines were put to work clearing the site. Following the macabre discovery of the body parts the police commenced the task of putting things together.

In March 1976 Elcock was arrested as he left work at the Forge and taken to Millgarth Police Station where he was interviewed by Detective-Superintendent Hoban and Detective-Superintendent Gilrain.

So, at the exact time that Elcock's wife was sitting in my waiting room her husband were openly telling the detectives as he put it, "exactly my association with her." He told them that he had met her early in 1974, had a date with her and then taken her to the home of a friend called Vernon St Clair Waldron, where they stayed together until March, and then moved to a flat in Sholebroke Avenue in the Chapeltown district of Leeds, where many people from the Caribbean had settled.

He then moved to Middleton, another area of Leeds, with Mary until she kicked him out. "Why did she kick you out?" asked Hoban, and he replied frankly, "Well, to tell the truth, I wanted to go and see Doreen, my other girl, and my baby, and if Mary had only accepted the situation I would still have been with Mary, and there would have been no trouble." Hoban was perplexed by this disclosure and asked, "What do you mean? Who is Doreen?"

It was strange that Hoban should be perplexed. He had served for many years in Leeds, and in particular knew the Chapeltown district well. Almost 20-years earlier there began an influx of immigrants from the Caribbean, an area which had in turn housed those who came from Lithuania in the early-part of the century, to the Poles in the immediate post-war period, followed by the Asians and then in very large numbers, the Caribbeans. The area had been transposed, night life had become vigorous, clubs had sprouted up and relaxed sexual attitudes had been manifested not only in the open increase in prostitution and the pimps who conducted them, the sale and use of drugs which had become endemic, but also with the equally relaxed family arrangements, which resulted in many of the young men having more than one family. The phrase "my baby's mother" would mean a girl with whom the male did not actually live, but for whose child he accepted or sometimes bragged about responsibility, and from time-to-time contributed to upkeep. In his reply to Hoban, Elcock indicated that Doreen was more than a casual fling, and his eventual plan was to marry her, so much so that he had bought her a wedding dress and already made enquiries about moving from his house in Pottery Vale to a larger one. "Doreen isn't very bright, she is a poor sort of girl, but needs me to look after her. In fact she has two children to me, she lives with her mother in Oak Tree Close, and to tell you the truth, I intend to marry her."

"So what you are saying," said Hoban, "is that you were moving between two homes, you had two women at the same time." Elcock stood up and stretched his back, for his was a large frame. "Look, Mary didn't want me to go and see Doreen and the baby, Mary knew about Doreen, but Doreen didn't know about Mary. I had a simple choice. One day, just out of the blue Mary said either go to them and stay, or stay with me and don't see them. So I said they win, and she kicked me out."

Elcock smiled shamefacedly, after all he was a big man, and here a rather small person was throwing him out, and he described how he took his few bits of furniture. But then Mary had to go into hospital and they both relented, and a short time passed by as she recovered, and he picked her up from the hospital and took her on holiday to Bridlington, a blustery fish-and-chips resort full of boarding houses on the East coast about a couple of hours' drive from Leeds. He described how the magic of Bridlington didn't last, and they returned to Leeds, but although he was helping Mary to recover, and, he added surprisingly, she was fun to be with, he really didn't want to stay with her, he wanted to get back to Doreen and the babies. He remembered that when they got back to Leeds from Bridlington, they found the house had been burgled. "As Mary was frightened to be on her own I stayed with her, and on 23 September we went to her mother, and borrowed some bedding in order to stay at the house in Throstle Square of which Mary had a tenancy. Later we went to the *White Swan* (a pub in the centre of Leeds), and it was there that we saw Mary's ex-husband Billy."

Hoban clearly saw a line to pursue when it became clear that Elcock had an innate wish to clear a way to return to Doreen, and he urged him to elaborate on his movements on that evening in September 1974. "We visited the Scott Hall, and from there Mary indicated she wanted to go to a club called the *International* in Francis Street, but I didn't want to go because the people there all smoked weed." The *International* was a club in a building, which had once housed a flourishing synagogue.

Elcock was asked whether at the end of the evening they returned to Throstle Square, but he said that was not so, they had gone to a flat in Sholebroke Avenue belonging to Keith Spooner, which was much nearer to the Scott Hall, to which Elcock had a key. He explained to Hoban,

"Drink makes me tired, and Mary was lively, she kept going on at me about going to the *International* and I just said no way, I am not going there, and she knows that when I say no, I mean it, so eventually I lay down on the bed, and the last thing I remember is that she was sitting on the side beside me."

Hoban asked, "Did you lose your temper with her?"

Elcock smiled and replied, "No I never lose my temper, I went to sleep, and when I woke she was gone."

"So what time did you wake up?" asked Hoban.

"Maybe about one o'clock, or later, I just do not know," he said.

He admitted that Spooner had not been at the flat that night, and he must have been at work, so it was just he and Mary alone there that night.

Hoban persisted:

" But Alban, didn't you go looking for Mary?" The answer was clear that he had not, and it seemed he didn't really want to know where she was. He had made his mind about Doreen and the babies.

Hoban changed tack, but just slightly, and raised the question of Mary's daughter Mandy. Mother and daughter had been pretty close, and of all people Mandy knew most about her mother's habits and was familiar with her various male friends. Mary had unruly hair, and her hectic vagrant lifestyle was not conducive to regular visits to the hairdresser, so she often wore a shoulder-length wig which did not look too bad at all. Some said it improved her appearance no end, and Mandy remembered that she had been present at her grandmother's house, when Mary, wearing a wig, had come to borrow the bedding. Moreover, and this was deemed of high relevance, she had arranged with Mary that she would come and see her the following day and take her to see about a job.

Mary did not come the following day, or the next. Mandy was asked about this, and admitted that she considered this most unusual, for no matter how disjointed their family contacts had been due to Mary's lifestyle, when she made a promise she usually kept it. This probably also explained why, when Mandy visited her mother's home on the three subsequent days, and despite finding no trace of her did not inform the police, believing that, as had happened on more than one previous occasion, "she had gone off with some man". Hoban asked Elcock directly,

"Did you tell Mandy that you thought she might have gone off with someone else, as she had in the past, and not to bother the police?"

Elcock thought for a moment and said, "Yes, I thought she might have done."

Hoban's next question was straight to the point.

When you saw all the publicity in the *Yorkshire Evening Post* and on the news about the discovery of a body," he paused, "did you not think it could be Mary?"

Elcock stroked his chin and without the slightest sign of concern slowly answered, " Well, her mother and Mandy thought she might be dead, but I couldn't digest this ... I never associated the two."

The detective pointed out that it seemed the body was wearing the clothing Mary had worn on the 24th. He looked directly at Elcock and slowly made the telling point, "When you were the last person to see her alive".

Having dropped this bombshell Hoban glanced over to Gilrain who gave a barely discernible nod. It was at this point that Hoban proceeded to repeat the caution to Elcock. It was delivered in the simple straightforward wording of that time: "You need not say anything unless you wish to do so, but anything you say will be taken down and used in evidence." Elcock took the caution in his stride. After all, he was not trained in the ways of criminals, not even self-taught, for he had no previous convictions whatever.

Hoban knew that I had been instructed to represent Elcock by his then wife, but at that time there was no legal requirement, as later introduced under the Police and Criminal Evidence Act, for a lawyer to be allowed, called in, or even provided to a defendant being interviewed in even the most serious circumstances. The police ruled the roost on such matters, but I would never have expected Hoban to use his powers improperly or to gain any advantage over an accused.

Elcock had experienced no more trouble with the police than any of the other immigrants who stood out in that grey industrial Yorkshire city. His dislike of the *International Club*, its habitués and those who smoked weed stood out. Instead of clamming up, he volunteered,

"Are you sure it is her I can hardly believe it? I can only hope you find somebody who saw her after me."

Hoban responded speedily, "Do you know of any such person?" but Elcock shook his head. The detective pointed out that strangulation appeared to be the cause death, and a tie, which was his, had been found round her neck. Elcock did not flinch:

"Yes, it's mine. You must think I'm right in it," he added. "All I can say is that Mary must have pinched it, and hidden it at Throstle Square, and whoever killed her has used it to make it look like me. I remember, after I had moved my stuff from Middleton I looked round and found she had kept and hidden a shirt and some slippers. I managed to get those back, but she could have hidden the tie anywhere."

He explained that he had kept the tie in a wardrobe, and it was ages since he had last seen it. He had worn a suit and tie when he went on the short holiday to Bridlington already mentioned. He explained that the tie belonged to a man called Lloyd Francis, with whom had shared a house in 1972. Francis had left the house to serve a term of imprisonment, and left his clothes behind, including the tie.

And then came the 64-dollar question:

"Did you kill Mary McCourt?"

"Certainly not. I knew she was sick, and if I wanted her dead, it was only a matter of time."

"But she was pressing you to live with her, wasn't she?"

"I know what you mean, I'm not silly, I know things look bad, and I was with her that night."

"But you don't appear to have made any enquiries after her disappearance, why?"

Elcock appeared to have no answer for this; he remained silent for nearly half-a-minute and then said, "You know, I have only just digested that she is dead."

Elcock was given time to rest and was offered food, but understandably he had no appetite. I was still not permitted to see him. After he had had a sleep, the questioning was resumed, this time by two different officers of the West Yorkshire Police Murder Squad, Detective Chief Inspector Smith and Detective Sergeant Cowman. They repeated many of the questions already put, and in the main received the same answers.

The theme of the tie was revisited.

"Were you wearing the tie on that day?" They meant the day on which Mary was last seen. Elcock seemed revived in spirit with a surprising mock enthusiasm for the questioning.

"Good, good, that's what I expected, to be given the third degree. I want you to ask me these kinds of questions. I know I am the main suspect; things don't look too good for me, do they?" His enthusiasm was uncanny, and provoked the next question.

"Well, was it you that strangled Mary?"

"No," he said: "I would not do anything like that, it's not my nature."

Smith sighed, " A lot of murders happen on the spur of the moment, and arise from some little domestic dispute that just gets out of hand."

Elcock again smiled: "I am completely innocent, and this is England, not South Carolina."

The significance of such a comment was not lost on the detectives. It would be idle to assume that they appreciated it, and just a trace of annoyance could be detected in the next comment.

"For a man being interviewed about the murder of a woman who was in reality your common-law wife, you give the impression of being very unconcerned about her murder, and frankly you give the impression of enjoying being interrogated."

This did not abash Elcock. "Good, good, I see what you are thinking, but why should I be concerned? I expect you to prove me innocent."

The two detectives made it clear that they believed otherwise, recounting once again that he was the last person to see her alive, that he had the murder weapon, the tie, and that they treated with disdain the theory that someone else had acquired his tie. Smith was becoming somewhat exasperated; he was a less patient man than Hoban, and struggled to avoid showing his true feelings. He leant forward, and in a barely discernible voice looked Elcock firmly in the eye:

"You said earlier that you thought someone might have used your tie to make it look as though you had killed her. If that is so, why should he hide the body?"

Elcock smiled. "That is a very good question, but I cannot answer it."

"What did you do on Tuesday?"

"We had something to eat, and I wanted to leave her at Throstle Square, but because she was frightened she wanted to come with me, so we went to the *Scott Hall* pub, and we stayed till about ten." He again explained that he had refused to go to the *International Club*, and he did not have much money left, so they went to Keith's flat in Sholebroke Avenue, and when he woke up Mary was gone.

Detective Sergeant Cowman looked surprised.

"But didn't you think it strange that Mary left you, after she had said that she was frightened to be alone?"

"I don't know, I just fell asleep, and when I woke up she was gone. Anyway if I had killed her surely Keith would have seen the blood when he came home."

"But why should there have been any blood?"

"When a person is strangled there should most likely be blood."

Cowman interrupted: "Can we have a sample of your blood?"

As was his right, Elcock said "No."

Cowman would not let it rest there. "Look," he said, "if I put my hand round your throat and strangled you, there would not be any blood about." Elcock was not to be outdone.

"If someone was being strangled they would be thrashing about, and would hit themselves, and would start to bleed."

"Maybe she was not killed in the house, but in your car?"

"In that case," said Elcock, "there would be blood in my car."

"No," Cowman persisted, "I just don't see why there should be blood when you strangle someone."

But Elcock had the last word: "I did not kill her."

Mary's wide circle of friends reflected her popularity. Since the age of 16 she had associated with a large number of men, she had been married three times, one husband was deaf and dumb and had been violent to her; she had given birth to three children, two of whom were adopted, and the third, Mandy, had spent a considerable period in the care of the local authority. The officers took an overview of all that they knew about her, the observations and opinions of various family members and those who had known the couple, all of which formed a pretty consistent picture.

Her mother had difficulty in keeping track of her, and she spent considerable periods away from Leeds. Sometimes she would write, and a brief note was the best that could be expected, but sometimes she would not be in touch for months. Her mother told the police that her daughter "was always clean and tidy, smart in her personal appearance, but she was violent and of ill temper when she drank spirits." Her father described her as "here today and gone tomorrow". Her brother, Anthony Parkin, told of having seen one of her husbands, Peter McCourt, who was deaf and dumb, "trying to strangle her".

Her association with Elcock began in early-1974 and they soon started living together at 5 Throstle Square. It was then that she bought a wedding dress and marriage was in the air, but it came to nothing for the simple reason that both she and Elcock were still married to other people. In September another man, William Donnelly, was living with her at Throstle Square, but later in September Elcock was back in residence.

On 23 September 1974 Elcock and Mary visited her mother, borrowed bedding, sugar, jam, a photograph and a sewing box and took them to Throstle Square. On the following day they again visited her mother, whom they asked to look after Mandy a little longer, and it was then that she wore the black wig. That was the last time Mrs Parkin saw her daughter.

Mandy became worried, but it was ten days before she told the police. On 3 October they forced their way into the house. They found the jam, the sugar and the sewing box. The wardrobe doors were open and all Mary's clothes except the wedding dress were missing. The bed was made up, and this was noted because Mary only ever made up a bed just before she got into it. Also missing was her newest handbag. Mrs Parkin and Mandy disposed of all the property at Throstle Square, and although they asked the Salvation Army to help trace Mary they did not make any further approach to the police for another six months, on 17 April 1975.

Elcock saw Mrs Parkin some four months after her disappearance, telling her he had no idea where she was. He said that he and Mary had been out on 24 September, they had had a quarrel and Mary just got out of the car and walked off. "It wasn't much of a quarrel, and she'll come back eventually because Mary and I were made for each other."

Mandy had lived with her mother and Elcock in Sholebroke Avenue, and said that the couple got on well, although there were arguments about the house, the furniture, Elcock's girl-friend Doreen and the fact that Mary was seeing other men. Mandy described that on such occasions Mary would shout and cry, whereas Elcock merely walked about and nodded his head.

She said the last time she saw her mother she was wearing a jacket, blouse and red skirt, and that the tie was like the ones Elcock wore, but maintained that the one she saw him wearing on the last occasion was a different colour from the exhibit.

When Mandy visited the house on 3 October most of the clothes her mother liked had gone, and Elcock said her mother had told him, "I'm no good for you," and had walked off.

Tony Dyer had helped Elcock move his furniture from Throstle Square after Elcock's earlier sojourn there, and that on that occasion Mary lost her temper and shouted at Elcock, who was calm and laughed as he left, saying, "I don't need an old bag like Mary when I have Doreen."

Janine Kelly, who had lived at Sholebroke Avenue at the same time as Elcock and Mary, said that later when Elcock was asked where Mary was, he had said, "I don't know, perhaps with another man, she disappears sometimes, you have to forget about her."

Late that afternoon the detectives retired to the office of Hoban which was on the top floor of the police headquarters in Mabgate, a modern building which had replaced the ancient Millgarth. The officers reviewed the statements that had been taken from all the witnesses and decided to send officers to Elcock's own residence at 56 Pottery Vale, where they placed into black bin-liners various items of clothing and a wig. The wig, to become Exhibit 47, was shown to Mary's mother at the trial, and when asked if it was her daughter's she replied, "I cannot be absolutely sure, but I am almost positive." The police accepted that the wig was shown to Elcock's second wife and she identified it as having once belonged to her, and there was no forensic evidence to support whether it had been worn by anyone else.

Following the search of his house Elcock was still bright, and readily agreed to help the police, "All I can". He was asked what clothing he had been wearing on 24 September 1974, some two years earlier, and he pointed to his black suit. He was asked about the wig, and replied, "It is my wig, I think it belonged to my first wife, I cut it down a bit... they all leave bits and pieces you know." In fact he meant his second wife.

At his trial Alban Elcock chose not to give evidence.

The main thrust of the Crown's case was the tie round his neck. It was fiercely argued by the defence counsel that the tie was never put round the neck as a ligature, and that the knotting of it, if the evidence of a forensic scientist, Dr Clift, was right, was how it would be if it was worn as a cravat. The judge had clear views on this theory. He urged the jury to consider whether or not it was originally worn as a cravat was not conclusive of the question whether it was used as a ligature. He pointed out that the prosecution had asked how anyone else apart from Mary could have got hold of that tie if it had been in the possession of the defendant. He also emphasised that there had been no sign of a struggle at Throstle Square, bits and pieces were left where they had been on the 23rd and 24th, and the bed made and not slept in. So how could anyone have got hold of the tie except the defendant?

The judge asked, why go to the risk of secreting the body on a site to be demolished if as Elcock had suggested in an interview that the tie was used by somebody else? The judge pointed out that the Crown believed Elcock had a motive. He was in a muddle with his two girlfriends, and this is what happens when you try to run two at the same time.

The judge made much of the fact that upon waking-up to find Mary gone, Elcock had not made any effort to go looking for her, though he pointed out that her daughter Mandy had not done so either, and that Elcock's answers to the police had been checked, were found to be truthful, that he was an honest man and had never shown any tendency towards violence.

In his summing-up to the jury the judge suggested that Mary's mother's reaction, described by a police officer, when she saw the wig, spoke louder than words. It had been the only moment she trembled. In his words, "She really lost it when that was produced, a sensible and composed woman, until what was for her, that dreadful moment." He said, as every judge says in each and every criminal case to the jury: "The facts are for you, you may think from what I say, or by the nature of questions I may have posed during the course of the case that I have views on the evidence; if you agree with those views then follow them, but if you do not then you need not follow them."

However, what the judge did not tell the jury was that there was no forensic evidence to link that particular wig with Mary, just as he had dismissed the point put forward at some stage in the case, which was that Elcock's second wife also possessed a wig. The prosecution had admitted that the wig had been shown to Rubalyn Agatha White, his second wife, and she had identified it as once being her property. This particular failure on the part of the judge was but one of 27 matters referred to in the grounds of appeal, but which the Court of Appeal rejected.

The jury was out for three hours and came back with a guilty verdict. Elcock was taken into custody, for until then he had been on bail. He was sentenced to life imprisonment. I went down to see Elcock in the cells. In his hands were the remains of a cricket ball; clearly they had not yet had time to search him and dispossess him of it. When you tear the leather off a cricket ball there are thousands of strands of elastic, and it can take a long time to disentangle them. He had clearly been working over a considerable period of time to take them off strand-by-strand, and he had almost reached the centre of the ball. As we sat there talking he sensed something inside the ball, and this re-energised his grappling with the rubber. Eventually I could see what was embedded inside. It was a tooth, either that of a human or maybe an animal, something that I learned later had voodoo connotations.

"Would you like us to give notice of appeal?" I asked.

He shrugged his shoulders and replied, "Mary must be laughing," and Norman Jones drafted the notice over the next few days.

There were three grounds: first, that the prosecution needed to prove three elements, that the remains were those of Mary McCourt, which was conceded; that she had been murdered, and had not died from any other cause, and that it was Elcock who had murdered her. The grounds of appeal showed that although the jury had accepted the last two elements, they were not in accordance with the evidence.

The second was that a submission made at the close of the prosecution case by Gilbert Gray QC was rejected by the judge, and that in doing so he misdirected himself. The third was that in his summing-up the judge committed a number of material irregularities.

The appeal was heard at the Royal Courts of Justice in June of 1978. Lord Justice Eveleigh delivered the judgment. He stated that there were 27 particulars in the grounds of appeal, and he described the arguments at trial as having been skilfully put by Gilbert Gray QC. The judge went so far as to say, dealing with the suggestion that the digger might have tightened the cravat: "Taken in isolation, that is perhaps a possible theory, if one were to admit into one's consideration the greatest speculation and possibility of the flimsiest kind. But one cannot take it in isolation, it has to fit in with the rest of the case, and there is overshadowing the whole of the argument of the defence on this aspect of the case, the fact that the body was there at all in the rubble, itself an indication of foul play, and that there were there in its neighbourhood, a sheet and plastic material. One asks why the body was there, of course death may have occurred by other means and the body laid there for some reason unknown, but that is highly speculative."

The judge itemised the 27 particulars, and stated that it was not the intention of the court to deal with every single ground in isolation, because they were typical of the kind of criticism one finds where the defence says that although the deficiency in one piece of evidence may not be fatal to the verdict when you take them all together, the totality of their weakness makes the verdict unsafe and unsatisfactory. However, in this case the court came to the conclusion that nothing was unsafe or unsatisfactory in the conviction and the application to appeal was refused.

CHAPTER 15

The Murder Where the Victim Was … the Judge

It was 1981 and I was at a concert at the Lounge Hall in Harrogate.

In other parts of the town the spring flower show was at its peak, and there were crowds everywhere. The teashops were full, *Betty's* as ever to overflowing, with the usual queue stretching down towards the Valley Gardens.

The concert had just reached the interval and like many in the audience I made towards the entry vestibule, but as I did I suddenly heard my name announced over the sound system. "Would Mr Barrington Black please make himself known at reception"? I sensed this was not a social call, but would in all probability be work and I made a snap decision that I was not going to miss the second half, or at least only if it was a really interesting call.

It was "Hello, Mr Black, this is Detective Inspector Slater from the Lancashire Constabulary here, I am actually speaking from Scotland, but we have a man here who is asking for you. It's up to you if you want to come up to Scotland, but there is little point because we will be bringing him down to Preston shortly. He will appear there in court tomorrow, and he is being charged with murder and kidnapping, oh and by the way, the person murdered was a judge."

I checked out what time they would arrive in Preston, where he would be detained, and the time and whereabouts of the court in question. I also asked if he had any family so that I might contact them at least so that they might make other arrangements for his representation, but he was single and of no fixed abode, though he did have a sister living in Burnley. I went back into the second half of the concert, but my mind was not on the music.

I would later discover that on the evening of the previous day in the police station at Hawick, a town in Roxburghshire in the eastern Southern Uplands, Detective Inspector Slater, together with Detective Chief Inspector

Meadows and Detective Constable Arnold, sat in the small interview room near the cells. Opposite them at the tiny chipped wooden table was John Smith, handcuffed to the detective constable. The interview was comprehensive, dealing with a number of aspects of the case, and John Smith was quite forthcoming. There were none of the "No comment" responses which were to become the norm adopted by interviewees over the ensuing years. Equally, at that time the law did not insist on the offer of legal assistance from the outset of such an interview. An offer would, however, be passed on at the conclusion of an interview, as John Smith was told by Detective Chief Inspector Slater.

"A solicitor has been enquiring about you."

Smith asked "Who?"

The DCI responded, "A Mr Howarth from Burnley, I think he's already representing you."

"Not on this he's not," snapped Smith.

"I don't want any fucking cowboys from Burnley; they work hand-in-glove with the police. If I go back to England I'll have Barrington Black."

The DCI paused for a moment, making a mental note on how that would affect the question of any delay before asking,

"You would want us to arrange that would you?

What if he isn't available?"

Quick as a flash, Smith smiled as he said, "He'll be available for this."

At the end of the concert I went home, and told Diana, who had not accompanied me because of a cold, about what had happened; she was not surprised. The call of course had been made initially to our home, and she had advised the caller where I was. We decided that rather than risk any problems with travel the following morning I should drive over to Preston and stay there the night so that I could have a reasonable amount of time to meet my new client before appearing in court.

While I was known in most police stations in Yorkshire, the desk sergeant at Preston was a shade more particular, and so I had to show some identification. I was then ushered into the interview room and to my great concern told that because of his violent nature a police officer would have to remain there during the interview "For your personal safety, sir." This was a situation I'd had to face on many previous occasions, but I persevered with my unwillingness for anyone to be present, and the officer withdrew.

A tall, well-built man of good physique aged about 30 was shown into the room.

"Hello, Mr Black, thanks for coming, I've heard a lot about you," he said.

We shook hands and I invited him to sit down.

"I'd rather stand if you don't mind," he replied, but the room was small and I didn't want him hovering over me.

"No, please do sit down, it makes it much easier for me, and I really do need to get to know you."

He relented straightaway, and this was the only time I would see him without a great pile of papers in his hands.

He spoke easily, almost non-stop. I had no need to prompt him. He knew what he wanted to tell me, and what I needed to know. He had been through this procedure with lawyers before.

"NFA," he said, which meant he was of no fixed abode, this was not unusual, and many of my clients were in the same position. "I have numerous convictions, the last one a year ago for assaulting the police, and they gave me 28 days." He did not, however, at that stage tell me about the most important conviction, the one which had led him to commit the act with which he was charged.

He did have next of kin, the sister who lived in Burnley, and he told me to visit her and go upstairs to the back bedroom, where under the floorboards against the far wall I would find two letters which would tell me why he had done what he had done. I noticed he was shaking, albeit slightly, and asked how he was medically. I learned he was on Valium, a tranquilliser, and Tuanil, a sleeping tablet. He had been on Valium for ten years and Tuanil for the previous two months; there were bottles in his property with the Burnley chemist's name. He told me the name of his GP, which I had asked for because in order to get the tablets he would have needed a regular prescription. He listed the various doctors he had seen in recent years and the establishments where he had been both an in-patient and out-patient. He volunteered that he had never indicated to any of the doctors his feelings about the penal system or the judge.

He paused at this stage, and got up and walked towards the barred window. I cannot explain this action because it was cloudy outside and he would not have been able to see anything, but it gave him the opportunity to avoid my direct gaze, which I had fastened on him when I paused in the writing of my notes.

"I was feeling like a powder keg as a result of that sentence," he whispered.

"Which sentence?" I enquired, though I had an idea.

"It was Judge Openshaw, he sentenced me at Preston Quarter Sessions in 1968, 13-years ago, to borstal training. There had been five charges, two of burglary, taking a vehicle, driving without insurance, and while disqualified."

"Any matters taken into consideration?" I asked.

"Nineteen," he admitted. He sighed and went on, "And I had to do 18 months, 18 bloody months. While other lads spent shorter periods there, I had to stay for 18 months."

I noticed a flaw in his argument even at that stage, but thought better about saying anything. In fact borstal at that time was an indeterminate sentence of between six months and tw2o years, and the exact duration would have been beyond the remit of the sentencing judge.

There were always some clients who could not wait to blurt out their version of events, what had happened, why they had done it, what they had done and how. I frankly found this much easier than the other kind, those who were silent or near silent, people from whom an account of their deeds needed to be drawn out with patience word-by-word. But this was not John Smith, who was one of the former.

He had taken a train from Burnley, where his abode was unfixed. It had not taken long to get to Preston; he knew the way because he had been there on two or three previous occasions, looking around the area. He had gone into a field, and came out near some houses round about one am. There was no hint of anyone being around; he arrived at the house which he knew was the judge's, for he had studied the electoral roll. He went into the garage, which was unlocked, and opened the car door. On the seat were some envelopes on which was written the judge's name. He closed the door, and moved towards a wooden shed where he lay down and tried to sleep, but he couldn't, because he had much on his mind and what was more, it was cold, so he walked around the area. Just as the sky lightened he entered the garage, climbed-up into the rafters and lay there, like a tiger, and waited.

It was just after eight am when he heard the noise of a door closing and the footsteps came nearer. He told me, "At this stage I was going to jump on him, I wanted to see his eyes and the expression on his face, so I pushed the knife forward, it was a big sheath knife, I lunged at him in the stomach and he fell back, I lunged again, this time in the chest and he fell back again, I caught him on the neck and on his head, I think it was about half-a-dozen times that I lunged at him."

The judge's wife had come out of the house. I later discovered this was because she could not understand why there had been neither sight nor sound of the car leaving. She saw the judge and shouted, "Oh my God!" Smith said that he told her to keep away, and tried to start the car, but it cut out. He ran towards the main road where he stopped a passing car, jumped in, and waving the bloodstained knife ordered the driver to take him to Newcastle. He told me that it was fortunate for the driver that it was an estate car, as had it been an ordinary car he would have put him in the boot. It was much later, many miles later, and after two tankfuls of petrol, that he ordered the driver into some woods, tied him up, left him and drove the car himself. That only lasted for quarter of a mile, for a police car that must have recognised the description and number chased him, and eventually the car had to stop. He paused, and said, "When they came to me I still had the knife on me." He looked me in the eye, and a conspiratorial smile was etched on his pale face. "Can I tell you something very important, Mr Black?" I nodded. The smile broadened. "I think they have charged me with the wrong offence." Many people confuse murder with manslaughter, and I half expected some observation to this effect, but I was certainly not prepared for what followed. "I think they should charge me with treason according to my reading of *Archbold*."

Archbold was the author of the *Bible of the Criminal Practitioner*, published first in 1824, and known by its full title *Archbold on Criminal Pleading Evidence and Practice*, now well beyond its 60th edition. Every judge and criminal practitioner refers to it daily and it is also the most well-thumbed book in every prison library. It was clear that John Smith had been one of its most avid readers. "Yes," he continued, "they should charge me with treason. When a justice is attacked it is treason, it is not necessarily murder." He paused, and gave a self-satisfied nod. I explained the true situation, but he did not quite seem to understand.

To be perfectly frank and to confirm what I was saying I had to open up my own copy of *Archbold*, which I always carried around as ballast. I did this because varied as my practice was; treason was not one of the most common offences with which I was acquainted. After all in those days it didn't crop up much at Halifax Quarter Sessions. However, my quick search confirmed something that had been at the back of my mind, namely, that by the Treason Act of 1351 *Archbold* clearly stated, "It is treason to kill a judge of the High Court being in his place doing his office." Leaving aside such arguments as might be mustered by some bright spark to point out the present distinction between judges of the High Court and circuit judges, a distinction not contemplated in 1351, there remained the clear interpretation of the words "being in his place doing his office", which I would translate as meaning actually being on the bench, rather than getting into his car at home, albeit on the way to work.

John Smith was just a little miffed by this disclosure, and I could not be sure whether he took in what I next said to him, and so I repeated the distinction between murder and manslaughter and I also discussed in brief what diminished responsibility was all about, in as simple terms as I could muster. From that first moment with him it was clear that he did not want to plead diminished responsibility, because, he said, if he was put over as someone who was unbalanced, "My message will not get across, nobody will believe me, they will think I am a crank." I did not know much about John Smith at that stage, having only been in his company for about 20 minutes and possessing only two sheets of paper, the one with the offences with which he had been charged, of which there were two, because in addition to the murder there was also a count relating to the kidnap of the hapless driver of the car, and the other sheet listing his previous convictions, but giving no details of their circumstances.

He satisfied my curiosity in this direction by his next outburst. "I climbed up Blackpool Tower in August 1980, and I got right to the top." His broad Lancashire accent and that particular phrase brought to mind a song from my childhood sung by George Formby. This exploit amplified an entry on his criminal record, which explained it in a more sterile fashion with the words "breach of the peace", that he had been bound over in the sum of £50 to be of good behaviour for two years. John Smith said there was more to it than just climbing a tower; it had been a protest against the police, against penal establishments and against the government of this country. He had written letters to Michael Meacher and to Robert Kilroy-Silk, members of Parliament who appeared to him to be concerned with the welfare of prisoners, and he gave me instructions where to find the letters and a statement that he had made, which I eventually duly discovered in the loft as he had described. Our interview was briefly interrupted by the arrival of the police surgeon who had been called earlier by the detectives, who had taken possession of his various pills. After examining him the doctor called me to one side. "He is addicted to these drugs, he is hung up on Valium, I had better keep him on them for the time being, and then the doctors at Risley can decide what they want to do." Risley was the Lancashire remand centre, to which he was clearly bound, because bail was obviously out of the question, and this he quite understood.

The initial hearing before Preston Magistrates' Court was brief. The prosecutor of what had befallen Judge William Harrison Openshaw gave an outline. He was the most respected and conscientious presiding judge over the Preston Circuit, and had been so for many years. Prior to that he had practised as a barrister on the Northern Circuit and was well-liked by all who worked with him. In the lobby of the magistrates' court was a young couple who needed no introduction, as they were clearly the son of the judge and a young woman who I later learnt was the son's wife. It is always a difficult moment to confront the victim's kin, and a moment the significance of which those two would have recognised, for each was a practising barrister. As I passed them I briefly expressed my sympathy, and I hoped that they understood that I was doing a job in which in other circumstances either of them might have been engaged.

Given the demeanour of John Smith on the day of the incident, Walter Hide, the driver of the car, was a very lucky man despite the terrifying experience he was to be put through. He was driving to work in his Austin Maxi having left home which was not far from that of the judge, but little did he imagine that before mid-afternoon that day he would be hijacked, kidnapped and compelled to drive over 100 miles at knife-point, be tied-up to a tree in a wood, and that his car would be sought by police in three counties in England and one in Scotland. His thoughts were purely on the work of the day as he moved in a slow line of moving traffic approaching traffic lights, when he saw a man running from the driveway of one of the houses on his left-hand side. The man was waving frantically and Hide's immediate reaction was that it was an emergency, and so he slowed down almost to a standstill. Then the man approached his vehicle, grabbed the nearside front door handle, opened the door, jumped into the front passenger seat and pulled out a large sheath knife from the left side of his trouser waistband with his left hand. He held it across his lap with the point towards the driver. His only words were, "Just do as I say and you won't get hurt." He gave directions to get on to the A6 towards the motorway heading North. He sounded agitated as he said, "I don't suppose you've been hijacked before—not a pleasant experience, eh?"

As they drove at 50–60 mph towards a service station the intruder said, "The guy had it coming to him, about 13-years ago he sent me down, to borstal." At the service station he said, "You fill it up, no tricks," but before saying this he picked up a blue sweater which had been on the passenger seat and covered the knife, which he held with the sweater. He got out of the car with the driver, standing next to him all the time as the car was filled, and ordered him to also buy some cigarettes and matches. Returning to the car, Smith said that if they came across any roadblocks he was to put his foot down and drive through them. He helped himself to Hide's sandwiches, explaining that he had neither slept nor eaten the previous night. "You won't mind me having these sandwiches will you, you probably had a lovely dinner last night, and I had nowt."

He lit a cigarette as they cruised along at 70 mph and he relaxed a little and rested the knife on his lap. Smith again said in a low voice, "He had it coming to him," but then turned towards him saying, "You'll probably know him, Openshaw."

He made it plain to Hide that the stage would come when it would be necessary to leave him tied up, probably to a tree. He did not like this idea and tried to talk him out of it by inviting his captor to just leave him somewhere and promising not to leave until half-an-hour had passed.

They reached Newcastle, did a detour, bought more petrol and made for the direction of Edinburgh. There followed a surreal discussion on the best way for the driver to be tied up, and with what. They settled on jump lead cables which were in the back of the car. They drove off the road and found a quiet spot. Hide's wrists and legs were tied, and Smith promised to phone somebody to tell them where he was. Before leaving he asked for his name, and Smith replied, "It's a bad thing to kill someone." Without another word he drove off in the car. Hide shouted for help as loud as he could, but no-one came, and after about half-an-hour he managed to free himself and make his way back to the road, where he found a house from where he phoned the police. Hide had resorted to remarkable calm, but later admitted to his fright. When taken into the woods he realised he was in grave danger of losing his life.

The police put out a call to all vehicles in the area, one of which sighted the car and pursued it, relayed the car number. It accelerated towards a police check point, was chased further and stopped. A man got out and ran across a field, and the police ran after him, tackled him and brought him down. The knife was seen protruding from his waistband, a second officer pulled it out, and Smith was arrested and taken to Jedburgh Police Station.

The trial

The first thing I did after the committal of the case from the magistrates' court to the Assize court was to endeavour to have it transferred from Lancashire. I have already explained that Judge Openshaw was well-known and respected in the Preston area where he sat. It would follow that he would be known by potential jurors who might have strong feelings about someone charged with his murder. It is not uncommon in such circumstances for an application to be made to have the case transferred to another area, and I had done that for example in the case of Donald Neilson, which had been moved from the Midlands to Oxford. In this instance the court could see the significance of my application, and without much trouble the hearing was transferred to Leeds Assizes. It was set down to be heard before Mr Justice Lawson and a jury in November 1981.

The more detailed instructions which John Smith gave to me merely amplified the brief instructions which I had taken when we first met, and they had prompted me to set in motion the need for medical reports on his state of mind as near to the date of the killing as possible. At that time there was no obligation to disclose what had been revealed in the medical report if the defendant did not wish this to be done, and it was not unknown for more than one report to be sought, to assess variations in the opinions of various psychiatrists. This was despite the instruction I had from Smith about his mental state. He made it clear that he was fully conscious of all the implications that might follow his actions. He was not "drunk or drugged to the eyeballs, falling about all over the place." He admitted that he might have had several drinks or taken a few Valium during the course of the evening, but he was not legless. In fact he said he was quite calm and composed; moreover, he had planned it over a period of months, so it was no spur-of-the-moment job. But I still had my doubts, and felt it my duty to investigate all possibilities.

He had been at least three times to look over the house and the surrounding district. On each of those occasions he had been unsure whether he was being followed, for he had innate suspicions about the police watching his every move. He had planned his actions for months, but nevertheless when he arrived on that morning he accepted that he had acted totally irresponsibly. This was a strange observation, because on the one hand he stated that he had committed the offence because he wanted it to be known that what he had done had in fact been done for his specific reasons, yet on the other hand he was deploring his lack of thought which would enable his own detection. He described how he went from one car to the other checking their contents, while at the same time leaving fingerprints all over their interiors. He even took a pullover from one of the cars and laid it on the floor as a pillow while realising that by so doing he would leave traces of hair or clothing which would lead to forensic detection. He also lit a couple of cigarettes, throwing the ends on the garage floor, which could have been sent for tests, and not only on the pullover, but also he knew his clothing fibres would be on the beams and footprints on the floor. He found it strange that he recalled all these little details even at the time, but nevertheless pursued his objective. He described the act in detail, and said it was like a nightmare come true.

I had never before experienced an accused actually use the word which he did. "I am a murderer. A cold calculated killer who deserves no sympathy and I ask for none. Nobody should be allowed to take the life of another in cold blood, and if it suits public opinion I would welcome hanging back tomorrow if I felt it would achieve anything. I would be prepared to die, it doesn't worry me now. What I have to go through in the forthcoming years is far greater punishment than any walk to the gallows, and I hope you will appreciate that fact."

He told me that he felt sorry for the family and that was why he was pleading guilty, that he didn't want to cause them any more distress by going through it all again. "They have suffered enough now. But everyone seems to forget about all the people he has sentenced in the past, some for long terms, some for short, who had been unable to stand the strain and stress of confinement, and who have either taken their own life or gone mad."

Smith recalled when he had been in Strangeways Prison awaiting allocation to another place, sharing a cell with a young boy of mixed race aged 15 whom Judge Openshaw had given five years for a knife attack. Smith considered this excessive even though he knew nothing of the circumstances and described him as being a victim of our feudal penal system. Smith argued that if someone so young had to be deprived of his liberty the sentence should have been more humane and civilised. He accepted that it wouldn't work with many who would never learn, but repeated that if he, Smith, had been treated better on his first sentence "it might have been different".

He argued that Openshaw could never understand the logic of giving someone a chance, saying that he always had to do things by the book and was blind to human reason, that he would not give on anything and was totally inflexible, so, said Smith, he paid for it with his life. "He took mine, so I took his."

Smith maintained that he had vowed after he had been sentenced that he would "get him when I get out", and that no amount of solitary or loss of remission would cloud his memory. He came out with the extraordinary admission that about four weeks earlier he had gone to London with the intention of killing Lord Hailsham, the then Lord Chancellor and head of the judiciary, but he admitted that when he got down there he just could not do it and threw the knife he was carrying into the Thames and came home.

In the light of these assertions it might seem logical that the senior medical officer and visiting psychiatrist at the place of detention, Risley, where Smith awaited trial found that he showed no evidence of any specific mental disorder, that he was fully in touch with reality and well aware of the nature and possible consequences of any charge against him; and that he had never been hallucinated, deluded or showed disorder of thought. He was closely monitored as a category-A prisoner and note was taken of the hostility and resentment expressed against the prison authorities, and although he continued to express paranoid ideas they were not considered truly delusional. In short, the doctor felt he was fit to stand trial.

The prison medical officer, who in turn concluded that he was not suffering from any mental illness under the Mental Health Act, referred him to a consultant psychiatrist, nor could he be rated subnormal, but he suffered from a distortion of personality. This was despite a review of the various indications of psychotic disorder revealed over the years, and the earlier making of a section 60 order following an occasion when he had threatened to jump off Blackpool Tower.

I instructed an experienced psychiatrist, whom I had worked with on many cases, someone who, if there had been a shred of evidence or act which might enable a defence of diminished responsibility to be put forward would have highlighted this. In the case of John Smith he was unable so to do, and having spent much time looking in great detail at the matters indicated by the two earlier medical experts could find nothing to contradict them. The most that could be said was that Smith suffered from a personality disorder.

No court or judge is happy, where the evidence is unchallenged, to proceed with a sentence, particularly in circumstances which lead towards a heavy disposal, without a clear examination of the evidence. The court was provided with just such an opportunity by the fact that when brought before the court and when the charges of murder and kidnap were put to him, Smith remained silent. When this happens a jury has to decide whether the defendant was mute of malice, that is deliberately, or "by visitation of God".

I had initially instructed Gilbert Gray QC, a barrister with whom I had worked on many occasions, including the trial of Donald Nielson, the Black Panther. But for some reason best-known to my client, and on the one and only occasion I can recall it happening to him, Gilly was sacked by his client. The trial was about to start, witnesses were prepared, the hearing all set to go, and I had been fortunate to find a respected counsel, Gerald Coles QC, to take the case, but once again Smith found no favour in his advice, and Coles was also dismissed after unsuccessfully telling the court that his client felt that first he had wrongly been charged with murder, and the correct charge should be treason, and second that the case should be tried by the International Court at The Hague, because Judge Openshaw was too well-known by all the counsels and judges in the English courts. Coles advised him of the error in his beliefs here, and so he left the case.

Smith still wanted someone of note to represent him, and the name of Sir Ivan Lawrence QC, MP was mentioned. Lawrence had received much publicity and a knighthood as chairman of the House of Commons Home Affairs Committee, and to my surprise was available to take the case.

Because Smith had still refused to enter a plea, a jury were empanelled to decide the issue of whether he was mute of malice. This largely rested on evidence that he had been quite prepared to speak until arraignment, that he had spoken to people in prison and to the doctors, so the jury had little trouble in deciding the mute of malice issue. Having decided this, the judge took the next perfectly proper step of stating that the action, or non-action, of Smith would be treated as a plea of not guilty and the evidence against him would be heard, whereupon Smith sacked Lawrence.

For a while he retained the service of the junior counsel, Louise Godfrey. He seemingly also had no quarrel with me, and I was asked by the judge, Mr Justice Lawson, if I would kindly sit in the dock, next to Smith, "to best explain the procedures to him, as he had no leading counsel," and said the judge, "Would you kindly implore him not to interrupt the proceedings, and conduct himself more appropriately, otherwise I will send him to sit in the cells."

There followed the worst few hours of my professional life, sitting in the dock during a murder trial, when the prosecuting QC called all the necessary evidence. In respect of each witness Godfrey was forced to say, "I am not instructed to ask any questions."

This lasted for one-and-a-half-days. During that time Smith sat on the floor of the dock, walked around it, pulled faces at counsel and witnesses, and somehow managed to smuggle a cigarette and match into the dock, and actually lit up and blew a large puff of smoke in the direction of the judge. That was the last straw; he was taken downstairs to the cells.

I remained where I was for about an hour. At last and at a suitable moment I raised a hand. The judge saw me, and over his reading glasses said, "Yes,

Mr Black?"

"My Lord," I said, "the defendant is now down in the cells ... do I really have to sit here?"

"Oh, no, of course not, I'm terribly sorry Mr Black; you can come out of the dock, and sit on the solicitors' benches."

The jury was out for a long time, and on one occasion returned with a question for the judge on the standard of proof required. However, eventually they returned verdicts of mute by malice on both counts.

The judge refused to allow Louise Godfrey to read out the statement that Smith had written. He said, "I have seen the document, and I am not going to allow this court to be used as a platform for his attention-seeking activities. He has already achieved this by murdering someone. He is a very dangerous man, and will remain so for a very long time."

So, on 19 November 1981 the judge sentenced Smith to life for the murder of Judge Openshaw and five years for the kidnap of Hide. He ordered that he should not be released for at least 25-years. As he left the dock Smith turned and shouted at Mr Justice Lawson, "I will not forget it; if I ever get out of here I'll be round to your house and cut your throat."

At this time, in 1981, Judge Openshaw's son, Peter, was a young barrister, who ten years later became a QC. He was appointed a High Court judge and knighted in June 2005, and his wife, Elizabeth Swift, was also appointed to the High Court, and made a Dame, the very first time such appointments had happened to a husband and wife on the same day. In July 2008, Mr Justice Peter Openshaw sentenced Daniel Breaks to life, with 30-years to serve for an offence of murder. The defendant shouted towards the judge: "I will escape and kill you."

At the time of writing about this case, in the spring of 2014, I thought it necessary to obtain Smith's permission which he granted, provided any royalties to which he might be entitled for this permission be distributed between the Red Indian Population of North America, and the Aboriginal people in Australia. I shall follow this promise by making a modest donation to an appropriate charity.

CHAPTER 16

Courts Martial

During my army service I did some Court Martial work. The tribunal was made up of three officers, the President usually of the rank no lower than lieutenant colonel, and the others no lower than captain. There was a legally qualified judge advocate or assistant judge advocate who dealt with matters of law and advice on sentence. The prosecutor would be an officer from the Department of Legal Services to the arm in question.

After leaving the army I remained on the list of those willing to accept defence instructions, and from time-to-time I was also instructed privately.

The end of the Second World War was dominated by the aim to reach Berlin, a race between the British and American armies on the west, and the Russian army on the East. It was virtually a draw, and the result was that under the ensuing occupation of Berlin, the Cold War aggravated the issue of control, and Berlin was an isolated divided compound within the eastern part of a divided country. That isolation was worsened as relations between the East and West deteriorated, and the railway running to Berlin from the West became subject to controls and inspections. The British, French and American section of the four-power occupation force were on one side of the Berlin Wall, built in 1961 and not pulled down until November 1989, and on the other side were the Russians. Due to the railway and road closures the British force had to be supplied by transport planes and these planes landed at Gatow Airport, which was manned by the RAF.

My client I shall call John, for that was his name, but there will be no further identification, for he was not my normal type of criminal client. I know not how he fared thereafter, for this case was in 1977. At that time he was serving in the Royal Air Force, ironically nearing the end of a short service engagement and therefore due for demob within days of the incident which was to delay his departure for civilian life. As a senior aircraftsman stationed at Gatow, he would be entitled to free time and there were no restrictions on fraternisation with the German population, so it was quite normal that he should have a German girlfriend, and that he should be free to visit any place within bounds in western Berlin. This included the *Pizzeria Guerrina* on the corner of Breiterstrasse and Charlottenstrasse, a small but busy eating and drinking establishment owned and run by Frau Nermin Elbers. The local police did not know the pizzeria, for its customers were mainly well-behaved locals who ate, drank, chatted and sang to the accompaniment of a sometimes rather loud jukebox.

There was, however an ominous structure in the area where the pizzeria was situated, a dark stonewalled and somewhat menacing large building but a few footsteps away. This was Spandau Prison. Built in 1876 as a military detention centre, after the Reichstag fire of 1933 it was home to the opponents of Hitler, holding them in a form of protective custody. It became the predecessor of the Nazi concentration camps. This was the prison in which those Nazis who were found guilty at the Nuremberg trials, including Rudolph Hess, were confined. The four occupying powers alternated control of the prison on a monthly basis, and the flag that flew at any one time was that of the force then controlling the prison. It was demolished in 1987 following the death of the last prisoner, Hess, to prevent it from becoming a neo-Nazi shrine.

But on 29 November 1977, when Rudolph Hess was no doubt safely locked in his cell but a few hundred metres away John and his girlfriend, Ursula Wasserzier, entered and sat down at a table in the left-hand corner of the pizzeria, where they ordered two pizzas, a coke and some water. While waiting for them to arrive John pulled some coins out of his pocket and went over to the jukebox and selected a few records. No sooner had he done this than a group of eight people came into the pizzeria, a plump, jovial crowd. Frau Edith Schultz, the proprietress of the *Zickenshulze* pub next door, together with her husband and the others sat down at the first table near the entrance. They ordered a bottle of Sekt and some food, and when the bottle arrived and was poured they all sang in German *Happy Birthday to You*.

The singing drowned the music from the jukebox, and thus began the preliminaries of a Third World War. Who started the scuffle was but one of the points to be analysed by a subsequent Court Martial, which explained my presence in Berlin some months later.

It seemed that rather sadly Senior Aircraftsman John had tucked in his pocket a handgun, and yes, somehow or other the gun was fired, and fired in the direction of the publican's husband, who was thereby caused injury to his face and upper body. John was charged with wounding with intent to cause grievous bodily harm (or GBH), an offence so serious that even in the civilian courts a conviction would attract a substantial period of imprisonment. There were other charges included in the indictment relating to the possession of the pistol.

I have described my days on National Service, and how during that time I was fortunate to spread my fledgling wings by appearing in Courts Martial. At that time I made certain contacts with the Army Legal Service which enabled me to have my name on the list of those to whom legal aid would be granted to conduct their cases, and the retention of my name on that list after I left the army, together with what I modestly call my own reputation, enabled me to travel to Germany, Northern Ireland and Cyprus to attempt to save soldiers from the somewhat draconian clutches of military law. I say this because it was natural that offences committed while on service, or even worse in the face of the enemy or potential enemy, should attract higher sentences, particularly when there was either a danger of distraction, or an example to be shown to others. After all you can't fire a gun with accuracy if you are sniffing coke, or if you place your comrades in danger by negligence, disregard or foolishness.

His case was to be tried by a District Court Martial composed of senior officers (in the RAF this would be a wing commander and two squadron leaders). A member of the RAF's legal service would prosecute the case, and although the defendant would be offered a defending officer because of the seriousness of the allegation, it was explained to him that he could choose a civilian lawyer on the approved list of those to whom a legal aid certificate would be granted. His father in the UK telephoned my office to see if I was available to take the case. Not knowing about the legal aid proviso he offered to pay my fees, but I was able to assure him that that would not be necessary, as the RAF would pay both the fees and my travel costs.

The hearing was due to take place on 9 May 1978 at the RAF station, Gatow. I flew in to Templehof, the commercial Berlin airport, and was met by the officer who had been appointed to assist me in conducting the defence, Flying Officer Malcolm Brown; we were driven in an official limousine to the officers' mess at Gatow, where I was to stay. This all brought back memories of my own army service at Aldershot, even down to being given a batman, though I did resist the temptation to ask him "And how's Robin?" I was handed a file of papers, which contained the summary of evidence and witness statements, which had been taken from the prosecution witnesses, and then introduced to the prosecuting officer, Squadron Leader Mike Price, an affable soul who was most helpful in filling me in.

He immediately told me about a problem with one of the witnesses, someone who although a prosecution witness he felt would be helpful to my case. The problem was that the witness was unwilling to come to the air force base where the Court Martial was due to be held in a couple of days' time. Moreover, I was told that as the man was a German civilian, and the Court Martial was of course being held under the provisions of military law, he could not be compelled to come in to give his evidence. "Well," I suggested, "then why can't we go to him?". And out came the military law books, or more precisely book, for there was but one.

I spent the next day meeting, and having a conference with my client. He was a likeable young man, who had never been in any form of trouble before, and who had been within days of completing his service when the incident happened. Since the incident several weeks earlier he had been under open arrest, which meant that he could not leave the base.

The gun, which he admitted carrying, although looking fearsome was really a starting pistol which had been altered to fire all sorts, and which he really used for sound effects in the discotheque, which he ran. He also carried it as a precaution against being robbed, because this enterprising young airman had for some time been running a successful discotheque, and his profits had mounted, but alas could not be banked, and so he carried around with him large wads of the local currency. He admitted having the gun, and that having been threatened by one of the Schultz birthday group he pulled it out, always pointing it at the ground, to deter any anticipated attack, in other words a self-defensive gesture. But the gun had gone off accidentally when he was touched by the other man.

The trial followed the course anticipated, the Schultz group supporting, albeit with some degree of differences, the complainant's version. Defence witnesses seemed short on the ground, if any at all existed. It came to the point where I needed them to call the evidence of the reluctant witness, but he was not there, and the court agreed with my submission that we adjourn to the *locus in quo*, in ordinary language the place where the shooting had taken place. We got into three cars, and accompanied by motorcycles drove through the city to the pizzeria, the tribunal, the lawyers and the prisoner with his escort. The only thing lacking to give it a totally surreal atmosphere was that the orderly did not bustle around carrying an oversized pepper mill. The equally bemused witness, although still not compellable did turn up, and gave evidence which justified the efforts I had made.

Whilst driving back to the RAF base and down the *Kurfurstendamenstrasse* our attention was drawn to a number of posters showing nude women with three large heart shapes obscuring more intimate areas. The driver said this was a new club called *The Lonely Hearts*. He said he had heard the music was particularly good there. The prosecuting officer suggested that if we had each finished our closing speeches by the end of the day's proceedings we ought to pay it a visit. I am not sure whether it was the incentive of a visit to *The Lonely Hearts* club, but strangely enough we each did in fact conclude our closing speech by the end of that day's proceedings, and consequently that evening we drove downtown to *Kurdamstrasse* in the squadron leader's MGB GT. The person who answered the doorbell looked at us and demanded ten franks each, in return for which we were each given a key. It was pretty dark inside and it took some moments for our eyes to become accustomed, but what I saw was revealing in all senses of that word. There must have been about 50 people in the small room, in the corner of which was a bar, where a band was playing traditional jazz. People were drinking, dancing or just sitting around listening to the music, but they had one thing in common. Not one of them wore a stitch of clothing. By gestures it was shown that the keys we had been given were to individual cupboards, into which we were expected to put all, but all, our clothes. I am a natural worrier, and recall being anxious about what I would do with the key if I had no pocket into which it might be placed. Nor indeed was there anything remotely attractive about the sight of 50 well-constructed Germans in their *Geburdenstag* suits. The wing commander was enthusiastically disrobing, but I couldn't take it, and I confess I let the side down by telling him I would make my own way back to base, and see him in the morning.

When we assembled back in RAF Gatow, it was for the final stages, and considering the evidence I did not believe the outcome to be unreasonable. John was cleared of the most serious matter of wounding with intent to cause GBH, but convicted of an alternative much lesser offence, of carrying the gun *per se*. He was also cleared on two other charges involving the breach of military standing orders and the actual deliberate firing of the gun. I made a *mitigation* speech on his behalf, and his sentence of 84 days' detention, uncomfortable as it would have been in a military unit, was not as bad as it could have been. I am sure that upon his release he led, and I hope still leads, a blameless and positive life.

The next available plane for my return home was not until some two days later and I was pleased when I received a message back at the mess from the tribunal chairman, that his return too had been delayed, and he invited me together with the other officers to make an excursion into East Berlin. Would I be at the front door at 6.30 pm in informal civilian dress? We assembled, and shortly afterwards one of the RAF unmarked police cars drew up, the driver saluted the wing commander and asked him, "The usual place, Sir?" The reply was a grunt, "Of course." We drove through the infamous Checkpoint Charlie with the minimum of fuss, and as we did we entered another world.

West Berlin, despite the battle of 35-years earlier, looked a normal thriving city, with busy shops, heavy traffic and a lively population, but as we passed the hole in the massive concrete wall that was the checkpoint East Berlin looked completely different. For the first five minutes we drove through an area which had been razed to the ground, with swathes of heaped rubble and bricks, seemingly as untouched as it had been immediately following the close of battle. This gradually gave way to one or two inhabited buildings, and then some large concrete blocks of dismal grey flats. We suddenly came across a street of more respectable and better-preserved houses, and the car pulled up at one of them. I was not sure what to expect, but my expectations rose as we approached the front door, and after ringing the bell, an extremely attractive woman of a certain age opened it. I tried to control the smile on my lips, as she said, "Hello, Colonel" to the wing commander, and invited us in. We were then beckoned through some dark red velvet curtains like the front of a stage; it took a moment for my eyes to become accustomed to the light, and my hope of a Bacchanalian orgy vanished. Instead, there were displayed on an array of tables and shelves a collection of sparkling cut-glass tumblers, wine glasses, jugs and decanters. They had all clearly been brought in from Leipzig, one of the world centres of glass manufacture, which had survived the war. I discovered to my delight that the West German marks, which I had brought had a much greater value in terms of the East German mark, and as the wing commander had previously discovered, one could acquire some true bargains in whisky glasses and decanters. We took our purchases back to the police car, and the driver advised us to put the boxes well under the car seats. Sure enough the guards on the friendly side of the checkpoint asked if we had anything to declare. "Yes," I responded, "I am truly relieved to be back."

A very different location

There followed various other requests to travel for Court Martial work, and although not particularly profitable I enjoyed a few days back in the atmosphere of the military system and staying in an officers' mess. They varied from various naval bases in the UK, to Maastricht in the east of The Netherlands, which was the HQ of AFSCENT, Allied Forces in Central Europe, and to Northern Ireland.

This was the time of the IRA insurrection and I admit I felt the risk of these visits, especially when advised that a low profile at arrival in various airports was necessary, only to find that on one occasion this was not possible due to being summoned by name over the loudspeaker system to make myself known in the military reception area.

But no trip was more emotional than an invitation to a case involving a soldier serving with the First Armoured Division stationed near Detmold, which was conveniently also the Court Martial centre for that part of Germany. The case itself was but part of this story, in fact I suppose the *raison d'être*, but it was the location which made it different. The officers' mess was a rather grand building; clearly it had survived the war and had been built for a power before the arrival of the British. The marble hall, the gilded ceilings, the glass windows and the heavy wooden furniture meant that it was not a bright building, and in fact it was quite dark.

It was arranged that the car would pick me up at 7.30 am for the drive to Detmold and my conference with the accused, a misty November morning, rather cold, with the dawn reluctant to break. We left the mess and soon were driving along a country road with trees on either side. The car slowed down as we went round a bend, and what I saw made the hairs on the back of my neck tingle. The words *Arbeit Macht Frei* were clearly written in metal letters on the arch above a large closed gate, those infamous words which had been the introduction for thousands, nay millions, to the concentration camps. The army driver sensed my discomfort, and I did not need to ask as he volunteered, "You know what that is sir... it's Belsen." He stopped the car, and I wrapped my coat tightly as he pushed the gate open, for there was no lock as there was nothing to secure, just a large clearing in the forest with mounds of grass-covered earth and a few small memorial stones, no buildings, no huts, no museum, just a clearing in the forest. It took several moments for the significance to sink in. My driver broke the silence. "And you realise, sir, don't you, that the place where you are staying is where their officers lived?" I had not realised that, but then it made sense, if sense can come of such an environment: the building, the décor, the figures painted on the ceilings and dingy corners of the room where I had taken dinner and had breakfast, a realisation which on my return became manifest when I discerned the odd swastika woven into the paintwork. Much later that day I vowed I could not eat another morsel in that room, nor could I sleep in that building.

But back to the moment of revelation, the thought which went through my mind as I stood there on that miserable morning, looking at the mounds which I now realised had beneath them the remains of more than just one generation, was had my forebears not persevered in their journey from Lithuania to England, then I might well have been with them under those piles of earth.

Chapter 17

A Sad Day for Justice

It was around this time that I was instructed to take over the representation of one of The Birmingham Six. I had not represented the man in question at the time of his initial trial.

My part in the case related to an action brought by the six against the West Midlands Police, and this was in 1980 some five years after their initial conviction alleging assault following their arrest and subsequent interrogation.

The pub bombings, at the *Mulberry Bush* and *Rotunda* in Central Birmingham resulting in 21 deaths and 162 people injured had taken place in November 1974, for which the provisional IRA were immediately believed responsible. The one I was instructed to represent was John Walker, who although born in Derry, had lived and worked in Birmingham for some 15-years. He and his friends were arrested whilst travelling to Belfast to attend a funeral, it is right to say that the deceased had been a member of the provisional IRA. The men were arrested as they were about to board the ferry, but unfortunately they did not tell the police the true purpose of their visit, and this did not help them.

They were subjected to lengthy interrogation, and they made admissions which were later repudiated and it was during the course of this they said they were assaulted, and indeed at a later stage following a remand to prison in Birmingham their allegation was supported by visible injuries. Fourteen prison officers were charged with assault but found not guilty.

At the trial of the six, circumstantial evidence relating to John Walker's association with IRA members was deemed by the judge to be admissible, and there was considerable argument as to discrepancies in the nature of the scientific evidence presented by the Crown. The trial heard their allegations of the violence which had been used to extract the confessions, allegations which the trial judge Mr Justice Bridge described as "bizarre and grotesque".

They were all six found guilty of murder in August 1975, and sentenced to life imprisonment. The Lord Chief Justice, Lord Widgery, dismissed their appeal in March 1976.

However they were not to be silenced and the following year they pressed charges against the West Midland Police. There came a time however when the issue arose of whether they should be granted legal aid to pursue these appeals. The Crown, on behalf of the officers said they should be prevented from proceeding, and this is where I was consulted.

I recall visiting John Walker, a tall slim, naturally white faced and extremely gentle person. I took him once again through the details of the case, and his version of events, by this time amplified by the experiences in the courts, with the judges, and in the various prisons, all of which taken into account made me think of him as a man to be believed. I know it is not for the lawyer to believe a man, but for the jury or the judge, but this man's resolution shone.

In contrast I have to say that I was bitterly disappointed by the words of Lord Denning. The very name Denning was revered by every law student and practitioner. He had come to the bench like a blast of cool, refreshing, air and his judgments were a delight to read.

I could barely believe his words in that case:

> "Just consider the course of events if their action were to proceed to trial [this is the action by the six against the police]. If the six men failed it would mean that much time and money and worry would have been expended by many people to no good purpose. If they won it would mean that the police were guilty of perjury; that they were guilty of violence and threats; that the confessions were involuntary and improperly admitted in evidence; and that the convictions were erroneous. That would mean that the Home Secretary would have either to recommend that they be pardoned or to remit the case to the Court of Appeal. That was such an appalling vista that every sensible person would say 'It cannot be right that these actions should go further' they should be struck out either on the ground that the men are stopped from challenging the decision of Mr Justice Bridge, or alternatively that it is an abuse of the process of the court. Whichever it is, the actions should be stopped."

And so they were.

I was happy to know that subsequently despite the fact that an appeal against the conviction was dismissed in 1988, the third appeal in 1991 when new evidence of police fabrication and also questions about the scientific evidence previously presented, must have weighed heavily upon those responsible for the prosecution and their case did not proceed.

That court described the prosecution scientific evidence as "demonstrably wrong".

The men each received substantial sums by way of compensation for their many years in prison.

This case played a large part in the revisiting of the law on evidence, admissibility, and police involvement in interviewing as the evidence against them was very much based on confessions. Much was learned about the need for this type of situation never to happen again. It is therefore ironic that we have witnessed the arrival of non-legally qualified Ministers of Justice who double-up as Lord Chancellor, and whose political ambitions depend upon adhering to financial constraints imposed by a Prime Minister and Chancellor which do not sufficiently take into account the protection of the vulnerable in the criminal justice system. I deal further with this problem at a later stage.

Chapter 18

Some Changes in the Law, and Mainly for the Good

On the North-eastern Circuit, which stretched from Sheffield in the South to Newcastle in the North, and which included Leeds and York, we were fortunately served by many talented and accomplished barristers.

Over the years I have watched the rise of many youngsters, who would happily be sent into the magistrates' court for a few guineas to deal with the excess of cases which came into my office, and with which neither I nor the seven solicitors working with me could deal.

I know there would be some firms who would take advantage of these youngsters, but this would be quite wrong. If we had to seek the assistance of counsel in this type of situation, first he or she would be paid a fair portion of the fee, and second they would receive properly drafted instructions, taken by my firm from the client. We kept an eye on these youngsters, and when we felt they were up to it send them to do proper cases in the Quarter Sessions or Assizes, or indeed as they became known after 1972, the Crown Court.

I would then see the more capable be given silk, that is become QCs, and then recorders and judges. In more recent years the senior judges, city recorders, were all people whom I had at one time sent scurrying into the magistrates' court.

I like to think that part of my skill in the choice of counsel for my clients was to decide upon horses for courses, for example the fiery orator for a case without legal merit, and a legal brainbox for the case that required a painstaking analysis of complicated figures and detail.

I began practice in the days when there existed the dock brief, which in simple terms meant that the defendant could choose any counsel sitting in court, who was expected to give of his services, talent and experience in exchange for literally less than a handful of guineas, and if he received more than over half a handful, he would be lucky.

Many times did I see busy barrister make a dash for the courtroom door when a likely candidate for a dock brief stumbled into the dock. These were usually reserved for fairly simple and straightforward matters where the involvement of a solicitor was unnecessary in the Crown Court, but was more important to a solicitor in the magistrate's court where their distribution depended on the whims of the magistrate or his clerk. The clerk was the person who decided to whom it should go, and there was usually great interest in who it would be if it were a murder charge. From time-to-time a person so charged was in a complete daze from the time of the act until the time of his or her appearance in court; someone appearing for the first time would have no idea about instructing a solicitor.

There was gradually introduced the legal aid system and it was sufficient for those who practised either criminal or matrimonial work, which I did. Both leading and junior counsel were always pleased to receive instructions which were legally-aided. I never ever came across a case where counsel's clerk gave even the slightest indication of preference for a matter to be privately paid, rather than by legal aid, and although there were cases where I heard of lawyers seeking a supplementary payment I would not countenance the thought of this. It would have been quite improper.

I recall one case which came from Bradford where seven Sikhs who all instructed me were charged with murder. There was no conflict between them, in that they all gave the same version of events. I received seven separate legal aid certificates, and at first blush it looked as though I may have to try to find Seven Silks for Seven Sikhs, but common sense prevailed and I divided them into three groups so that each of their interests could be properly looked after.

There can be no doubt at all that the service which a defendant who was in receipt of legal aid obtained was in no way inferior to that given to a paying client. There were no constraints and I found that I was allowed to use my judgment when it came to matters of expenses incurred in the course of the preparation of a defence. Quite clearly the Legal Aid Fund, administered by the Law Society would not countenance lavish and unnecessary expenditure.

In some cases there was no end to the demands of a defendant up against what was a realistic avenue of enquiry. There were rates of payment, both on a time basis and on an assessment of the skill of the expert involved, medical, forensic or legal. I rarely had disagreements about my fees and counsel and expert witnesses knew that I would put their requests fairly to the fund. It would often require no more than a phone call for consent to be obtained.

An example of this was a domestic shooting incident. I was called upon to represent a man who took a gun to his wife, whom he believed was associating with another and who had told him that she was leaving him. The man who was quiet and timid had been depressed for some time; he had previously overdosed on anti-depressants. The facts of the case he admitted, and it appeared clear to me that it was necessary for him to be examined by medical experts as soon as possible. I put this into effect straightaway, and a report was obtained that he was indeed suffering from a mental illness, which substantially diminished his responsibility. For such a plea to succeed it was necessary to obtain reports from two properly qualified psychiatrists to this effect, and this I had done.

Counsel was Gilbert Gray QC, and Arthur Myerson, then a junior counsel, but later to become a QC and judge.

This was a prime example of a man receiving the same expert professional help from the medical and legal profession in a speedy and professional manner, which could not in any way have been improved by having been a paid case.

They agreed with the reports I had obtained, and the case went before Mr Justice Boreham and a jury, who found the defendant guilty of manslaughter through diminished responsibility. He was sentenced to a hospital order, though without restriction of time. Despite that he only spent one year in the confines of Broadmoor.

☙

There have been considerable changes in many aspects of the criminal law and criminal procedure since I began practice, in some ways improvements, and some rather renegade steps in the name of progress.

At first blush the creation of a separate prosecuting authority, in this case the Crown Prosecution Service, would give the impression of an independent view being taken so far as prosecuting a case was concerned. Before my time the court of first instance in criminal matters was called the police court and was often in a building adjacent to or closely connected to the police station. A single blue lamp illuminated the exterior of both buildings. The prosecutor would be a police officer, usually an inspector or chief inspector, but often a sergeant, each of them uniformed lest any mistake be made about who they were. The list caller, that is the person who decided in what order cases would be heard, was sometimes the most important person in the court, at least in the eyes of defence solicitors eager to have their cases heard. Both lay and stipendiary magistrates were independent, though from time-to-time their true allegiance slipped out.

When an offence was detected the culprit would be marched to the police station, and the arresting officer would hand him over to the station sergeant and be expected to tell the sergeant what the person was to be charged with. Somewhere upstairs in the police station would be either more senior officers or solicitors employed by the police or local authority to prosecute, and they would then have charge of the conduct of the case. The staircase to their offices was always open for the officer in the case to discuss progress, and take advice upon witnesses either to be called, or who yet needed to be sought. The securing of a conviction was the aim, and there might be a speedy decision as to whether the original charge was too severe or too lenient, and an immediate amendment made.

The Crown Prosecution Service was established in 1986 with the responsibility of providing legal advice to both the police and other investigative agencies, to decide whether an accused should face prosecution and conduct such prosecutions in magistrates' courts and Crown Court. The Attorney General superintends its work, but the person with executive responsibility is the Director of Public Prosecutions. The criteria are whether there exists sufficient evidence for a realistic prospect of conviction. If there is, then the Crown Prosecution Service will conduct the prosecution, using their in-house lawyers at the lower level, and instructing counsel at the higher level. The advantage is that there will be an independent review of the evidence, in that the file will not just remain in the hands of the police, and decisions will be made with all due regard and in an unhurried fashion.

The problem here of course is that the decision may take time, and there may be many discussions. It follows that delay exists, and this may not be fair to an accused, who in an extreme case may be held in custody for a lengthy pre-trial period.

A case which illustrates the advantage of the earlier, speedier system involved a fight between two men. Again I shall not use names because those involved would no doubt wish it to be put well behind them, for it happened getting on for 40-years ago. The defendant was a thoroughly decent young man of 20-years who visited a public house with his friend, and then travelled on to a nightclub. He had not had much to drink, and there was no suggestion of misbehaviour on his part. In the club he had a discussion with a bouncer, a largely built man. The discussion was friendly, and referred to the sponsoring of the bouncer at an event involving a display of strength. My client willingly agreed to this, and in fact handed some money over. A little while later my client noticed his drinking glass was chipped, and turned to the bouncer who was standing near the bar, and asked if he would mind changing the chipped glass. The bouncer took umbrage to this, stating that was not his job, in fact he was paid to fight. It was said that the bouncer developed the discussion about their comparative strength, and he challenged my client to sort it out by having a fight. My client and his friend made to leave, and went to the car park, whereupon the bouncer again repeated his invitation to a fight, and they both went behind a wall. The evidence of the various witnesses was somewhat convoluted, but there was an indication of blows being struck by each. My client's version was that he was approached by the bouncer, and pushed him away a couple of times. In short the bouncer fell backwards, hit his head once against the floor and sustained the injury from which he died shortly afterwards.

This is where the question of speedy action by the police requires a story. The incident happened at about 2 am on 13 May 1982. A post-mortem examination was carried out at 7.15 am on 13 May, and thereafter the defendant, who had been arrested, was charged with murder and appeared at a special court held many miles from Leeds where he was represented by another local solicitor. He was remanded in custody for four days, during which I was instructed to take over the case. I immediately obtained an independent pathologist's report and upon its receipt expressed it to the police.

I appeared on 18 May for him, and applied for bail, which was granted by the magistrates with stringent conditions of residence and curfew. To the credit of the police, immediate consideration was given to my report and my representations that this charge should not be one of murder but of manslaughter at the worst, and even that would be contested. The police prepared the file within weeks, and committal took place and the case sent to the Crown Court.

The judge on Assizes was Mr Justice Peter Taylor, who later became Lord Chief Justice. As a QC I had known him well, and instructed him several times. For the defendant I instructed Gilbert Gray QC with Elizabeth Baker. The judge tried the case in his usual exemplary fashion. After less than two hours deliberation the jury acquitted our client on the remaining charge of manslaughter, and he walked free. I doubt that such a swift disposal could take in the somewhat convoluted procedures of today.

The distinction between murder, a common law offence, and manslaughter, under the Homicide Act 1957, enabled a finding by the jury to bring in a verdict of manslaughter, even if a person had been charged with murder. This is what happened in 1978 in a case which I dealt with, also having instructed Gilbert Gray QC.

I shall again mention neither name nor location, for I hope that the person concerned is still around. All I will say is that this arose from a dispute between two brothers, the problem being an attractive Scandinavian girl who came into the life of one brother, and this resulted in the loss of the life of the other brother. This was somewhat like the Genesis story, though there the older Cain killed the younger Abel, and here it was the other way around. But the reason, though not described in Genesis but ascribed by the commentators, was the same, jealousy and anger over a beautiful woman.

The case was tried by Mr Justice Boreham. The jury took longer than in the previous case I mentioned, and they were out for some seven hours. They returned a verdict of not guilty of murder though guilty of manslaughter, and the defendant was sentenced to five years.

It will probably be realised by my appreciation of the results of the last two cases that I am a strong supporter of the jury system, and there were many other cases in which I was happy for the fate of my client to have been left in the hands of 12 strangers, who until they came to court and saw the defendant had never previously clapped eyes on him. This is a view which continued during my subsequent judicial career, and indeed I was frequently grateful that the ultimate decision was not in my hands, but theirs.

There are certain exceptions, which I shall deal with later, but the simple straightforward decision, for example, necessary in the case of a defendant pleading self-defence, is one far better left in the hands of the 12. A straightforward example of this was shown in what I termed "The Christmas Domestic".

Many of our Yorkshire friends would go away over Christmas, and as the Christmas holiday became prolonged, stretching from Christmas Eve until the day after New Year, it eventually became a two-week holiday. But not for me, nor, alas my family. The Christmas holiday period was always a busy one, and it was inevitable that I would be called out to one if not more police stations around the West Riding. The close confines and strains of familial gatherings coupled with the ingestion of alcohol which that time of year called for often resulted in violence, and on more than one occasion fatality.

The call came on Christmas morning in 1977; it was from Bradford Central Police Station, so I knew it would be serious, and it was. The accused had been charged with murder, a stabbing, and the victim had died on the spot. It will be noted that the accused had been charged before I arrived, arrested, interviewed and then charged, for this was some seven years before the Police and Criminal Evidence Act had come into effect. This act ensured that a defendant was told he was entitled to legal advice virtually the moment he stepped into a police station, most certainly before he was interviewed. He could have a solicitor present at the interview to advise him, and if he did not have a solicitor then a duty solicitor would be provided. In 1977 it was only the savvy accused who would say that he would not answer any questions until he had seen a solicitor, and then if one was not readily available, or if the interviewing officer thought it would interfere with the proceedings, even that could be refused. But this defendant was not savvy; his only previous experience with the courts had been over motoring matters, and so he had already spoken to the investigating officers and told them his side of the story.

In this case, that was probably to his benefit. It impressed the jury. For here was not someone seeking to hide behind the curtain of legal protection, or as happens so often since the Act, obscure the normal progression of a search for the truth by answering "No comment" to all and any police questions. Here was a young man, 30-years-of-age, caught up in the most terrifying circumstances, and accepting responsibility for a man's death — if not his murder. But murderer he was not, as I advised him when his tearful story unfolded.

He had been an adopted child, had an uneventful education and trained for an apprenticeship but failed to secure qualifications due to a minor illness. He worked constantly, though his employers changed, and he again sought to advance his skills and had just qualified as a joiner before the tragedy. His stepfather died leaving him a sum of money, and this spurred him into a marriage which lasted weeks. He became friendly with his estranged wife's sister, whose husband was sent to prison as a result, among other things, of his violence, after which the two became more than just friendly. Her husband's time in prison was nearing its end, and he had sent threats to get my client. He told his wife that he was coming home and she suggested that my client left until such time as she could pluck up the courage to say she was leaving her husband. She dreaded this because of his temper, but she did not wish to abandon her home and chattels, and there were two young children to think of. Ironically she was concerned that if he did not have a home to come to he would need to spend a further four months in prison.

My client therefore left the house and lived elsewhere, but the two maintained contact. She told him he had agreed to a separation in front of his probation officer, but later he got drunk, kicked her out of the house and ripped all her clothes, and when the police were called would only attend when three officers were available, because of his reputation.

The two of them found an alternative address, but heard that her husband had "put out a contract for £500" on my client. Their hiding place was discovered, her husband forced his way in and after a struggle threw my client on to the floor and punched him. The police were called and he left. The pair moved yet again, and once more he found them.

Being Christmas Eve, and the current job finished, my client brought his tools home, and as was his habit the toolbox was in the bedroom. At 2 am on Christmas morning there was shouting outside. My client asked, "What do you want?" The response was, "I want you," and he started kicking down the door. His fist came through the door window and he ripped out chunks of glass and threw one at him. My client lifted his arm for protection, and the glass hit his elbow. There was blood all over the place. The man's other hand reached through for the latch. My client was petrified, his throat dry, he could not utter a word, fearful not only for his own safety, but that of the woman. The man tried to climb through the hole in the door, my client looked round and was but a few paces away from the toolbox. He grabbed the chisel, intending to injure the man to keep him out of the flat, and jabbed him twice in the chest. The two stabs did not stop him, and the man tried to get hold of my client who swung out wildly with the chisel, not knowing where he hit him. The man stopped as if he had had a sudden change of mind, turned to walk away and fell down.

This was the version accepted by all the witnesses, clearly a case of self-defence, clearly a matter for a jury to consider.

On the following morning, which was Boxing Day, a special court was held. I decided to tell the court the full story, and made an application for bail. Most unusually in a murder case, it was granted.

I instructed Arthur Myerson QC, leading Robert Bartfield. Self-defence can be pleaded if a defendant takes such steps as he or she believes necessary at the time to protect himself or herself from an assailant, and it is for the prosecution to prove that it was not self-defence. The jury was out for less than hour, and returned a unanimous verdict of not guilty.

There was one occasion when I felt able to take immediate steps even before receiving the prosecution papers, to avert that seemingly indeterminate period that someone charged with murder has to wait in order to see the strength of the case against them. I can think of no worse experience.

My client who told me she had just been arrested for murder called me into the police station. She gave me no further particulars, but clearly the police officer dealing with the case felt that she needed support because he had permitted the call at such an early-stage. I quickly made my way to Millgarth Police Station and was surprised when introduced to my client. She was a 65-year-old African-Caribbean, who looked a far cry from the usual sort of people inhabiting that particular room. Through her tears she stammered, "He told me he would break my neck and throw me through the window."

I discovered that this retired tailoress lived in a shared house with a communal kitchen. She had been preparing her meal and was peeling potatoes, and had a knife in her hand. One of the other occupants, an 18-year-old boy, came in and said to her, "I will break your neck if you don't give me my knife back." He then counted to ten and shot his fist out at her, she slipped on her back, still holding the knife and the boy knelt down over her, pushing her shoulders back. She lifted her hand with the knife in it, catching him, and she knew it had done harm because he spat out blood.

It may have been the fact that she washed any blood from her face and at the same time washed the knife, which caused the police to consider that there had been premeditation, but they did and then charged her. It probably didn't help that some four years earlier she had received psychiatric treatment and had required in-patient treatment for hallucinations.

I appeared for her the following morning, and persuaded them that this case was different from the normal run of stabbings, and she deserved bail with certain conditions, which they granted. I decided then that rather than wait for the papers, I would obtain an independent pathologist's report, which came back in double-quick time. It confirmed that death had resulted from that single wound, the track of which had been five and half inches long, and had not been obstructed by any bony or cartilaginous structure and could have been caused by someone running on to the knife. The knife being withdrawn, and the deceased then collapsing or jack-knifing forward to the point of the knife, still being held by the assailant, could have caused a second wound.

I expressed this report to the Director of Public Prosecutions, and after a few days received a call that the director was not intending to proceed with the case and the charge would be dropped.

My practice was clearly a specialised criminal one, and I am a fervent believer in the need for specialist practitioners.

The day of the high-street practitioner who is a jack-of-all-trades is long gone. There are few left because the law has become more complex. It is true there may still be some such practices where the mainstay is domestic conveyancing, and often allied to that will be an element of probate work. One can go a little further perhaps and follow Mr and Mrs Happy, who having bought their house might need a solicitor due to a matrimonial dispute before one of them dies, and so divorce might be added to probate, but that's about it. Anything beyond needs a specialist. I have seen the odd family solicitor come into a criminal court when one of the happy family transgresses, but they are like fish out of water.

And so it happened that other practitioners referred criminal cases to me, it was a natural sequence. Sadly, however, from time-to-time I had to pick-up the debris of a badly handled case and attempt a resurrection. I was therefore quite accustomed to people making an appointment to see me to discuss a case already tried upon which they sought a second, if somewhat late, opinion.

I discouraged this because often there was little I could do, and if they were persistent the only course was to quote a fee, which I hoped might send the enquirer in another direction. Some of these requests, however, did interest me, and although unprofitable I would examine them in outline. One such request for an appointment related to a murder case which had been heard in another city some years earlier. This was a case in which I had played no part; other solicitors had acted for the accused and at his subsequent appeal.

A couple had parted, the husband had a record of violence against his wife, and her departure was understandable. She obtained a matrimonial order against him, which he steadfastly refused to pay and she took up with another man who came to live with her in the matrimonial home. The husband's lack of interest abated, and he would turn up at the home often after the pubs closed seeking unreasonable late-night access to the children to whose welfare he had otherwise failed to contribute. His interest increased once he realised another occupied what had been his bed. On one occasion he threatened to kill the "other gentleman", who eventually quietened him down.

Having regard to his previous behaviour an iron bar that had been part of some derelict building in the neighbourhood was brought into the house and stood just out of sight near to the front door. Sure enough, once again after pub closing time along he came, accompanied by one of his drinking companions. Because of the noise they made the terrified woman handed the iron bar to her co-habitee as they opened the door. The visitor demanded to see his son, but he was told it was too late, and started to leave, but then changed his mind and repeated his demands. A scuffle occurred, the co-habitee used the iron bar, and the estranged husband struck out once with a knife, an implement which at the trial he described as using for cutting meat, it was that one knife stab which caused the death.

The trial had required the jury to exercise their minds on the convoluted question of self-defence, and the distinction between murder and manslaughter, but they had returned a majority verdict of murder. An appeal was heard, but criticism of the judge rejected. There was one important aspect, however, relating to the evidence at the trial. When the incident occurred there were only three people present, the woman, her new best friend and the estranged husband. The new best friend was the deceased, and therefore unable to give evidence. The wife, for that she still was, despite being estranged, could not be compelled by the prosecution to give evidence against her husband, and the defence at that time could not be sure what her evidence would be, so chose not to call her. Mark the words "at that time" for they are important.

So the estranged husband, the defendant, was the only person whose voice was heard at trial. Quite clearly the evidence of the estranged wife would be pivotal. The husband's trial took place in May of 1969 and his appeal was heard a year later.

It was two years later, in July 1972, that the wife came to see me, accompanied by her sister-in-law, the sister of the accused, and an outline of what had happened was presented to me. However, one important fact was not disclosed to me, and that was that on the day after the incident, having made a statement to the police she returned home and found the iron bar lying in the grass near to where the two men had been fighting.

This she disclosed only at a later interview which she sought, having thought further about the matter, and it having no doubt preyed on her mind. She was introduced to one of my assistants, Jasper Mann, a retired detective chief inspector, and made a full statement to him. She indicated that the iron bar had been picked up by her and left in an outhouse in the garden. She had not mentioned anything in her statement to the police about this, and surprisingly said that the police never asked her if her co-habitee had any sort of weapon. She had withheld this information because she was bitter about her husband's earlier conduct towards her.

It took several months for the Home Office to give consideration to this vital, yet previously unheard, evidence and in November 1972 they granted a legal aid certificate for me to act for the man in an appeal against the conviction for murder. In February 1973 at the Court of Appeal, before the Lord Chief Justice, a verdict of manslaughter was substituted, with a sentence of seven years, of which the defendant had served nearly three years.

Chapter 19

Murder Within the Walls of a Prison ... and Other Places

One of the reasons for punishment by imprisonment is to deter others from offending. Of course there are other reasons, such as the protection of the public and therefore keeping criminals off the streets for a time, but even for the most serious offences it is only the occasional person who is sentenced for life meaning life. Deterrence is the name of the thought that passes through the mind of a potential offender and stops him or her in time.

Unfortunately, for many people a period of imprisonment is the price they have to pay for the life which they have chosen to lead. Every few years they will leave their spouse, partner or children for a variable period of time during which they will be housed, fed, rested and provided with the company of their peers, all at the expense of the state, but to the relief of its more honest citizens. The length of that period will depend upon two things, first the skill of the lawyer whom that very same state provides them with, and second the mood of the judge who has the task of deciding whether, and if so, for how long, that housing, feeding and resting will last.

Apart from their peers, the only company each of them will have for that period are those whose task is to supervise and ensure their secure retention. I have the utmost admiration for those who take up the career of prison officer, but often wonder what makes people do so.

I have an unsubstantiated belief that some items forbidden by the rules are subject to a blind-eye acceptance and considered a safety valve for an otherwise explosive situation. The cursory search of visitors indicates a degree of toleration, for how otherwise, despite the electronic equipment, the body searches, the sniffer dogs, would it be a known fact that drugs do find their way into prisons? Then there is the use of rice remains, potato peelings and other items to manufacture with patience and care hooch, an alcoholic fermented drink. And then also there is the knowledge that there are bookmakers, wing bookmakers, bookies' runners and all the paraphernalia of gambling, which indicate that this is a difficult industry to control. The best that the authorities can do is search for the wealth, in the form of the coin currency which is an integral part of gambling.

The governor deals with an offence committed in prison, if a breach of prison rules. There used to be a board of visitors, but since 2003 it has been replaced by an independent monitoring board. The governor deals with discipline. His or her power is to award loss of privileges and if necessary loss of remission, although the more serious internal offences are reserved to a visiting judge whilst others would come within the normal criminal law and be dealt with by the courts.

Murder within the prison does not happen all that often, and the two cases I dealt with were the only ones committed during those years. The first arose through a dispute over betting. Where there is little else to occupy the mind it is easy for those who have more than an amateur knowledge of the turf to specialise and devote even more attention to the horses. After all the radio and newspapers were available, so they could continue their studies. Strangely enough small currency, a shilling, sixpence and suchlike (for this was pre-decimalisation) were more use than a pound note or a fiver. The money would be originally smuggled into a loved one in the form of a note, for this was easier, but that note would lose quite a bit of its value in the course of being changed.

Wakefield Prison was no exception, a long-term prison in the centre of the city, running along the main London to Leeds railway line, and housing a considerable number of lifers and long-term inmates. The head bookmaker was an important member of the community, and he had held that position for many years. He employed a string of associates, two on every wing, and their runners. The last mentioned were extremely skilled because it was forbidden for people to move from wing-to-wing.

Not even the prison officers had any concrete evidence as to how or why the death had occurred, because the deceased did not expire for some days and he was not discovered in his cell, but wandering the corridors naked, but with blood streaming from his head. It was the prisoner who first summoned help who was eventually charged with the murder, for it was he who stated that he came across the victim in the corridor "hissing and gurgling. Quite unable to speak." Blood was found on that man's bed, not only his own, but also a trace of that of the man who had seen him. There was also discovered a bed leg with a bloodstained cloth attached. The man remained in a comatose state for several days, and it was necessary to operate on his head, but he died. The prison officers stated that they "believed it to be a betting dispute" and that it seemed bets had been made, and the betting slips put in after the race had been run. I suppose that when conditions are not ideal these things can happen.

The other prison murder was more poignant. The narrow windows of the cells at Wakefield have even narrower ledges. The windows open slightly, but the iron bars make the question of escape unthinkable, although it seems that if your arms are fairly skinny you can reach out to the ledge. Even the most parsimonious prison meal results in some odd scrap being left over, and the pigeons of Wakefield know that here they can find a spot of lunch. Pigeons are creatures of habit, and even if untrained as homing pigeons there is something in their genes that will encourage them to call in at the same place for lunch each day. Jenny the pigeon would call upon this particular prisoner each day, have a few pecks at what was laid out for her and coo her thanks to the gentle soul who was serving a life sentence. Jenny and the prisoner became the talk of the wing.

But the inmate who occupied the cell immediately above Jenny's provider had a wicked sense of humour. Although he could not see this daily procedure he could hear it, and for some irrational reason it annoyed him. It is amazing how simple items are easily secured in prison, but this man somehow had a long piece of strong cotton, and at the end he tied some wire in the shape of a loop. He spent a few weeks befriending his neighbour, and at the same time secured a temporary job in the prison kitchen. He regaled his new friend with all the advantages of his access to the kitchen, and how as a special treat over the next few days he would cook something for him and bring it down to his cell. He kept to his word, and a few days later carried a prison plate covered in silver foil along to the man's cell. Needless to say, the man was overcome, as you don't often eat *à la carte* at Wakefield. He tucked heartily into his meal, but could not understand why his benefactor then burst out laughing. When his laughter subsided, it was confession time. "You've just eaten Jenny."

The cook was dropped in one fell blow. The charge was murder. I could make some facetious comment about getting even more bird, but I won't.

The Boarded Barn Murders

It sounds like something from Rumpole, "The Boarded Barn Murders", but this was something far more dreadful than anything that John Mortimer might have conjured up. It was also a case which indicated to me that true remorse can be shown by an accused, and that in view of the strength of the evidence a realistic attitude can sometimes be adopted. Quite often such remorse and acceptance might well result in some advantage in sentencing terms, but not so in this case.

I had been called in to represent one of three men charged with aggravated burglary and the murder of two women who were doing nothing more than clearing out the cottage belonging to the mother of one of them. One of the men was also charged with rape. The cottage was in an isolated position, and there had been some newspaper publicity of the sum received by the elderly lady for the sale of her husband's business. Ironically this type of scenario had also been the prologue to the Lesley Whittle murder in which I had been involved some four years earlier.

The three men were attracted to the prospect of obtaining a lead on where the resulting wealth was kept. I shall not dwell upon the bloody mayhem in which their venture resulted. Suffice it to say that there was an abundance of forensic evidence and enough confessions to make even the most habitual defendant use the time-honoured phrase, which is like music to a detective's ears, "Caught bang to rights." Indeed, the confessions went so far as to include among the answers given in the course of the interrogations, "I will get 40-years for this." It is most unusual for such a pragmatic attitude to be even hinted at.

Quite often, even in the face of considerable evidence, a defendant will maintain a plea of not guilty. I believe that many actually talk themselves into the fact that they are not guilty. The best one can do in those circumstances is what is known as putting the prosecution to proof, or testing the evidence, hoping that in some vital point their case will fall apart, or that by tackling each and every point the cumulative effect of such an attack will give the impression of weakness to a gullible jury. This does happen from time-to-time and I became more conscious of it when I became a judge.

I found the attitude of my client refreshing. From the start he admitted his part, as he had to the police. He could not understand how civilised the police had been.

There is no real joy in presenting a hopeless case, I always realised that my duty was to my client, but one could not help but feel a considerable degree of sympathy with the victim, where they were still alive, or the family of a victim in the alternative situation.

But with a guilty plea, there would be no parading of the family of the loved and lost, and those were the days before the "victim statement". This was introduced comparatively recently, and I have some misgivings as to the propriety of such emotive displays. One judge was criticised for saying, "We don't take much notice of them." That may well be, but he should not have said it. It is often a perfectly proper safety valve.

The judge at Chester Crown Court was Mr Justice Philips. I once again instructed Gilbert Gray QC, an appropriate choice for I knew that the only hope for my client to have his inevitable sentenced shortened would be by a reasonable recommendation on duration. Life shall mean life would not entirely be out of the question having regard to the nature of the offence. Gilly did his best.

The defendants appeared in court in blue boiler suits. I can still hear some of the phrases with which Gilly in his lucid and mellow voice silenced that ancient courtroom with a mitigation speech creating bricks with the minimum of straw. The boiler suit he likened to sackcloth and ashes and he explained the defendant "felt no right to ease the comfort of his appearance". There had been the motive of robbery, but his panic had been "ineffable", that is too great for description in words. So this was now his "public confession, well-motivated and valid, abject, utter and complete was his self-recrimination." The man was "dim, not a leader, but one of the led." He pointed to him, and said, "Look at the loneliness of this inadequate." And he finally described his immediate confession as an indication of "guilt without guile."

The judge did not distinguish between any of the three men. There were sentences of life for each of the murders, ten years for the aggravated burglary, 12-years for the rape, with a recommendation for release not to be considered within 30-years. So this was just a little less than the figure Gilly had anticipated.

The death of a policeman's mother

When the elderly mother of a serving police officer is discovered with two stab wounds in her home one might reasonably assume that when a suspect is brought into custody by the son's fellow officers, some prejudice may be revealed. It was refreshing to realise that in the course of that investigation there was not one single indication to make me think that might be the case. Prejudice in those days was carefully avoided in another important respect, the law on which has now been changed. I refer to what is known as evidence of bad character. In those days the law was careful to try a person for the specific offence upon which he had been charged, and upon the evidence in that case, and that case only. In summary this meant that a defendant could not be asked questions about his bad character unless he had impugned the character of a prosecution witness.

The law was changed in 2003 so that the much more sensible course would be followed of allowing a defendant to be asked about his previous convictions, subject to various sub-rules stipulating that it or they bore striking similarity to the instant charge which he faced. This would mean that a man charged with burgling a house occupied by an elderly lady and indecently assaulting her in the course of that burglary could be asked about this if he subsequently faced a charge in which the facts were similar. I would emphasise, however, that in the instant offence there was neither evidence of nor suggestions of any indecent act. Nevertheless, the prosecution took care not to have the previous offence of the accused brought up.

I received a phone call from the defendant's mother, asking me to represent him the following day in court at Bradford. He was 18-years-old, and had a physical disability. His reports from psychiatrists, psychologists and probation officers described him as "not all that bright". In these days someone of such a description would most certainly have a lawyer or an appropriate adult present at the police interview, but not so in 1982. The 18-year-old spoke quite openly to the police officers. Initially he denied knowledge of the flat, or that he had ever been there, but he later accepted that he had, and relied upon repeating that the stabbing had nothing to do with him. There was nothing harsh, no bullying by the officers who interviewed him. If they felt disgust at someone who had allegedly killed the mother of one of their colleagues, they didn't show it.

He had met someone whom he knew, whom he named and vividly described, and quite openly stated that the other person had suggested the old lady's house be robbed, that he had gone along but that it was the other man who did the stabbing. And even though the knife that did the stabbing was not found, the police had found the key to the lady's flat and items of her jewellery in his flat, no blood relating to him had been found in her flat. Yes, there was a bloodstain on his coat, but that was shown to be his own blood. His fingerprints were found in her flat, but that was no surprise as he had admitted that he had been there. Yes, he had been there but without any previous indication of having that in mind. The other man had stabbed the woman, though afterwards it was he who had taken the knife out of her body, and simply taken it back home. He maintained they had simply gone there to steal.

The police visited a man with the name given by the defendant. He had been at school with him, but the man said he had not seen the defendant for some three years prior to some six days before the incident occurred, when they bumped into each other at a local café and they had spoken to each other. The suggestion by the prosecution was that what the defendant had done was recall that he had seen the man with the name given, and had put together that name together with a description of various other people to form an imaginary person, and that in truth the only person involved in the burglary and murder was the defendant.

To his credit, notwithstanding his low intelligence, the defendant maintained throughout the lengthy interviews that he was not responsible. As might be expected given the background information which I had of his upbringing, I deemed it necessary to have him carefully examined by two psychiatrists and a psychologist, and there was nothing from their conclusions which might assist in a plea of diminished responsibility. He was deemed fit to stand trial and understand the proceedings.

I instructed Wilf Steer QC, a highly respected senior counsel from

Newcastle Chambers, the same chambers which spawned Lord Chief Justice Peter Taylor, and as junior, Robert Smith. The judge was Peter Beaumont MBE, known as "Bashir Beaumont" from his days in the colonial judiciary (the "Bashir" was often misunderstood to mean "Basher" for his sentences were rarely light). In this case however, there could only be one sentence, life.

The defence had been restricted to the issue of joint enterprise, that there had been another man, and that the 18-year-old did not know that his companion would resort to murder. The jury were out for quite a considerable time, and I mused then, as I do now, would they have been out for quite so long if they had known of that one previous conviction, which because of the law at the time was kept away from them?

An open-and-shut case

The phone call came when I was at home. "Good evening, Barry, there's someone here asking for you." I recognised the voice straightaway, so I had a good idea what it was about. It was Detective Chief Superintendent Dennis Hoban, the head of the West Yorkshire CID.

Some two or three days earlier there had been the news in the local newspapers and radio of the discovery of a body of a woman on a grassy embankment in Mabgate, not far from Leeds Parish Church. The area also hosted several public houses and in the crypt of the church was a soup kitchen for the vagrants who frequented the pubs and visited the nearby labour exchange. The police search for the suspect had ended when he actually handed himself in at Settle, a small town in the Yorkshire Dales.

Hoban and I were about the same age, and I had watched his rapid progress through the ranks. We had done many cases together and I had a great respect for his ability and integrity—something which I hoped he returned. I realised that if the chief phoned me, it must in all probability be about that particular case, and I was right. "Matter for you," he continued, "but I don't think there's any need for you to rush, he's coughed-up to it, so we should be able to get him before the court in the morning."

Though I respected his assurance, I made a habit, when someone faced a particularly serious charge such as murder, that I would see them straightaway, and I drove over from my home in Harrogate to Leeds Police HQ that night. Hoban had left the charge sheet for me, and also the single sheet which my client had signed when seen by him.

"I killed this woman … and lost control of myself. She called me a Geordie bastard and I got hold of her throat and went berserk … I know I am guilty and need some sort of treatment to help with my drinking, and to keep off the tablets … I thought it would be best if I gave myself up in the hope to get some treatment."

He was huddled under a blanket in that grim, small cell, ever grateful to me for having come out that night to talk to him. I did not tell him then that I thought the case was hopeless, for I could not, I did not know enough about the evidence, nor enough about him, though I feared that over the next few days if not weeks, the jigsaw of forensic evidence and the circumstances of his rapid departure from Leeds, to say nothing of the words he had openly used in his confession statement would limit any area of defence. The factors of the alcohol and drugs habit needed probing, as did my discovery that he had been hospitalised in the past for bouts of depression. More problematic was his previous record, which included a lengthy prison sentence for a serious offence which I could not disassociate from the instant one.

I was my duty to examine the only possibility, which was diminished responsibility, but that would need support from psychiatric evidence. I approached a specialist in that field, and although sympathetic to a degree he could not put all his force behind such a finding, and although he tried his best in court to encourage the jury to come to such a conclusion, the force of the expert evidence called by the Crown proved too damning. He was duly sentenced to life imprisonment. At that time there was no recommendation on duration to be made, and as with many other cases his liberty would be decided by a parole board which would have the ultimate responsibility of deciding whether to recommend to the Home Secretary whether he was fit to be released back into society (a responsibility that now falls to the Justice Secretary).

CHAPTER 20

A Little Nostalgia

Hair today, but gone tomorrow

Although we spent the first 22-years of our married life in Harrogate, it now seems a world away. We made some wonderful, close and highly amusing friends; we had great times, went to fine parties and gave many ourselves. Our first address was College Barn, Linton, followed by Bilton Dene, Harrogate and then Longlands, Harrogate, so I mused that it was only when we came to Redington Road in Hampstead that we could afford to have a house with a number. The Morrises, Laxes, Farnells, Lesters,

Springalls, Arnolds, the "other" Blacks, were all great party people. We were all bright young things, some now a little more tarnished than others.

Harrogate enjoyed a great Liberal revival, initially of the 40 or so council seats, all of them Tory, Rodney Kent made a great breakthrough and gained one for the Liberals. I was persuaded to do likewise, and sure enough gained a seat, and eight new Liberal seats were gained. There was still a Tory majority, by far, but at least there was now some debate at council meetings. After my first year on the council, there came along a general election. My name had become quite well-known in Yorkshire because by this time I was appearing regularly on television, a programme called *Calendar* with Richard Whitely (later of *Countdown*) and Austin Mitchell (later to become the MP for Goole). They would call me in to speak or be interviewed on legal matters, and I was also invited by the BBC *Look North* programme on a similar basis. In view of this fame I was selected as Liberal candidate for Harrogate in the general election. Harrogate of course was a safe Tory seat, and the member was part of a well-known brewing family. The Labour candidate was Edward Lyons QC, who had been a friend at university, and whom I actually instructed from time-to-time. Although not elected I received a pretty respectable vote, and came second, beating Lyons into third place. Maybe I should have persisted. Eventually Harrogate became a Liberal seat largely due to the efforts of the candidate who was a highly respected local headmaster, who is now in the Lords. However, I was a little restless about the Liberals on the council pandering to the Tories, and moved over to the Labour party. I was the only one, and something of a one-man opposition party. The Tories loved this.

I raised the question at a meeting about the state of the road near the level crossing at Starbeck. "Ah," said the Tory leader, "Does the Labour member find it makes his Bentley rattle?" I have to admit, but did not do so then, that that was precisely my fear.

Then it was time for the next general election and I believed a parliamentary career still beckoned. I was selected for the short list in the Rother Valley constituency. This was an area between Doncaster and Rotherham, where there was a labour majority of about 20,000 and for years their member had been a former miner. The local party were somewhat disenchanted by his performances in the House, and were looking for someone who could put them on the map a little more. Being on the short list meant that I had to visit the many mines and miners' welfare clubs in the area, and visiting the mines meant going down into the depths of the Earth to talk to those wonderful men who spent their lives in that subterranean hell hole. However I deemed it expedient, having done my court work in the morning, to drive the Bentley home and swop it for Diana's Mini Clubman which would look better parked in the grounds of the miners' club.

All went well over the months, the others on the short list looked quite beatable, but on the very last day of the campaign it became clear that the choice was not to be me, rather the constituency party secretary. In some ways it was to my regret that they chose him, for he went on to win the seat, enjoy a fulfilling career in the Commons, and end up in the Lords.

Once again, I mused, if only. But at least I never had to tell Diana of the firm promise I had made that if selected we would leave Harrogate for the family home to be removed to Maltby. Initially she had misheard, and thought I had said Malton, a rather smart town in North Yorkshire, in fact the county town of North Yorkshire. She went into shrieks of disbelief a few moments later, when I clarified that it was not Malton in North Yorkshire, but Maltby the one next to the Maltby Main colliery between Rotherham and Doncaster.

In each of my cases I was the defending solicitor. This meant being at the receiving end of the initial instructions, be they from the accused or from a member of that person's family, or occasionally from the magistrates' clerk whose duty it was to allocate legal aid cases. A list was maintained in each court of local solicitors willing to take matters under legal aid, and although the list was important to those who had set their stall out to deal with crime, this did not apply to everybody in practice in the area. There were solicitors not wishing to depart from the more remunerative departments of the law, the property conveyancers, the commercial lawyers, the corporate or family lawyers. Among these were some who in the course of what they felt to be public duty allowed their names to remain on that list, and accordingly were allocated the odd high-profile murder. Once they had such a case many were not quite sure what to do with it, and were dependent upon counsel for what steps to take. This must have proved more expensive to the legal aid fund than handing the case over straightaway for the sole determination by a solicitor who knew his way along that particular path.

Virtually all my cases were legally-aided, and those responsible for assessing costs, who initially were the Assize or Quarter Session clerks, knew who was and who was not a time waster. The Law Society on a pretty fair basis to those who did not attempt to overcharge dealt with the run-of-the-mill cases before the magistrates.

Friends would ask, "How can you make legal aid pay?" The simple answer was that it was fine if you had enough of it, so you were not just going to court with one or two cases and spending the morning waiting around, which would hardly be worthwhile. It was different if you had up to 30 cases and were able to time and space your way around all the courts. It was after all not just clocking up minutes in court, but the time which had to be spent on the preparation of the cases.

Not all matters I dealt with involved murder. Many of the names of the day were people with whom I came in contact, for instance Viv Nicholson of "spend, spend, spend" fame, but she had spent most of it when I saw her, Lord Kagan whose sombre home in the Lake District I visited more than once, and I was convinced he invented the Gannex because of that cold house, and the well-known chairman of an international printing company who was receiving unwelcome overtures from Robert Maxwell.

The practice was quite successful, and this enabled me to have one particular indulgence.

I loved motor cars, and my particular favourite for several years was the Jensen Interceptor. It became quite recognisable around the courts of the West Riding, and indeed further beyond. Although the car was capable of a fair speed, my licence remained clean until one November day an officer in an unmarked police car with a radar gun caught me. His reading was 56 to 58 mph in a 40 limit. I clearly had to plead guilty, but was concerned about having an endorsement, and it was this that required me to attend court to add substance to my letter which read

"The unmarked police car had followed me for two miles and I was stopped, the first words by PC 814 were 'Well, well, well, if it isn't Mr Black.'" Can I be blamed for suspecting the worst, especially as only a day or two earlier I had secured the acquittal of a man charged by Leeds Police with an armed bank raid. However these things are sent to try us at the best of times.

"I would clearly have loved to plead not guilty but I don't suppose I would be eligible for legal aid and I certainly could not afford to pay the sort of fee that I charge. Please be gentle—wife, four kids, and a very slow Jensen to support".

I then went into the witness box and asked the magistrates not to endorse my licence. I explained that on that particular day I had 18 cases in Leeds Magistrates Court, and other new clients to see in the cells that morning. I had dug up an old case, the message of which was that work of her majesty's courts should not be delayed, and so I concluded by saying, "One works to a very tight schedule and the traffic delay was worse than usual. Your worships would not have taken kindly to being held up by not getting to the court on time." My audacity paid off, and although I was fined £10, neither did they endorse my licence for those "special reasons".

I had noticed a reporter in court, and am obliged for the recollection of the exact words in that case from the headline report in the *Yorkshire Evening Post* of that date, a report picked up by many other newspapers and one copy was sent by a friend who saw it in the *International Herald Tribune.*

By 1969, having been a partner in Walker Morris & Coles for some ten years, and seen the Leeds office grow, from my two rooms to become a firm dealing with company and commercial law, and with many partners and staff I decided that my specialised work did not really fit in with a firm which had such a commercial nucleus that we needed two waiting rooms, like first and second class. You couldn't have Bill Sykes the burglar sitting next to Sir William Sykes, Bart, and the trustee.

Some offices became available in South Parade, and I departed with a few members of staff. The departure was quite amicable and worked smoothly, and Barrington Black & Co was established. I had some articled clerks, or as they are now called trainee solicitors, who came with me, qualified and to whom I subsequently gave partnerships. The practice flourished during the time of the various cases I have described, and we had a staff of about 20.

In 1984, after having been involved in advocacy for some 27-years I received a phone call from the Lord Chancellor's Department. It was from a lady called Miss Lorrimar, whom I was later to refer to as Miss Moneypenny, for she looked and spoke like that character from the James Bond films, and as I was later to discover, her office in the bowels of the House of Lords was just as depicted in the film. When I eventually went to see her, I had to stop myself spinning my hat towards her coat stand. She was the secretary to the Permanent Secretary to the Lord Chancellor, Sir Thomas Legge, and he was the kingmaker in the world of judicial creation. She asked if I was able to help them. It seemed that they had an enormous backlog of cases in the magistrates' court in Birmingham, and wondered if I might spend a couple of weeks there sitting as a deputy stipendiary magistrate, and if so would I mind coming to London to see her and Sir Thomas.

"Like in the morning?" I ventured. "Oh no," she said and mentioned a date far in the future, well at least in the following week. I shuffled a document or two, to make a diary-like sound, and we agreed a time and date. I put the phone down, and sat back. This would clearly be a first step on the ladder towards a judicial career, something which I had secretly hoped for from and even before the start.

I didn't say anything to Diana at this stage, but went off to London in due course. They were both quite charming, and knew a surprising amount about me. After all, these were the days of the old nudge and a wink, the discreet enquiry in the right place, the practice which had been tried and worked over years and which had provided incorruptible, albeit sometimes irascible benches of judges for a system which ran smoothly, and which did permit the odd grocer's son to make his mark, though only if his name was Denning. It was a far cry from the present-day adverts in all sorts of papers, almost, but not quite including, the *Poultry Dealers' Gazette*.

And so it was that I sat in Birmingham. The work was straightforward, I'd been on the receiving end for 27-years, and required no tuition on how to dish it out. I realised that if I wanted to do more, then there would no doubt be reports sent to Miss Moneypenny, and they had to be good. I had heard a rumour, and it seemed logical, that the people to be nice to were the ushers and car park attendants, because the chief clerks to the justices who sent in the reports first sounded them out, for they saw the real you. The reports must have been good, because more calls came in to help out in Birmingham, and then in London as a deputy metropolitan stipendiary magistrate. I did quite a few of these in different parts of central London, and quite understandably my partners realised that at the age of 52 I would have to make a decision.

Indeed later that year decision time came. The call from Miss Moneypenny this time was, "Mr Black, Sir Bryan wonders if you could come to see us, as he would like to discuss your career with you." Sir Bryan Roberts QC, a distinguished senior civil servant, had taken over from Sir Thomas Legge in the Lord Chancellor's department, and at a later stage he would become a personal friend. The phrase "to discuss your career" was a euphemism for either to sack you (unlikely) or to offer you a job. Happily it was the latter, and from the point of view of my age, and considering my ultimate judicial ambition, it could not have been better. So once more off I went. The meeting was a friendly one, they were well pleased with me, and offered me an appointment as a metropolitan stipendiary magistrate, to sit initially at Bow Street. The pay was not as good as my earnings at the time, but if I had any hope of a judicial promotion and pension I would have to take it. It meant more regular hours of work, no night time or weekend call-outs by desperate clients.

I said I would have to discuss it with Diana, for it would mean leaving Harrogate and living in London. For Diana this was a difficult and painful decision. She could see what I was striving for, and the extent to which I did not cherish the life of a magistrates' court hack as the years advanced, but she was happy in Harrogate, we had a spacious albeit expensive home, she had her parents there, had many friends and a full social life. She was most unhappy, but we decided to try it for a while with me commuting Monday to Friday. I cannot underplay the stress which accompanied her eventual agreement to move to London. It was not easy and I shall always be grateful to her for the sacrifice she made.

I gave the practice to my partners, who by this time had developed other aspects of the law than crime, and there were matrimonial, family, conveyancing and commercial departments. I was interested to see that shortly after I left they amalgamated the practice with two long established Leeds Firms, William Bateson Coates & Co, and Harrison Jobbings & Co. and that the amalgamation was called, and still practices as "Black's", they occupy two buildings and practice in all aspects of the law except crime!

And so we moved, the children were quite happy about this because they were either at school, university, or starting work; to them London was a great challenge. I suspect they would have moved there in any event. We found a lovely apartment, spacious, arboreal, with a nice garden and outlook, and although it took a little time, made many friends. Diana became a London travel guide and joined the City of London bench.

My advancement in the law proceeded. In due course I became an assistant recorder and then recorder, and in 1994 a circuit judge sitting in the Crown Court at Southwark, Snaresbrook, Inner London and then Harrow for eleven years, retiring at 72, but thereafter was invited to sit for half-a-year till the very day of my 75th birthday, when the condition of being statutorily senile set in. To my amazement even more judicial activity however, was to follow.

CHAPTER 21

Deuteronomy Chapters 18–20

"You shall appoint Judges and Officers in all your towns in the land that the Lord your God is giving you, and they shall judge the people with righteous judgment. You shall not show partiality, you shall not accept a Bribe. Justice, Justice, shall you pursue…"

Yes, it goes back a long way, and although these were God's words, when it came down to brass tacks the appointment to metropolitan stipendiary magistrate by tradition was the direct gift of the regent. Clearly the sifting was done by the men and women in the Lord Chancellor's department and the actual note would read, "Should Her Majesty be minded to invite you to take the position would you be prepared to accept?" They couldn't risk a "No thank you" directly returned to Her Majesty.

The history of the courts in London is well-known, particularly that in the past they had been tarnished by the fact that there had been several misunderstandings about the suggestion that it would be nice if the justices tried hard not to accept a bribe.

London was probably no different from any other large city. The keeping of law and order has been a gradual process. "The poor are always with us," and so are thieves and felons, and the more wealth acquired by some in the population, the greater was its attraction to others.

At first as the city grew, each male was expected to do his bit towards maintaining the safety of his home, however humble. The male was expected on a rota basis to act as night watchman, but it did not take long for that onerous duty to be sub-let to a deputy, privately hired and paid to police the streets. Eventually the residents in each parish were taxed to pay the salaries of a force of watchmen. The aim was more for protection then detection. Suspicious people were held overnight and then brought before a justice who would decide, without much paperwork, if they should be freed or sent for trial at the Middlesex Sessions or the Bailey.

Justices had been around since 1361, not only in London but throughout the country, never paid for by the government but also entitled to charge a small fee for their services. In the country they were mainly the landed gentry, but in London those with more influence and wealth were the merchants, who soon grew tired of their powers and weary of the demands on their time, and so more tradesmen were appointed. Unfortunately they did not do a particularly good job, and corruption was rife, and because they profited from the status and drew a not inconsiderable income they became known as trading justices. Crime was not their only duty, and they also acted as arbitrators for the small tradesmen in the area, and again drew fees from this. The Middlesex Justices Act eventually eliminated them in 1792.

But in the meantime how did they get over the problem of administering good, true, incorrupt justice? There is an antique door with a highly polished brass handle at the side of Bow Street Magistrates' Court, in Broad Court, just past the statuette of a "Young Dancer" and beyond three red telephone boxes, and as I entered that first morning I thought of those who in the early-18th-century had walked through that same door, though it was only later that I realised it had also been used to admit many young ladies who had earlier appeared in the dock. In place of the corruptible justices there had been people like Thomas de Veil, Henry Fielding and subsequently his half- brother John Fielding, who were deemed by the government to be reliable, and would carry out the government's instructions with care. They were in fact more like local administrators than purely justices.

Thomas de Veil was the first, conducting his business from the front room first of all at his house in Leicester Square and then in 1740 in his house in Bow Street, at that time on the opposite side to where the court would be, and nearer to the present site of the Royal Opera House. He later moved across the road, gathered various titles relating to different duties and conducted his business from the present site. It was he who at the same time as breaking-up gangs of robbers with the aid of his private force of Bow Street Runners was at the same time consorting with prostitutes, who knocked on the door through which I had entered. Henry Fielding and then his half-brother, the blind John Fielding, followed De Veil.

I broke the news that I had been offered a permanent appointment to my partners, all of whom had been articled clerks, who received a partnership in my firm (obviously not a full one), and had remained to form a reasonably substantial firm, dealing mainly in crime, family law and house conveyancing, and consisting of a general practice about 20 strong. I gathered them into my office, and finished my news by saying, "So chaps, Barrington Black & Co, it's all yours." They were not entirely surprised because over the months I had been called upon to sit with growing frequency. Within a few short years they had amalgamated with three other quite old-established firms of solicitors, though the one firm so created is practising still under the name Black's, a now a far larger firm, mainly commercial.

And so, for me, to London, where the first stop was to the Law Courts in The Strand and into Court No. 1 for the swearing-in ceremony before the Lord Chief Justice, whom as a QC I had frequently instructed and indeed crossed swords with when as leader of the North-eastern Circuit he prosecuted the more important murders. I took the oath, and he smiled and whispered, "Well done, Barry."

Some time later in 1996, we went to a piano concert at Middle Temple and the pianist was Peter Taylor. This was not the first time I had heard him, because as a High Court judge sitting at Leeds Assizes he stayed at the judges' residence, Carr Manor, and whenever he was there a well-tuned grand piano also went into residence and a favoured few were invited to hear his talented playing. It was said that had he not entered the law he could have followed a promising career either as a concert pianist or a professional rugby player, having captained his county of Durham. That concert was poignantly memorable. He played with his usual skill and received rapturous applause. On the way home I switched on the car radio to the late-night news, and was shocked to hear that within the past few moments his resignation as Lord Chief Justice, due to illness, had been announced. He had timed it that the announcement would be made after the concert, so that it would not distract from the tribute to another judge which was the reason for the concert. He died within the year, but shortly before that we were attending an event at Trinity House and as I approached the staircase, heard a faint voice calling me over to give the speaker assistance to climb it: it was an unrecognisable Peter Taylor.

His memorial service took place before a packed congregation at St Paul's, and although conducted in the main by non-Jewish clergy, there came a time when his son stood up to recite the Kaddish memorial prayer in Hebrew, and as he did, many of the people there, including myself, pulled out the traditional small skull cap and joined in the responses.

After the swearing-in, I took the family to lunch at The Savoy, and then made my way to Bow Street. I was rather nervous that first afternoon, a condition that gave a whole new interpretation of the phrase "A Bow Street Runner". Having been met and given my case list by Joyce Farley, known as the headmistress of Bow Street court, though her official title was chief clerk, I was then welcomed by Sir David Hopkin, the chief magistrate, a Dickensian Welshman. He was also president of the British Boxing Association, a rough-and-ready character if ever, whose personal pugilistic appearance belied a beautifully modulated voice. Among his other traditional duties and titles, for chief magistrate was a personal royal appointment, were the obligation to sit on the Court of Green Cloth, and act as the Clerk of the Queen's Kitchen, the Groom of the Great Chamber, the Page of the Back Stairs, the Lord Steward and Master of the Ceremonies. He never spoke in great or indeed any detail of the decisions of state made at these fascinating meetings, though they were held regularly, and meant that on those days I would often sit in Court No. 1 at Bow Street.

I shared duties with two other stipes, a genial former barrister called Ronald Bartle, who immediately asked if he could put me up for the Garrick Club, which was but a few hundred yards away. It was not the fact that he told me that it would take about 12-years to reach the stage of membership that worried me, but that it did not admit any ladies, though it did allow homosexuals and alcoholic. So I replied, "Would that it was the other way around," and the invitation was never repeated.

The third stipe was Quentin Campbell, a larger-than-life character who sported a magnificent black cape and a large black fedora hat, both of which he wore on the non-railway part of his journey each day from just outside Oxford to Marylebone, which he travelled on a bicycle. The bicycle spent much of its time chained to the railings outside the court, and so naturally was referred to as "Pankhurst".

The four of us worked a four-day week because it included sitting on a

Saturday morning in a rota of one in four. Thus if you worked Monday, Tuesday, Wednesday, Thursday, you could have an extra-long weekend by working the following week on Tuesday, Wednesday, Thursday and Friday. Saturdays, or indeed other days, could be swopped with your colleagues.

For this reason among others it had always been a gentleman's appointment. Most of the earlier stipes had been barristers, in fact QCs who had opted for the gentler life.

As one who had been steeped in the criminal courts I found it quite easy, as the job meant that I had neither juries nor other members of the tribunal to consult. In fact a stipe probably had as much power as a High Court judge sitting as a judge of first instance; he alone made the decision, and sometimes that could be a powerful one, as for example if dealing with the committal on say a murder charge. If dissatisfied with the evidence, you could stop it at that stage.

And so, on that fateful day in 1984 I entered through that particular side door, and was shown to the room, which I would share with Ronald Bartle. It was a beautifully furnished room, with polished woodwork, leather chairs for work by the desk and a more comfortable leather easy chair upon which to rest for a few sobering moments after lunch. A crisp copy of *The Times* sat on the desk, on top of which sat the day's list of miscreants.

To my surprise, on that first day I was then ushered into Court No. 1, the history of which shimmered before my eyes as I looked at the dock in which many historical characters had stood. The enormous wooden chair in which I sat, propped up by several red velvet cushions, knew nothing about theories of lumbar support, and I jump slightly ahead by reporting that it was a matter of a couple of weeks before I was looking-up a list of physiotherapists. She must be qualified, I insisted, having had to deal in court within an hour of arriving with a long line of enthusiastic amateurs.

My anticipation of Court No. 1, Bow Street, was perhaps aimed too high. "Bow Street," I thought, "it will be a succession of spies, Class 1 murderers, those involved in political misfeasance, and those who trespass into the royal palaces."

It was nothing like that. Bow Street covers what most people consider to be the centre of London, but that works out to be Soho, Piccadilly, Charing Cross and The Strand. Thus, when the cell door was opened, it regurgitated a line of tarts, touts and transvestites who engage in the night life of central London, and the shoplifters from all walks of life and every spot on the globe, who ply their trade by day.

I was later to discover that the more sophisticated criminals were sent to Horseferry Road, Marylebone, or the City of London courts, and an even more sophisticated class of tarts, touts and transvestites to Great Marlborough Street.

The third case was called by the police officer, or to give him his official title, the list caller, a stout figure approaching retirement age (his, not mine) with a clipboard. Solicitors and counsel needed to be kind to the list caller because he had the choice of calling their case on straightaway or making them wait ages. I found the name which he called on my list, and it was only when he repeated "Sharon" that something made me look up. She was smiling in my direction, and I immediately recognised her as one of the troupe working for a Caribbean pimp who I had represented more than once as a solicitor in Leeds. Pimping was serious in those days, and could earn a five-year sentence, so this man had invariably pleaded not guilty and proved quite a profitable client. Several of his girls were reputed to operate in London, and as cheap away-day tickets had been introduced by British Rail between Leeds and Kings Cross, they had been dubbed the "have it away-day girls".

I didn't think I should smile back, but by the time that thought manifested itself I had done so. "Oh dear," I said, "I think we know each other, don't we?" Almost every counsel in court looked-up, and realising their interest I blurted out, "But only on a professional basis." Even those who had not looked-up the first time did so then as I hastily explained, "My profession, not yours." Happily she pleaded guilty, and I evidenced no favour by depriving her of the usual £50, with time-to-pay, that time being the period long enough for her then pimp to open his wallet and shuffle in the direction of the fines office.

The more interesting cases, which were trials, some of them not so insubstantial, were usually timed for the afternoon session and as the lunch break in court was from 1 pm to 2.15 pm, I decided to go for a little amble around Covent Garden, particularly as I had learned that one of the perks of the job was the ability to park one's car in the evening in the adjoining Bow

Street Police Station car park, useful if one was visiting the opera. On the way out I passed the three telephone boxes in Broad Court, and was rather puzzled by the large number of photographs pinned-up inside them showing a number of attractive girls in various stages of undress. Their names were shown and in large print a telephone number. I asked about these when I got back to court that afternoon, and was told that one of my predecessors, perhaps influenced by the habits of the original stipes, had actually attempted to contact some of them. He had returned to the court, picked up the phone and dialled one of the numbers, asking if that was "Candy", and could they meet up at 7 pm. "I am sure you can, Sir," was the reply, "but could you first dial 9 for an outside line?"

Every month a stipe was expected to spend a dreary afternoon dealing with the road traffic offenders' list. There would be about 300 names and one ploughed one's way through it. Occasionally the culprit turned up to argue his or her case. One of those was a historian whose name I recognised as a notorious holocaust denier. He was charged with going through a traffic light at red, and as with all those who pleaded not guilty, his case was put off for witnesses to attend. "When it comes up I don't think I had better deal with it, Mr Irving," I said, "there is just a chance you are going to say that the traffic light never ever existed." He smiled wryly.

There was a relaxed attitude about swopping days with colleagues, so if for instance one wanted to go to an exhibition one could swop one's day off with someone who would take your list. This way I managed to sit at many of the other courts in central London, where the diet was not so entrenched as at Bow Street. I loved the rough and tumble of Marylebone, which included Kensington and Notting Hill in its bailiwick, and Great Marlborough Street for its rarefied gentleman's club atmosphere.

All new stipes spent their first few weeks under the watchful eye of Sir David Hopkin, and were then moved on to other courts, but he quite enjoyed my company and I stayed there for a year and a bit before being moved on to Marylebone.

The family connection with Bow Street did not end there, because my younger son, Jonathan, represented Jason Handy as a solicitor, the very last defendant to appear at Bow Street before it finally closed down on 14 July 2006. Handy, a 33-year-old from Kirkcaldy, could not believe his luck, when after being dealt with in a lenient manner to mark the occasion, he emerged from the court surrounded by cheering jailers and security staff with his hands held high above his head.

The closure ended 267 years of legal history at a court which played host to characters as diverse as Oscar Wilde and the Kray twins.

Marylebone was a very different establishment, which housed family and youth courts as well as a busy criminal court. There were two stipendiary magistrates' courts and my fellow stipe there was Sir Bryan Roberts KCMG, QC who had served in the artillery during the war, then became an Attorney General and magistrate in Nyasaland before joining the Lord Chancellor's department in the UK; on retirement from that appointment he finally secured appointment himself as a metropolitan stipendiary magistrate. He had in fact been the first person to interview me for judicial appointment.

There were also about five courts manned by lay magistrates, who have been drawn from a wide spectrum of Debrett. They were delightful and highly conscientious people, and I particularly enjoyed the company of Lady Kitty Giles, the wife of Frank Giles, then editor of the *Sunday Times*, Susan Baring OBE, of the banking family, Lady Elizabeth Cavendish, a daughter of the Duke of Devonshire, and a close friend of John Betjeman and Lady Elizabeth Williams, who had been secretary to Winston Churchill.

None of the defendants were anywhere near as interesting, especially Boy George. I had no idea who or what he was, when one morning he appeared before me on a drugs matter. "Lot of traffic outside," I mused to the clerk. "Yes," she said, "it's Boy George", which meant nothing to me, and my response was "Well, shouldn't he be in the juvenile court then?"

At that time there were about 20 metropolitan stipendiary magistrates, all based in London, and six or seven other stipendiary magistrates spread around England and Wales (there are now many more). The Scots of course had a completely different system involving sheriffs. The lay magistrates in many parts of the country were cautious about the infringement by stipendiaries on to their particular patch, not least being that the stipe would take the more interesting work and leave them the dross. On the other hand, it was sometimes necessary for a stipe to be flown in to an area which did not have one and where there was a particularly sensitive or legally-complicated case to be dealt with. From time-to-time I was selected to be a flying stipe.

One such case involved John Cannan, who had been suspected of involvement in the murder of Suzy Lamplugh, an estate agent who had disappeared after arranging a meeting with a client known as Mr Kipper. The police were never able to charge him with that offence, but they did charge him with the murder of Shirley Banks, and another rape, and the committal was to be heard in Bristol, an area that did not have a stipe. The case had attracted a considerable amount of media attention, and I did not wish to stay in a hotel in the city, so selected a Wolsey House establishment. These are private homes which have rooms available to take a paying guest, named rather ironically after Cardinal Wolsey who roamed the country staying at private homes, though in his case without paying.

I did not tell my host why I was in town, other than that I was a lawyer, but to my chagrin, that evening was invited by them to their drawing room to watch television, and there clearly for all to see were shots of me arriving at the law courts. My cover was blown. The case itself was extremely interesting, and I could understand why the police had thoughts about him being a potential suspect on the Lamplugh case. However, I was not concerned with that, but in my examination of the evidence, although I committed him for trial on the main charges, there were other charges about which I was not satisfied, and duly cleared him. Some weeks later I received a letter from him, thanking me for being the only person who had ever listened to his side of things, and asking if I would take over the conduct on his behalf of the murder and other charges upon which I had committed him. I politely responded that this would not be possible, and subsequently noted that he had been convicted by a jury and sentenced to life. However, he was never charged with the Lamplugh murder, nor indeed was anyone else.

One other instance was a request to travel to Leamington-on-Sea to hear a case involving fraudulent repair work to the homes of elderly people. These were particularly nasty offences; the crooks would make use of the motorway network to travel far from their homes and search for houses inhabited by the elderly. They would persuade them that work was necessary to the roof, seek extortionate payment and examine the house for any items of value. This case involved a number of such victims and was so serious as to merit committal to a Crown Court and I had to hear the evidence.

I found a nice hotel overlooking the sea, and went down for the first morning of this three-week case to be told that the defendants had agreed to a committal without taking the evidence. I looked at the witnesses and wondered whether some of them would last another few months, and had certain doubts. I have to admit I also thought of the nice hotel overlooking the sea on that summer day, and how pleasant those three weeks might have been. I made an executive decision, "No," I said, "I don't think a committal without evidence at this stage would be appropriate; the witnesses are here, they are prepared to give their evidence, let's hear it." I made this decision realising that if some of the witnesses did not last for the next few months, then at least we would have their sworn depositions to place before a Crown Court in time to come.

A far less pleasant experience, also at a place called Leamington, was being flown in to deal with poll tax refuseniks. I was later to deal with the rioters in the Crown Court, but these were the non-payers, and there were thousands. The court at Leamington designated to deal with many of the Warwickshire non-payers was some distance from the town itself, in fact it was quite isolated. The demonstrators were mostly students from Warwick University, and they turned up in their hundreds, surrounding the court building. It was sometimes difficult to hear the proceedings and sometimes disconcerting to hear the repeated chant of "Two, four, six eight, we all hate the magistrate!" This was one of the few occasions I actually needed police protection.

It was while sitting as a metropolitan stipendiary magistrate that I was first invited to sit as an assistant recorder in the Crown Court. A recorder is a part-time judge and part of the judicial selection process, moving on if satisfactory after about 18 months to the designation of full recorder.

I was sent on a short three-day residential course with about 50 others, and we learned the ropes, and play-acted the trial scene, being shown how to deal with at least some of the problems not necessarily explained in the textbooks of what could happen during jury trial. I sat at the Inner London Crown Court in Newington Causeway, and felt that if all went well I could be on track for a judicial career.

CHAPTER 22

The Circuit Bench

I had been a stipe for about eight years, when I opened a brown envelope with the magic stamp of the Lord Chancellor on the envelope. It was a short letter telling me that they had sent me a previous letter, some six weeks earlier, to which they could not trace any reply, had I received it? I most certainly could not recall having received any such letter, but rather than admit this to be the case decided to make enquiries at home.

I have mentioned earlier that Diana had been a qualified Yorkshire tour guide and that when we moved to London she decided to continue her career as a freelance guide by qualifying for the London and southern regions. This she had done with no small effort and study. The qualification is not unlike a degree course, taking some three years and including the history, geography and economics of the area as well as all other matters of an artistic and political background. She enjoyed the challenge and as freelance could work as and when she pleased, and subject to family demands. The telephone table in the hall was her cornerstone, and it was also the repository for uninteresting and therefore unopened letters. The envelopes were usually brown and sometimes useful for jotting down the odd telephone number, usually relating to her guiding bookings.

When I arrived home that night I made straight for the pile of unopened envelopes with Biro jottings, and sure enough one with such marks relating to a family of Japanese tourists wishing to visit Westminster Abbey when turned over was clearly addressed to me, marked "Strictly Private" and with the Lord Chancellor's logo. It wasn't all that important, only an invitation for my name to be put to the Queen for elevation to the circuit bench and become a Crown Court judge. I was just on 60, normally the age limit for the appointment, so I hastened with my letter of acceptance down to the House of Lords just before they brought the portcullis down to do whatever it is that noble lords do on a Tuesday evening. I must admit it had been my ambition by accepting an appointment as a stipe earlier that as a solicitor rather than a barrister it would be an easier path to the circuit bench. In later years this was not impossible, but in my time it was more likely.

An appointment for a "job", as it is known in the trade, only came about as a result of a nod and a wink in those days or a "tap on the shoulder", depending upon what your co-professionals and the judges thought of you. For a solicitor this was not easy, because although the rights of access to the Crown Court had become possible, it was not sensible to devote time which might otherwise have been occupied dealing with clients in hanging about the Crown Court waiting to have one's cases heard. In any event cases were restricted to conducting appeals in which one had appeared before, or committals for sentence by magistrates. In short one could not conduct a full-blown jury trial. Moreover, there was undoubted antagonism from the bench, made up then of former barristers, so progression through the magistracy to recordership was more sensible, and it worked for me.

I was therefore very happy when Her Majesty forgave my delay in responding to that original letter telling me that she was thinking about appointing me, but the matter was confidential. My mother at the time was in her nineties, and I would have liked to tell her, just in case… But I kept to the directive, and waited till the Queen had spent her holiday mulling over the idea, and told me she was going for it.

A trip to Ede and Ravenscroft, the legal outfitters in Chancery Lane, and a measure-up for the purple gown with lilac silk arms, the red team leader's sash and the velvet knickerbockers seemed to be devouring the handsome cheque I had been given as a clothing allowance. I cheated a little on two items. First, the patent-leather shoes with silver buckles would have cost about £300, but I found some high-heeled shoes I had worn once or twice in the "Sweeney" era, worn then as evening dress and to match my side locks and flowing hair. I bought a pair of silverish buckles at John Lewis and glued them on to the shoes.

We were due to pay a short visit to a relation in Australia before I was to be sworn-in, and that involved a stopover at Hong Kong. I recalled a Mr Raja advertising his services as an inexpensive tailor. I took some photos of the traditional court jacket, then costing about £1,000, but which Mr

Raja put together for about £150 in around six hours. There remained the question of the black silk tights which one needed to wear with the velvet knickerbockers and black patent shoes. I couldn't believe that Mr Ede and Mr Ravenscroft wanted £50 for a pair. Diana suggested a visit to the ladies' underwear and stocking department at John Lewis. I hung about behind a pillar when she was asked by a young girl if she needed any help, so she asked to be shown some black silk tights. The girl pulled some out, and Diana said "No, I want much bigger ones." The girl looked perplexed and said, "But madam, you surely take the smaller size," whereupon Diana pointed at me skulking behind the pillar, and said, "Oh no, they are for him." I am told that my blush was several shades more crimson than the red sash.

As a recorder, which is an ancient and part-time judicial appointment, I had sat at various inner-London courts. The part-time aspect was that I performed this duty in tandem with my work as a metropolitan stipendiary magistrate. It was a duty which a QC was expected to perform, and aspiring but experienced junior barristers were expected to perform because it was considered an essential step on the judicial ladder.

The first Crown Court at which I sat was Southwark, a modern building presided over by Judge Gerald Butler QC, who coupled being an excellent judge with being a determined administrator, who wanted to ensure that not one moment was lost, so that the machinery of justice whirred along non-stop. On the first day I was told that no adjournment should be granted in any case the file of which bore his initials in red ink. Sure enough there was an application in my first case, and that was one in which the file bore his initials in red. An application was made, and without a trace of hesitation I granted it. The following morning I arrived bright and early, and the only other car in the car park was that of Judge Butler. To my surprise he was standing at the outer door, arms folded. I said, "Good morning," and his reply was, "Why did you take that case out of the list?" "Because," said I, "the defendant had died." His look softened.

I pushed my luck. The judges' dining room overlooked *HMS Belfast*. And just to the left, on the other side of the river was the Tower of London, As we all stood there, later that morning, nursing a glass of pre-lunch sherry, for after all this was not the Old Bailey, and lunch was consumed with a sherry glass, not a bottle of claret, *HMS Britannia* came into view and a several-gun salute was fired from the Tower. Some innocent recorder, unaware that it was the Queen Mother's birthday, asked, "What is that for?" In a voice that alas came out much louder than intended, I responded, "I think a jury at Inner London Crown Court have actually convicted somebody." After that I got on quite well with Judge Butler.

I also spent some time dealing with the aftermath of the London poll tax riots; these had blighted the centre of London around Trafalgar Square and The City. It meant spending many hours watching and re-watching the video footage of the police on horseback charging down The Strand amid the hurling of scaffolding poles and equally wicked missiles at the poor horses. The juries in these cases showed good common sense: political violence is one thing, but injuring animals is another. They convicted and I sentenced, and the Court of Appeal agreed with my feelings.

I was then directed to sit at Snaresbrook, a vast *Palais de Justice* dealing with the ineptitudes of London's East End and its environs. This was not the easiest place to get to because they were rebuilding the North Circular Road and it took over an hour to get there from home. That didn't worry me, but something else did. I had been there a year and was often summoned to sit next to the then presiding judge at lunchtime. I soon knew most of his stories by heart, since lawyers are notoriously repetitive in their anecdotal amblings. However, on one occasion he made a comment although not directed at me I found unacceptable, and I sought a transfer. This was immediately granted, and I was asked to sit at Harrow Crown Court. That judge's comment had proved to be a blessing in disguise, because now I was in court about 20 minutes from home, with travel against the rush both in the morning and late-afternoon. Moreover, the building, about three-years-old, had been carefully constructed with high-quality furnishing and high-quality security. It was because of the latter that it took a considerable amount of heavy overflow work from the Central Criminal Court. From my room I had a panoramic view from the steeple of Harrow School church across the landscape towards The City. I was very happy there.

I was given a rape ticket, which meant that sex played a prominent part in my diet, though there were cases of violence, drugs and all other things reflecting the vicissitudes of life

I was able to work speedily because as I had been able to type since my days as a student I transferred happily to the use of a word processor, and was pleased when they became standard issue. I could take down the evidence in cases as it was delivered, with no need for pauses whilst the witness "watched the judge's pen" and this considerably reduced the time taken in court.

The quality of counsel who appeared was something I soon began to evaluate and in the main I was blessed with a competent selection, which over the years I was able to note would progress, and in the main they did. Unfortunately there were those who did not have the nuance to take up and benefit by criticism, but those who showed determination, ability and that they had in fact prepared their cases were usually the ones who did not waste time and concentrated on the important issues.

Although called Harrow Crown Court, and situated in that borough, we dealt with cases from all over North-London in addition to those sent from the Bailey, with cases as unusual as the largest producer of fake Viagra, who I gave the longest sentence recorded for such an offence. He had made much money over the years by creating this unsupervised imitation, and the likelihood that he would eventually be punished was something which I described as having stood out a mile.

One day a charming old lady, looking like everyone's favourite granny, appeared before me. There had been doubts over her attendance on health grounds, and when the case was called on she was in a wheelchair and accompanied by a uniformed nurse. There were pipes and tubes going in and out of all parts of her. She was charged with running not one but a whole string of brothels and employing an entire force of willowy eastern European blondes in that trade. I read the papers, absorbed the photographs and admired the detectives from the vice squad for having so diligently and painstakingly pursued their enquiries seeking evidence down to the last detail. Less interesting were the pages from the evidence of those officers engaged in calculating her profits and wealth from this trade, but the result was amazing, running into several millions. I decided that there was little point in sending this elderly offender to prison, particularly as the millions were still intact and accessible for payment of a massive fine and costs. I was minded to do this even before I knew who her counsel was, and there he appeared, none other than my old friend Gilbert Gray QC.

She pleaded guilty to each of the 20 counts on the long indictment, and each time she spoke the word it was with an air of incredulity, though she resisted actually mouthing the phrase, "And what's a nice old lady like me doing in a place like this?"

Gilbert rose before me, one hand raised to the heavens and the other with the black gown falling away like the wing of a giant bird, and without looking me in the face said, "Your Honour, I can only plead old age and infirmity." "Maybe, Mr Gray," I found myself replying, "But what about your client?"

At Harrow the listing officer was a hard but at the same time understanding taskmistress, who ensured that my list was always full and there was never a slack moment. Her skill in assessing the duration of cases was uncanny.

I found the resident judge at Harrow a different kettle of *gefilltefisch*, for she was Her Honour Myrella Cohen QC, one of the first women QCs and certainly the first in the North-east, and she ran the court like a mother hen who would angrily peck at anyone who disturbed her brood. She was a no-nonsense judge loved by all.

She was eventually followed by His Honour Judge the Viscount Colville of Cullross QC, a judge with a title so long that his court list needed to be posted lengthways. He was a former planning silk who had appeared in many notable enquiries, and had in his time also been a Home Office Minister in the government of Edward Heath. Mark Colville had no grounding in criminal law, but this was not totally unusual. Many High Court and eventually appeal court judges who had little criminal experience had small difficulty in picking it up, but in addition it is not beyond reasonable deduction that his government service assisted when he came to the judiciary and almost immediately was appointed resident judge. He was a very pleasant man, caring of the staff and compassionate to the criminal, but when necessary he could be hard. He liked to relax at lunch-time with a glass of dry sherry, and was sometimes just a little late in resuming his place in court.

On one occasion he gave a six year sentence the recipient of which was not the happiest person in court, and as he was led down the stairs of the dock he was heard to hurl a four-letter obscenity at the judge, who heard it and called for the man to be brought back, firmly held by the prison officers.

"Mr Robinson," he said, for Mark was always polite, "it could be," he continued, "that after you have paid your debt to society, and are released, we may meet socially, and if that be the case, and you once again wish to address me, will you at least get my title right, and remember that there is an 'o' between the 'c' and the 'u'."

Judge Roger Sanders, an experienced former criminal barrister and stipendiary magistrate, highly respected by the bar, adored by the staff, who made a fine resident judge, followed him. One day in court his eyes fell upon a vivacious woman barrister whom he invited into his chambers to discuss a legal point. The discussion went well, a good result for both parties, and they have been happily married for many years.

I sat at Harrow for eleven of my twelve years as a circuit judge, and of course had been a stipe for eight years previously, and was due to retire in August 2004 at the statutory age of 72, at which point my colleagues and members of the bar, totalling to my astonishment, over 200 solicitors, barristers and judges actually paid good English pounds to come to my retirement dinner held in the hall of Middle Temple. Sixty defendants also asked whether if they came it would count against their community service orders. Gilbert Gray and Roger Sanders made very flattering speeches. They also arranged, knowing my love of opera, for an opera group to perform in that ancient and beautiful hall.

However, I did not look forward to the idea of retirement, so I made an application to the Lord Chancellor for permission to sit for the next three years, until the absolute age limit of 75. Should that permission be granted, and it was quite rare, then I would be allowed to sit for half the year for the simple reason that as my annual pension was generous, that is one-half retirement salary, then should I earn more than half-a-year's salary I would exceed that amount enjoyed by my younger sitting brothers-in-law, and that would never do.

It was while waiting for the Lord Chancellor to make up his mind on this that I received a phone call. It came from a fellow judge, one who had also progressed from being a fellow stipe, Judge Jeremy Connor. Jeremy was one of the most popular judges, so laid back that he was almost horizontal, a lover of opera and music in many forms, a collector of art, who lived in a beautiful white Regency house in Regents Park and drove an elegant Porsche. He was unmarried. The message was simple. He knew that I was due to retire, and as Jeremy was a focal point of bar gossip, he had heard that they were looking for a judge in the Bahamas "to clean things up", would I be interested?

What a question. Visions of blue skies, white beaches, palm trees, dusky maidens catering to most of my whims, floated before me. In the words of my old school song, "Where could I be 40-years on?" I had hardly put the phone down after saying "Yes" than it rang again. This time it was actually from the Bahamas. I soon discovered that two genial Englishmen virtually ran the Grand Bahamas. Sir Jack Hayward, known as Union Jack, not because he organized groups of workers, but because of his love of the flag, and Edward St George had together virtually built the economic, structural and shipping success of this Commonwealth realm. They were on friendly terms with the government and their advice was sought in all spheres, and one problem at the time was the independence of the judiciary. It seemed a change was called for, a new broom to do a bit of clean sweeping, and I seemed to fit the bill.

I said I would be delighted to come out and have a look, and within a couple of hours an upper-class Virgin Airways ticket via Miami was couriered to my court. This was convenient because I was due to take some leave the following week. The flight was one of the most comfortable I had experienced, with a change to a much smaller plane for the last lap to Freeport, where there was a warm welcome, a cool car, but alas no luggage, because it had never been to Miami, and decided to stay there. However, the car took me to a fabulous beach house, with two staff to look after me, though unfortunately no change of clothes. A few moments later came a knock on the door, and a beautiful young blonde woman announced herself. She was Henrietta, the wife of Edward St George. She told me that Edward had been delayed in the US, and having heard of my clothing plight would I, in the meantime, accept one of his old polo shirts and a pair of khaki shorts. I said I would be delighted and she smiled and disappeared.

I met Edward and Sir Jack the following morning. They filled me in about the legal problem of the islands, and I would have a small plane to fly me around the various areas, which were not inconsiderable, and I would end the day by meeting the Prime Minister, Sir Lynden Pindling, who welcomed me warmly and explained that there had been a problem over drugs and gambling, oh, and visiting gangsters from Miami.

The time came for me to board the little plane back to Freeport, and I noticed that the pilot had taken off his jacket and hung it over the back of his chair. A folded copy of the local newspaper was peeping out of one of his pockets, and I asked to read it and he said, "Sure." I froze. The main story was about a recent happening. It seemed that the judge's home had been attacked, in fact sprayed with bullets from automatic weapons, and fatalities had occurred, one of which resulted in the creation of the vacancy I had been invited to fill. My meeting with my hosts that evening was short. I suggested it would have been nice to know about the peremptory demise, and other events leading up to the circumstances of my visit.

I needed to say no more, and indicated by that silence that I was no longer interested in the position. Sir Jack mentioned that he would be travelling to London on the same flight as myself, and I found that I had been allocated a seat described by one of the cabin crew as Sir Jack's favourite seat. Moments later he entered the aircraft, and I immediately offered to change seats, but he said, "Oh no you have the comfy corner, it's the least we can do!"

There was, however, some consolation upon my return in that the Lord Chancellor had made up his mind on an extension and invited me for the next three years to sit half-time, that is for 26 weeks as and when needed, which was a happy arrangement. This would be till the very day of my 75th birthday, when the condition of being statutorily senile set in, and alas, I was then compelled to retire and hang up my wig, or so I thought.

Supreme Court Justice Gibraltar

Chapter 23

Recycled for an Unexpected Second Innings

As William Cowper wrote many years ago, "God moves in a mysterious way, his wonders to perform", and none more mysterious than when he looked down upon me one afternoon in late-August 2011. I had been retired from the bench for four years, and although I still avidly read court and law reports in the newspapers and the gossip in the legal papers, this did not abate my appetite.

The three-and-a-half-years of my voluntary job in the field of religious worship had been demanding in terms of the type of people I had to deal with, and the resolute belief of many of them that they had better ideas and could most certainly do the job better than I could. And as I had been around for but ten years I was still the new kid on the block, daring to interfere with the way things had been done for ages. I felt that I did some positive things by regularising the spiritual level, and modernising those earthly basic requirements such as new bathrooms, kitchens, and meeting facilities, and ensuring more people were in 'the loop', in retrospect I believe they appreciated my input.

And so it was that not on an occasion when I was involved in prayer, but on a weekday, when out of the blue, the message came. I had a reputation for being a quick operator, who suffered neither fools nor delay. At Harrow I would work my way through a long list of cases, with a dispensation not of, but with, justice. I seemed to get on well with my fellow judges and with the members of the bar, nor did the punters seem to complain much, as I was rarely, if ever, appealed.

And now, it seemed that I was needed in a foreign field, where the sun shone, and I love sunshine; moreover, it was not all that far from home. The call came from Gibraltar, a Crown protectorate, a promontory rock stuck on the end of a peninsula from Spain, at the gateway to the Mediterranean, not, as fondly believed by many, an island, but with similar problems of access and egress. Fought over by the Moors, the Spaniards, the Dutch, the French, the English and in its time by many others, but now, following the War of the Spanish Succession, the battles of 1704 and since the signing of the Treaty of Utrecht in 1713 firmly in the hands of the Queen of England. Article 10 contained one little problem: it forbade Moors and Jews to have a home in Gibraltar. Article 10 is famously unobserved, as we will see.

Gibraltar has been known as Britain in the sun, full of little Englanders, or rather, as one can't help noticing as one walks down Main Street, large Englanders, red telephone boxes, letter-boxes with the royal arms and policemen in blue uniforms with round helmets who do not carry guns.

The law, although distinctively called the laws of Gibraltar and with the Crimes Act and the Criminal Procedure and Evidence Act being the main current ones, generally follows English law, with barristers and solicitors, though often practising together, and their law courts and system run just as in England, with wigs and gowns for the barristers, red gowns and full-bottom wigs (on ceremonial occasions) and M'Lord-ing it for the judges.

The call I received told me that Gibraltar had a problem. There was a large backlog of untried criminal cases, and defendants for the more serious ones had been sitting in jail for up to a couple of years waiting to be heard. There had been a large volume of civil and commercial cases, many involving the financial affairs of insurance and shipping companies, all of which had made Gibraltar, with its benign tax attitudes, a busy commercial and legal centre, not just in Europe, but also in the whole world. There had not been court accommodation to hear all the cases. However, a recent programme of refurbishment had been completed and they would now have another permanent court to hear criminal matters. But they needed another judge. The High Court in Gibraltar is called the Supreme Court, and they wanted to appoint a Supreme Court judge whose main purpose would be to clear the backlog of criminal cases. Would I be interested? They suggested an appointment for two years, as an additional Supreme Court judge to the two they had already, as well as the Chief Justice. The financial inducement looked attractive, there would be generous tax concessions available and I could be granted non-resident status in the UK.

I was astonished and responded,"But do you realise how old I am, I'm coming up to my 80th birthday, surely you have an age limit?"

"Oh yes," they said, "We know, and we do, but as it would just be for two years, and your appointment would be as an Acting Supreme Court judge, and for that there is no age limit!"

There followed immediate discussions with Diana. She knew I was bored by retirement, and that my voluntary job was one from which I was ticking-off the days until it concluded. I had not resigned because that would give the opposition the gratification I would not willingly allow them to enjoy. However, for an appointment in Gibraltar I would have cause to stand down rather than resign. Quite understandably Diana could not entirely share the attractions of that place in the sun, for after all it would be away from the children, the grandchildren and her beloved bridge tables, but realising that I considered it a great opportunity, and after I pointed out that she and the family might enjoy a trip out there, and what is more somewhere she might just discover a bridge table, she relented.

And so, on 15 January 2012 I flew from Heathrow for about two hours and 20 minutes and arrived along a runway which straddled a busy road, or was it vice versa? And behind it that famous large piece of limestone, which I understood to be the home of several families of Barbary apes. I was met by the chief executive of the legal services, Alan Davies, a man who for the previous three years had been supervising the refurbishment of the law courts alongside his other duties.

Within minutes of arriving Alan suggested that I should buy myself a car. "Gibraltar can be very confining, you will need to get out at weekends, into Spain." I asked him where I could buy a decent second-hand car for such a purpose, and he suggested I should go to one of the main dealers called Bassadone. Now I have always had difficulties with names, in fact there are people sitting in prisons all over England who shouldn't be, just because I got the name wrong. And so of course when I phoned I asked to speak to Mr Berlusconi.

"I'm afraid we don't have a Mr Berlusconi here, but what exactly do you want?"

"Well, I'm after a model, not too old, but with decent bodywork, a bit of a go-er, and I rather like a noisy response when I press the pedal."

"In that case," was the reply, "it probably is Mr Berlusconi you want."

We stopped briefly at the apartment which Diana had helped me select on an earlier brief inspection visit. Only five minutes' walk from the Supreme Court, which would be my workplace, it was a spacious penthouse overlooking the marina, with views over to Spain, and in the distance the Atlas mountains in Morocco. The only noise came from a mysterious but constant conversation between the gulls and the odd ship's horn. It was so refreshingly quiet because only a few apartments were permanently occupied, the majority being held as a base for those who sought to register residence in Gibraltar and thereby take advantage of the tax delights of that jurisdiction. Provided they were resident in Gibraltar for at least 183 days a year they could ask themselves the following short questions. Estate duty or inheritance tax? What's that? VAT? Don't even think of it. Capital gains tax? No thank you. Income tax? 25 per cent, if you don't mind.

The people of Gibraltar have good reason for being there, sunshine, all those benefits and a free bus service for all residents. And two other things, free university education in the UK for their children if they passed admission requirements, and free UK hospital specialist treatment for serious illness.

After a brief call at the apartment I was whisked to see the governor to be sworn in. His residence is called The Convent, for that is what it once was, a colonial-style building with uniformed soldiers of the Gibraltar Regiment at the gate, spacious rooms, and a wonderful garden. Vice-Admiral Sir Adrian Johns had been appointed at the conclusion of a distinguished naval career, during which he had been head of the Fleet Air Arm. He was a man of great charm, respected in all parts of Gibraltar, who devoted himself to accepting virtually every invitation from organizations great and small, a man of the people who together with his wife Susie made a point of walking the full length of Main Street each Saturday morning and chatting with all who sought his company. On more formal occasions he would take the salute, resplendent in the various uniforms and decorations to which he was entitled. He was driven in the shiniest Jaguar and accompanied by a bevy of police outriders on the product of a certain Mr Harley Davidson. I gasped when I first saw this procession at what was called the Ceremony of the Keys, and little did I then realise that on two occasions during my period there I would enjoy such an escort.

I had brought my own *Testament* with me, upon which to be sworn, though when I was taken to the desk for the swearing-in, was shown a beautifully bound *Torah* as he described it, and which had been presented to the governor by the Jewish community. The ceremony lasted long enough for me to be introduced to some of the local dignitaries, including the Chief Justice, the Minister of Justice, the chairman of the Bar, the Attorney General and the police commander.

The Supreme Court was just across the road from The Convent.

If you tried to form a picture a colonial court building, then is immediately the one which would come to mind: a white building in a jurisdiction where the British system of justice had operated since 1720, with a green, green garden of palm trees and hanging fuchsia, coloured birds and orange flowers, opening through tall iron gates from the bustling Main Street, and the Union Jack proudly fluttering in the breeze.

I hit it off with my fellow judges from the first moment. The Chief Justice was Anthony Dudley, an affable Gibraltarian and a capable and distinguished lawyer who seemed to know everything about everybody and anybody in Gibraltar. Educated at university in the UK, he practised at the Bar in Gibraltar, and then after a spell as stipendiary magistrate and a Puisne Supreme Court Justice he moved with deserved speed to the post of Chief Justice. He was dealing with some of the most complicated civil and commercial actions for which Gibraltar had often been made the venue of choice. His room and desk were strewn with the numerous ring-bind folders which these cases often demanded, but he would always have a few moments for a chat or to answer some of my over-simple questions about local going rates for sentencing, customs, policy and how to deal with them, that is, the crooks as well as the Bar.

There were two puisne judges. The word "puisne" originates from the title given in a Supreme Court to any judge other than the Chief Justice, and not necessarily "small and weak" as I had understood the word to mean.

Mrs Justice Karen Prescott had followed a similar career, with university in the UK, and then the Bar and acting stipendiary magistrate, before being appointed at a young age to the position of puisne judge in the Supreme Court. She was an elegant woman, and indeed many of us were sad on days when she appeared in court in red legal robes. A quite formidable personality, she could no doubt instil fear into those who displeased her in court, but she also delighted us with her witty observations of the less capable advocates.

Mr Justice Christopher Butler was the other puisne, and his remit was the family court. It may well have been the confinement to The Rock which caused many marriages to decrepitate, and he had a full list of cases most days. He was very British, had practised at the Bar in England and still returned from time-to-time to sit as a recorder there. He had made many friends in Gibraltar and was well-known in business circles. I was grateful to him for introducing me to the Gibraltar culture, like the monthly concerts by the Philharmonic Society at The Convent and the meetings of the Gibraltar Society for Fine Arts.

My own work, as previously explained, was to deal with criminal matters, and in particular a criminal backlog which had been the result of a lack of court space, now resolved by the refurbishment of the building, and the demands upon the judges of the heavy commercial, shipping and insurance divisions of the law. This had meant that there were people waiting two or three years for their cases to be heard. There were about 40 such cases, and of course fresh cases coming along, and it was estimated that this would take the two years of my contract. In fact the backlog was cleared within eight months.

There had been one case looming over the entire criminal and indeed, by way of ancillary civil matters, the total calendar. This was the *Marrache Case* in which Benjamin, Isaac and Solomon Marrache who had run one of Gibraltar's largest law firms were charged with conspiracy to defraud. Prior to my arrival in Gibraltar, having read a short article in *The Times*, I had a scant knowledge of the outline of this case, but absolutely nothing of the detail. I knew that it concerned three brothers who were concerned with, if not partners in, a substantial firm of solicitors in Gibraltar. I knew that they had been arrested and that the running of the firm had been suspended. I knew that they had been charged with offences linked to the fact that between £30 million and £40 million of clients' money was no longer in their client account. It also became clear that this was a case which would occupy much time of a judge, jury, and the criminal court in Gibraltar. There had been no mention of this case by those who had explained the reason they sought my services in Gibraltar, and I was rather worried about the type of work which had been described, and in particular the need to dispose of the infamous backlog. There was no way a judge dealing with that particular case would be able to deal with the backlog, because no matter how speedy the judge, it was destined to be a long-running case.

On my first meeting with the Chief Justice and chief legal executive I was assured that in any event it would be some time before that case would be heard, because of its complexity and the stage of preparation it had reached, and there was much else for me to get my teeth into. Two days later, however, I saw that very case was in my list, albeit on a purely procedural matter, an application by one of the brothers to change his condition of bail. When originally arrested, all three had been remanded in custody, but when it became clear that there would be a considerable passage of time before the case could be heard, they were allowed bail albeit with the condition that they did not leave Gibraltar and that their travel documents were impounded. After all, there was over £30 million unaccounted for.

They had been released on bail some months earlier, and they came before me, represented by an experienced QC whom I knew quite well in the UK, and asked that this restriction be reconsidered as they found it rather confining in Gibraltar and had family in other parts of the world. I was told that their assets had been frozen, and that they and their families were entirely dependent upon the generosity of their local community. This of itself set alarm bells ringing in my mind, as I had received even within just a few days several invitations to enjoy what may very well have been the perfectly innocent hospitality of some very welcoming Gibraltarians. These I declined out of an abundance of caution, for it would have been untenable to sit at their tables, or even worse find my fellow guests had been the financial supporters of those who appeared in front of me. I also declined the persuasive tongue of the QC, whom I reminded that I had 30 million reasons not to comply with his request.

There was one change to the laws of Gibraltar that I did speed along. I discovered that for serious matters of crime the solicitors of Gibraltar would look to London and fly out a QC with expertise. However, the arrangements for legal aid were somewhat primitive, and payment for such an exercise was made by the solicitor adding the QC as a necessary expense to their own application to the government for payment. In other words, I thought a satisfactory system of legal aid to deal with complex cases was not in place. I discovered that there had been discussions in government circles and draft provisions debated, but none was then in force. I adjourned the case, for the case management of which I would be responsible, for two weeks for a satisfactory legal aid system to be brought into effect, and it was. I had been assured that I would not have to sit as the judge when it came to trial.

In addition to my having helped put the legal aid system into operation there, I also assisted by advising the registrar who was responsible for assessments under the very high costs (VHC) system which operated in the UK.

Legal aid systems now having been put into operation, solicitors were able to instruct counsel from the UK who were highly experienced in matters of commercial fraud. This was at a time when restrictions and cuts introduced by David Cameron's choice as Lord Chancellor and Minister of Justice, Chris Grayling, were severely limiting rates of legal aid and other services available in England resulting in genuine concern about the prospects of those at the Criminal Bar and in particular there were restrictions on the grant of legal aid for leading counsel. Although the Gibraltar Bar was undoubtedly competent there were times when I was asked to advise on specialist counsel from the UK, which I happily did and to the satisfaction of the defence.

As to the *Marrache Case* itself, money missing from the clients' account of solicitors is always serious, and when it is over £30 million, extremely serious. The case eventually started in the Supreme Court on the 14th October 2013 with three days of jury selection, it was tried by a retired High Court judge, Sir Geoffrey Grigson, and lasted eight months. There were several breaks for aspects of the case to be determined, and it will enter the history books, amongst other reasons, for being the first case where the jury tampering provisions were brought into operation, where if there is a suspicion of this happening, the judge can continue the case alone, carrying out the functions of both judge and jury.

Among other things, the judge had to consider whether there had been an intention to deprive clients due to an honest expectation that money would be repaid and much of the defence case was based around lack of criminal intent, and that each was not personally responsible for what had occurred. The only defendant to be fully cleared was an employee, Leanne Turnbull who was represented by Ann Cotcher QC, who took over in November, a month after the case started.

Following the allegation of jury tampering and the jury being discharged with the judge taking over, because of this, in November there was an application for his recusal, which failed. In January 2014, a submission of no case to answer failed. Abuse of process applications were made in February, which also failed. In March, a constitutional motion by Benjamin against the judge's appointment failed, as did his further application for judicial review.

In the event, the brothers were found guilty in July, Benjamin being sentenced to eleven years, and Isaac and Solomon to seven years each. But due process meant that this case was by no means over. In September an application for extra funding, beyond that previously allowed was rejected by the Supreme Court but accepted on appeal to the Chief Justice. In October, Benjamin's appeal on constitutional grounds was dismissed, and a week later the full appeal of all the brothers was also dismissed. An application to appeal to the Privy Council was turned down.

Several millions pounds were paid by the government in respect of the defence of all the defendants, and a further sum in respect of the appeal. These included the costs of the various ancillary submissions to the court, and the constitutional and judicial review submissions of Benjamin Marrache, made on the basis that the appointment of the judge was incorrect.

☙

I had asked, and was often asked myself whether there was much crime in Gibraltar. The surprising answer was yes, or at least certainly enough to keep me going. During my stay, I dealt with a murder, an attempted murder, several rapes, many woundings, some robberies, an arson or two, fraud, theft and many Class 1 drugs cases.

One of the main problems in getting the hearing of a case off the ground was the selection of a jury. Gibraltar is a small place with some 30,000 inhabitants, and nearly everybody knows everybody else. They have been to school together, played for the same football and other sports teams, married into each others' families, lived in the same apartment blocks, or been a close friend of a member of the family of the accused or one of the witnesses. Only nine people were needed to form a jury for most cases; for murder it would be 12, but to find those nine (or 12) from the 100 or so who had been summoned to form the jury could sometimes take over an hour.

In the main I found the jurors to be dedicated, punctual and industrious in application to their task. I cannot help denying that I was somewhat surprised on occasion by their generosity to an accused, but then, as I had told them, the facts were for them to decide upon. The notes which they would send me requesting further explanation were to the point and in the main understandable. I mentioned generosity to the accused. This perhaps is another way of saying that I was astonished by the proportion of acquittals, sometimes in the face of what I considered to be overwhelming evidence, though occasionally because of what I deemed to be a failure on the part of those investigating the matter. Examples were an acquittal on a charge of arson for a man seen loitering near shortly to be burned down premises, playing with a cigarette lighter to boot. There was a murder charge which I instructed the jury to throw out because the deceased had died well beyond the year-and-a-day rule of homicide law which still applied in Gibraltar; a large drugs case where the defendant believed his car was stacked with cannabis, not cocaine; and another case involving smuggling when I had a chance encounter with a smiling jury foreman as I left court, who quite uninvited told me as I passed him, "Of course we all knew he was as guilty as hell, but we couldn't put our hands on our hearts and say the prosecution had done their best."

Cases were timed on arraignment to a date or days in the future convenient to witnesses and for preparation for both sides, but there was one interesting difference from the UK. They were timed to start on a Monday, but on the basis of being told they would last five days, ten days, fifteen days and so on, really in terms of a working week. Of course not all cases would survive an earlier plea of not guilty. It is a universal habit that the nearer the hearing date and the more application to the evidence a defendant will hear, or give, the more does the reality of the situation sink in, and a plea of guilty seem the better course.

Equally a case deemed to last five days could be hurried along by an agreement between the parties over certain parts of the evidence, and in those circumstances the case would finish by Wednesday instead of Friday. In the UK there would be a list of floaters, that is, cases which should be ready to be called on at short notice, but not in Gibraltar. If a case finished on Wednesday there were two days vacant, though I would sometimes bring in a sentencing matter for a morning.

The Attorney General would prosecute the more serious cases himself. Ricky Roda, QC was a man of considerable experience in colonial justice. He had sat as a stipendiary magistrate in Hong Kong for some years, and also in other parts of the Commonwealth. He was supported by an extremely capable QC called Robert Fischel and a young team of counsel who were most keen and helpful.

The local Bar was mainly concerned in commercial cases; some would do criminal cases. Three or four were particularly good and experienced; I shall not name them for fear of inadvertently leaving others out. However, the main bread-and-butter work was commercial, and those who took on criminal cases did so more out of a sense of community duty, having regard to the disparity between the fees earned in such commercial work and the normal legal aid fees for crime.

However, if there was a particularly complicated criminal matter, then the local solicitors—and remember it was a fused profession of solicitors and barristers—would instruct counsel, usually leading counsel, to come out from the UK. This fused bar seemed to work well. There was no backbiting, fighting over clients or similar practices which I had known in the UK, and there was an easy attitude to helping each other out to ensure cases were heard promptly. There were four large firms, one in particular, Hassan's, being by far the largest and best-known, Triay & Triay, Triay, Stagnetto & Neish, Isolas and about 17 smaller firms, with partners in number ranging from eight to single practitioners. I found them all most polite, and I hope I was able to afford a little advice and assistance to any budding advocate.

The law certainly flourished and was visible in Gibraltar. You would see barristers striding down Main Street with their wing collars and white tabs, sometimes gowned, and many of them were also politicians. I found it mildly amusing that the Chief Minister and leader of the opposition, judging by the newspapers and radio, were ever at each others' throats, though in real life they were partners in the same legal practice.

During the earlier period of my stay in Gibraltar there was little difficulty in driving in-and-out at weekends, and there were visitors from London to show lovely towns such as Cordoba, Jerez and Malaga and even Tangier, 45 minutes away by ferry. There we found Mohammed, who on several occasions met us off the boat in his Mercedes and once showed us the main synagogue in Tangier. My friend Professor Mike Baum and I were pleased to make up the quorum or minion for prayers, only to find the proceedings disrupted by a man who at a point chosen by himself decided to stand and say a prayer for a deceased relative. We soon realised that the Arabic epithets being hurled at him were, "Not now, sit down." He refused and a struggle began, with a few more people coming in to make up the team, so we left. It seemed he was from Casablanca, and that is the way they did it in Casablanca, but not according to the customs of the Tangerines.

Eventually the Spanish made it a little difficult to get out of Gibraltar; it meant waiting in a long queue at the border post. They searched cars and motorbikes, even pedestrians' bags, with a toothcomb, supposedly looking for smugglers. The smuggling was not only cocaine and hard drugs, but also cigarettes. Spaniards are in the main heavy smokers and tobacco carries little duty in Gibraltar, so it is worthwhile buying cheap and then stuffing a few cork tips up your exhaust, as there were limits on what the Spaniards could take through.

The real reason for the fuss was Pedro. Pedro was a fisherman who complained about the interference he was getting from the Gibraltarian police whenever he took his boat out, which was every night. He had a favourite spot for finding young crustaceans and that is where he trawled his net at night time along the floor of the sea. The trouble was that Gibraltar considered that particular area of sea floor to be completely Gibraltarian, and even the crustaceans were therefore Gibraltarian and not to be disturbed in their activities. It was not as though the Gibraltarian fishermen were being deprived of a tasty catch because there are no Gibraltarian fishermen. However, there is nothing that angers a true Gibraltarian more than having his sea bed trespassed upon, and the Spaniards, who have had sleepless nights since that day in 1713 when the Treaty of Utrecht put an indelible stamp on the future of Europe and Gibraltar in particular, had a similar approach. So when Pedro was approached one night as he was gently trawling his nets and told that he was doing so in Gibraltarian waters, he shrugged his shoulders, sympathised with the Royal Gibraltar policeman in his powerful launch, and carried on trawling his nets. This happened several times, and on some of these occasions he was given a summons to appear at the Gibraltar magistrates' courts for illegal fishing. Pedro declined the invitation. A few more incidents followed and Pedro found he was spending more time arguing with the Gibraltar policemen than actually disturbing the crustaceans. A few Spanish politicians took up his cudgel and their Foreign Minister instructed the *Guarda Civil* to be a little more awkward with those who travelled over the border, be it into or out of Gibraltar.

Following Franco's time the border had been completely closed from 1969 to 1985, and thereafter there had been sporadic searches for smuggling reasons. However, despite occasional flurries of officialdom the flow was reasonable, especially to the benefit of the 8,000 Spanish workers who come in to Gibraltar on a daily basis, an oasis in the Spanish desert of unemployment.

And so it was that after Pedro they became awkward, sometimes stopping one car in seven for a thorough search, and sometimes every car. Motor cyclists and foot travellers did not escape; the waiting times for cars hit eight hours at their worst, one-and-a-half hours frequently, and rarely less than half-an-hour to an hour. The position was not improved when Gibraltar's Chief Minister decided to jettison 30 large blocks of concrete on to the seabed. "The reason," said the Chief Minister, "was not to prevent Pedro fishing there, but to eventually form an artificial reef and encourage sea life and fauna." The Spanish Foreign Minister promptly ordered the stopping and searching of more and more cars and travellers. The truth was that frustrating as it may have been for Gibraltarians seeking an escape from the confines of The Rock, it was even more annoying for all the workers who came in. Another period of lengthy queues followed the issue by the Chief Minister of defamation proceedings against a Spanish left-wing trade union.

This process only prevented me following my Sunday arrangement of driving into Spain for lunch on only one occasion. I avoided the crowds by going out and coming back at what was an early-hour by Spanish (and Gibraltar) standards.

In the 300-years since the treaty the place had grown from what was really just a garrison town to a thriving commercial, financial and legal centre. When cruise ships called, Main Street was thronged with people, occasionally with two ships on the same day jettisoning a total of 4,000 visitors. This meant excellent trade for the shops, and even without the ships the daily coach trips from the Costa brought in customers for the wine and alcohol, perfumery and electronics purveyors, and those who yearned for an M&S were not disappointed. Catholics, Muslims, Hindus and Jews lived peacefully side-by-side, the last having entered, despite the prohibition in the Treaty of Utrecht, from Morocco where they had sojourned following expulsion from Spain during the Inquisition.

There were many official gatherings to which I was invited, and they gave a wonderful insight into colonial life: the governor's garden party at The Convent, with the uniforms, the panamas, the summer dresses. The Ceremony of the Keys in Casemates Square was not unlike the one at the Tower of London, with the Royal Gibraltar Regiment proudly marching and counter-marching. Then there was the opening of the legal year, when the judges were all resplendent in red robes, lace bibs and long full-bottom wigs and were driven around Gibraltar in large black shining cars with motorcycle police outriders, who if they didn't impress the Spanish certainly impressed me. Then we went to the cathedral to pray that we dispensed justice with mercy — though not too much of the latter — and then back to the court garden to drink cava with the great, the good and the occasional bad, who had borrowed (or stolen) a collar and tie, learned how to put it on and had gate-crashed.

One of the attractions of my period there was that although the government did not offer me accommodation, or indeed any direct allowance for it, I was able to choose my apartment, and because the tax situation was so beneficial made sure it was a decent one. I overlooked the marina and most evenings went for a walk admiring the various yachts. One evening as the sun was just about to set I decided to stroll before changing, and must have stood out among the people gathering in the various restaurants along the water's edge. As I passed one spectacular vessel a tall man was edging down the gangplank. He looked at me and said, "You must be a banker or an accountant." We bantered and I eventually justified my presence. He introduced himself as Michael Ashcroft, whose full title was Lord Ashcroft, he of the Tory Party, fund-raiser and treasurer, but who had in addition hit the headlines as the target of numerous labour back-and front-benchers because despite these high political offices he was classed as non-resident for tax purposes in the UK. He asked if I lived in the rather smart apartments nearby and I said I did, adding how low taxes had assisted in my choice. "Aha!" he said, "then you are a tax avoider!" His full background had clicked into my mental processes by then, including the ownership of the smart yacht from which I had seen him disembark, and he appreciated my response, which was, "You, of all people can talk like that!" We met once or twice over the next few days, spoke of certain mutually known party supporters, and I was flattered to hear that both the Governor and First Minister had praised my input in their talks with him.

I found the work in Gibraltar well within my capabilities, and I was able to cut a swathe through some of the customs which had previously taken up quite a lot of unnecessary time, and I don't mean such small details as providing the jury with food and water through their deliberations, since they got on with the job much quicker without. I cleared the backlog and continued to deal with all the criminal matters for the remainder of my contract.

Gibraltarians themselves I found absolutely charming, especially those whose families had been there for a long time, who possessed an old-style laid-back elegance. Although all true Gibraltarians speak English, there creeps into their English conversation Spanish words in every second sentence, and vice-versa. And there are some strange little customs, such as blocking Main Street with their baby buggies, and rarely walking along it with less than five astride. They had come from Spain, Italy and Malta to Gibraltar, and brought their accents, names and foods. The Jews who have been there since about 1700 have built four synagogues, one in 1720, and are in the main pretty orthodox. The British who remained after service in the forces over the years are recognised by their names, their red hair, the pubs and the fish-and-chip shops. The Indians are recognised by their electric equipment shops.

This was a period of work which I thoroughly enjoyed, and I was fortunate to work with and meet so many truly nice people. I felt honoured that when approaching the conclusion of my two year contract the Minister of Justice asked if I would like to stay another year, or even two years, and continue to deal with the criminal calendar. There were responsibilities at home that needed my attention, and I regretfully declined, though I did agree that a further three months, which would take me to a date after 6 April, would be an attractive idea. My colleagues gave me an excellent farewell dinner at the currently best restaurant, and the bar paid kind tributes in court. And so, in his 82nd year, the blackbird flew home.

◊

So here I found myself, once again, with time on my hands and sitting at my word processor.

One of my extra mural pursuits had been writing letters to *The Times*, who have been particularly kind in that they have rarely failed to print what I regard as one of my gems. *The Telegraph*, *Guardian* and *Jewish Chronicle* also proved hospitable. The secret is to keep it short, and I graduated from the bottom of the last column three liner, to more recently, the ones in the square at the top of the page.

A reliable source informed me that drawing attention to the little-known Abuse of Honours Act 1925 in one of my letters, for it had not recently been mentioned in print, precipitated questions by a Parliamentary backbencher in the 2006 furore over "Cash for Honours". My feeling was that where honours had been bestowed upon people who had either given or secretly "loaned" money to a political party, and there was a strong indication that someone concerned with that fundraising had dealings with the House of Lords Appointments Commission, then there may well be some inferences drawn, and it seemed to me the existence of circumstantial evidence relating to an "unambiguous agreement" merited investigation.

I appreciated the fact that the Prime Minister might have been involved in such deliberations did not minimise the merit of an investigation, at least, it was known he was anxious to increase the number of Labour working peers. There had, after all, been much publicity of the "friends" of the Prime Minister and those active in securing funding for the Labour Party.

In the event an enquiry was held, it delivered it's report which explained the burden of the DPP before commencing proceedings as to the percentage likelihood of success, and more particularly the difficulty in proving that a sum given was "as an inducement or reward for procuring... a title of honour."

The investigation was focused upon whether there was any agreement between two people to make and accept a gift in exchange for an honour and that in the circumstances such precise evidence was unavailable.

The Labour Party is not the only political organization which has come under public scrutiny for failure to comply with the strict requirements of the 1925 Act, and the subsequent 2000 Act, though the public is still entitled to be mystified.

In recent years several honours have been awarded to political party "donors" and frankly, if this is not a pay-off for giving money, then I don't know what is. Are we really to believe that there are people so generous that they will give hundreds of thousands to a political party without some expectation? If they are so charitable then there are many more deserving and needy causes, which could greater benefit from their benevolence. It should be sufficient to satisfy the ego of such donors that in return they are invited to dine at the table of the powerful, but to give titles and more disgracefully allow them to enter the chamber of power so as to make it look as if this may have been in return for donations is absolutely unacceptable.

One wonders whether Assistant Commissioner John Yates might have been able to delve a little deeper, it was, so it transpired, he who resigned some five years later following criticism of the review he carried out into the 2006 police investigation into the *News of the World* phone-hacking scandal. Or was it simply that the Metropolitan Police were stretched to the limit trying to investigate in high places?

It is equally interesting that David Perry QC, one of the independent counsel who advised the CPS concerning no criminal proceedings in the honours case, did advise a reversal of the Lord Janner decision by the DPP, a matter about which one of my letters in *The Times* explained in simple terms the two stage course the DPP should have taken in that fitness to plead procedure, a course which eventually, was in fact followed.

In numerous letters over recent years I have indicated concern at the appointment of two recent Ministers of Justice, who have thereby assumed the mantle of Lord Chancellor. Whilst appreciating that the Minister of Health does not have to be a doctor, nor the Minister of Transport a train driver, the tradition has for centuries been that the Lord Chancellor was a lawyer, and usually a distinguished one, though I did wonder that the downward path began with the appointment of Lord Derry Irvine, whom it was unkindly said owed his appointment largely to having been a former flat mate of Tony Blair.

The fact remains that the subsequent appointment of Chris Grayling precipitated an abandonment of one of the traditions of that office, for how else can one describe the acts of a man who virtually tore up a legal aid and advice system which worked well, and provided assistance to those most in need. He has been followed by Michael Gove, another non-lawyer. In the first month or two in office Gove showed a willingness to meet representatives of the professional bodies, and although he expressed an understanding of their problems nevertheless has maintained that he is bound by the dictates of the Chancellor. He appears to have shown more sympathy to the Bar than solicitors, indicating the need for a "pipeline" towards judicial appointment, and the need for a strong Bar, and at the same time as his government accepts increases for MPs amounting to eleven per cent, they continue to cut legal aid, and reduce payments to solicitors by a further eight per cent.

David Cameron of course is responsible for each of these appointments, the modern trend is towards a legal service headed not by lawyers, but by people who are expected to act like the sales manager of some questionable commercial firm, with salesmen expected to hit sales targets, rather than provide an adequate legal service for the public, and one of which this country used to be proud. However and surprisingly one small but positive move occurred in response to legal challenges and public protests by a normally sedate profession, in which my son Jonathan Black was active as President of the London Criminal Solicitors Association, when at the start of 2016 Michael Gove announced that plans to drastically reduce the number of firms allowed to deliver criminal legal aid at police stations and magistrates' courts had been dropped and that an 8.75 per cent cut to legal aid fees had been suspended for 12 months.

I was fortunate to have been a legal aid lawyer during a time when it worked, and those who worked in it could concentrate on what they were trained and proud to do, and know that at the end of the day they would receive reasonable reimbursement.

My earnest hope is that it is not too late for common sense to prevail and for the reputation of our courts and our sense of justice built over so many years be restored, so that there should be no denial of proper independent representation to all in need who cannot otherwise afford it, in other words that the cuts in legal aid availability end.

For this would mean that the step-by-step, stage-by-stage, training ground in the lower courts where experience is gained by young advocates is revived. This allows students, and then probationers, to perform the minor work which traditionally provides experience leading to the fully qualified practitioner from whom the judiciary will eventually be chosen.

Otherwise, I ask, where will the judges come from?

Index

Abuse of Honours Act 1925 *212*
abuse of process *75, 142, 205*
admissions *141*
adrenalin *79*
Africa *18*
air-raids *18*
alcohol *102, 167*
Aldershot *52, 59, 62, 136*
anecdotal amblings *190*
anxiety *80*
appeals *95, 117, 188*
arbitration *178*
Armley Prison *68*
army *92*
   Army Cadet Force *26, 50*
   Army Legal Service *64, 135*
Arnold, Det Con *120*
arson *205*
articled clerks *173*
arts *28*
Ashcroft, Lord *210*
Attorney General *148, 184, 201*
audacity *173*
Australia *188*
Austria *43, 57*
backlog of cases *198, 202*
bad character *164*
Bahamas *194*
bail *97, 125, 150, 153, 203*
Baker, Elizabeth *150*
Banks, Shirley *185*
Bar Mitzvah *19*
barracks *61*
Barrington Black & Co *173, 179*
barristers *28, 82, 125, 145–147, 181, 182, 191,*
   207
Bartfield, Robert *153*
Bartle, Ronald *180*
Bathpool Park *88*
Baum, Mike *208*
BBC *18, 27, 54, 82, 170*
Beaumont, Judge Peter *166*

Belsen *140*
Ben-Gurion, David *23*
Bennett, Alan *27*
Bentley *171*
Berlin *133*
   Berlin Wall *133*
   East Berlin *138*
   West Berlin *138*
betting *161*
Big Ben *76*
Birmingham *174*
Black, Abraham *19*
Black, Diana *72, 187, 199*
Black, Jonathan *183, 214*
Black, Louis *21*
Black Panther *81*
Blackpool *10, 124*
   Blackpool Tower *130*
Black's *175, 179*
Blair, Tony *214*
Blenheim Barracks *52, 60, 62*
blood *165*
   blood samples *75*
bombs *17*
Boreham, Mr Justice *98, 106, 147, 150*
Bow Street *27, 175*
   Bow Street Magistrates' Court *178*
   Bow Street Runners *178*
Bradford *27, 68, 84, 146, 151, 164*
Brash, Minnie *21*
Breaks, Daniel *132*
bribery *76, 177*
bridewell *35, 68*
Bridge, Mr Justice *141*
Bridlington *108*
Bristol *185*
Britain's most wanted man *94*
British Expeditionary Force *15*
Broadmoor *147*
brothel-keeping *191*
Brown, Malcolm *136*
Bucharest *42*
Buckingham Palace *76*
Budapest *44*
Buller Barracks *56–60*
bullying *53, 63*

burglary *92, 108, 162*
Burnley *121*
Butler, Gerald QC *189*
Butler, Mr Justice Christopher *202*
Cairo *18*
Cameron, David *204, 214*
Campbell, Quentin *180*
Cannan, John *185*
Cardiff *15, 30*
Caribbean *98, 107*
car park attendants *174*
Carr Manor *179*
Cash for Honours *212*
Catholics *210*
cells *82, 98, 167, 181*
Ceremony of the Keys *210*
Chancery Lane *188*
Chapeltown *107*
    Chapeltown Police Station *99*
Chappell, Peter *76*
Charing Cross *181*
Checkpoint Charlie *138*
childhood *9*
Churchill, Winston *18*
circuit judge *176, 187*
City of London *190*
    City of London bench *72, 176, 182*
Civil Defence *13*
class *15*
cleanliness *59*
Clerk of the Queen's Kitchen *180*
clerks to the justices *174*
Cleworth, Ralph QC *70*
clients' money *202*
Clifford's Mount *73*
Cohen, Myrella QC *192*
Cohen, Reverend Aaron *19*
Cold War *133*
Coles, Gerald QC *130*
Colville, Viscount *192*
commercial work *68, 207*
Communism *41, 58*
community duty *207*
compassion *192*
concentration camps *134*
confessions *141, 143, 162, 167*

confidentiality *84*
Connor, Jeremy *193*
conspiracy *77*
conveyancing *179*
corruption *178*
costs
    very high cost case *204*
Cotcher, Ann QC *204*
Court of Appeal *76, 77, 88, 117, 157, 190*
Court of Green Cloth *180*
Courts Martial *63, 133*
Covent Garden *182*
Cowman, Det Sgt *112*
Cowper, William *197*
Cox, Carl Clement *103*
Cox, Philip QC *89*
cricket *41, 50, 75*
crime *92, 178*
    crime in Gibraltar *205*
    perfect crime *84*
criminal damage *77*
criminal law *34, 35*
criminal work *146*
Crown
    Crown Court *150, 176, 185, 186, 188*
    Crown Prosecution Service *148*
    Crown protectorate *197*
Cyprus *135*
Czechoslovakia *57*
Daily Mirror *83*
Daily Express *91*
Darrow, Clarence *67*
Davies, Alan *199*
Davis, George *75*
Davis, Rose *75*
debating *39*
defamation *209*
delay *149, 173*
delusion *130*
demobilisation *64*
Denning, Lord *142*
dentistry *15, 27–29*
Department of Legal Services *133*
depression *167*
detachment *94*
detection *177, 191*

deterrence *159*
Detmold *139*
De Veil, Thomas *178*
Devlin, Lord *76*
Dickinson, John *106*
Dickinson, Mary *106*
Dick, Uncle *14*
diminished responsibility *124, 130, 147, 165, 167*
Director of Public Prosecutions *148, 154*
divorce *155*
dock brief *145*
donkey wallopers *54*
Donnelly, William *114*
Downing Street *76*
drill sergeants *63*
drugs *107, 159, 167, 184, 190, 194, 208*
Dudley, Anthony *201*
Dudley (West Midlands) *83*
Dunkirk *16*
Eastern bloc *46*
Ede and Ravenscroft *188*
Edinburgh *126*
Egypt *24*
Elbers, Nermin *134*
Elcock, Alban Beresford *97*
Elcock, Margaret *97*
Ellerby Avenue *100*
Epstein, Jacob *23*
evacuation *15, 17*
Eveleigh, Lord Justice *118*
evidence
 circumstantial evidence *102, 141*
 evidence test *148*
 fabrication of evidence *143*
 identification evidence *75*
 scientific evidence *143*
 suppression of evidence *75*
 testing the evidence *162*
experts
 medical experts *147*
extortion *185*
family cases *179, 202*
Farley, Joyce *180*
Farnborough *53*
felony *177*

Fielding, Henry *178*
Fielding, John *178*
Fischel, Robert *207*
Fleet Street *76*
Florrie, Aunty *15*
Fonteyn, Margot *40*
forensics *85, 89, 105, 117, 128, 147, 162, 167*
France *15, 43*
Francis, Lloyd *111*
Franco, General *209*
fraud *185, 204, 205*
Freedland, Michael *54*
freedom *45*
Gallagher, Thomas *70*
Gallipoli *23*
gambling *160, 195*
gangsters *195*
Gannex *172*
Garrick Club *180*
gas-mask *14, 18*
Gatow Airport *133*
George, Boy *184*
Germany *14, 17, 134*
Gertrude, Aunty *14*
Gibbs, Sergeant *69*
Gibraltar *197–211*
 Gibraltar Society for Fine Arts *202*
Gilrain Det Supt *107*
Godfrey, Louise *131*
Gove, Michael *214*
grammar school *26*
Gray, Gilbert QC *39, 42, 95, 97, 117, 147, 150, 163, 191*
Grayling, Chris *204, 214*
Great Marlborough Street *182*
Green, Dr Michael *104*
grievous bodily harm *135*
Grigson, Geoffrey *204*
Groom of the Great Chamber *180*
Guildford *63*
Hailsham, Lord *129*
Halifax *124*
Hampstead *169*
handgun *135*
Handy, Jason *183*
Harrison Jobbings & Co *175*

Index

Harrogate *17, 72, 84, 119, 166, 169*
Harrow Crown Court *190*
Hassan's *207*
have it away-day girls *182*
Hawick *119*
Hayward, Jack *194*
Headingly *41, 76, 83*
heart valve *99, 102*
Heath, Edward *192*
Hegyeshalom *43*
Hess, Rudolph *134*
Hide, Walter *125*
Hitler, Adolph *13*
Hoban, Dennis *98, 106, 166*
Hobson, Jim *98*
holocaust denier *183*
Home Affairs Committee *131*
Home Office *157, 192*
Home Secretary *167*
Homicide Act 1957 *150*
Hong Kong *188, 207*
hooch *160*
hopeless cases *163*
Hopkin, David *180, 183*
Horseferry Road *182*
hospital order *147*
House of Lords *173, 187*
Hughes, Professor *34*
Hull *23*
Hungary *44, 57*
idealism *9*
independence *194*
instructions *145*
integrity *166*
interrogation *141, 162*
IRA *139, 141*
Iron Curtain *43, 57*
Irvine, Lord *214*
Isolas *207*
James, Professor Philip *34*
Janner, Lord *213*
Japan *19*
Jenkins, Roy *77*
Jensen Interceptor *81–82, 172*
Jews *13, 19, 73, 180, 198, 210, 211*
Johns, Adrian *200*

joint enterprise *166*
Jones, Norman *98*
judge *187–215*
   judge advocate *133*
judicial career *174, 186*
jury *87, 94, 98, 117, 150*
   jury tampering *204*
justice *9*
justices *177*
   historical fees *178*
   trading justices *178*
Kagan, Lord *172*
Kaufman, Gerald *25*
Kelly, Janine *115*
Kent, Rodney *170*
Kenya *92*
kidnap *86, 91, 119*
Kindertransport *14*
Kramer, Jacob *27*
Kray twins *184*
Labour Party *170, 212*
Lamplugh, Suzy *185*
Lancashire Constabulary *119*
landed gentry *178*
law *33, 145*
   criminal law *147*
   law and order *177*
   law in Gibraltar *198*
Lawrence, Ivan QC *131*
Law Society *146, 172*
   examination *49*
Lawson, Mr Justice *127*
Leamington-on-Sea *185*
Leamington (Warwickshire) *186*
Leeds *9, 64, 76, 145*
   Empire Theatre *36*
   Leeds Assizes *31, 97*
   Leeds CID *98*
   Leeds Town Hall *68*
   Leeds University *34*
legal aid *67, 82, 83, 135, 142, 146, 203, 204, 214*
Legge, Thomas *174*
Leicester Square *178*
Levi, Jack *65*
Levy, Soloman *11*

Liberals 170
life imprisonment 117, 142, 166, 167
listing officer 192
Lithuania 12, 22
Lloyd George 29
London 14, 64, 174, 177
   London Electricity Board 75
Lord Chancellor 129, 173, 177, 187, 193, 195, 213
Lord Chief Justice 97, 142, 157, 179
Lord Steward 180
Lorrimar, Miss 173
Loy, David 70
Luftwaffe 17
Lyons, Edward QC 170
Maastricht 139
magistrates 72
   lay magistrates 184
   magistrates' courts 63, 68, 145, 146
      Gibraltar magistrates' courts 209
   stipendiary magistrates 148
Mann, Jasper 156
Mansion House 72
manslaughter 124, 147, 150
marching 56
Marrache Case 202–205
Mars-Jones, Mr Justice 87, 95
Marylebone 182
Mason, Perry 67
Master of the Ceremonies 180
matrimonial work 146, 154
Maurice, Uncle 15
Maxwell, Robert 172
McCourt, Mary Jean 99
McCourt, Peter 102, 114
Meadows, Det Ch Insp 120
media 91
medical reports 127
Megarry, Robert 35
Megiddo 23
mental illness 147
merchants 178
mercy 210
   prerogative of mercy 77
Mick, Uncle 18
Middlesex Sessions 178

Middle Temple 193
Middleton 102, 107
Millgarth Police Station 98, 107
miners 171
Minister of Justice 213
miscarriage of justice 75
Mishcon de Rea 64
Mishcon, Victor 64
Mitchell, Austin 170
mitigation 163
Mons Officer Cadet School 50, 58
morality 15
Morley 71
motive 90, 116, 163
mugging 70
murder 75, 79, 83, 97, 119, 124, 146, 149, 205
   murder in prison 159
Muslims 210
mute of malice 130
Myerson, Arthur QC 147, 153
National Service 49, 82, 135
National Union of Students 41
Nazism 134
Neilson, Donald 81
   balaclava 90
   disciplinarian 91
   high level of planning 86
   meticulous individual 91
Newcastle 126, 145
   Newcastle Chambers 166
Nicholson, Viv 172
North Africa 23
North-Eastern Circuit 179
Northern Ireland 135, 139
nostalgia 169
Nuremberg trials 134
oath 179
officer 61
Old Bailey 36, 98, 178
Old Testament 15
Openshaw, Judge William Harrison 122, 125
Openshaw, Peter 132
opera 42, 193
Orient Express 42
Oxford Crown Court 81, 87

Page of the Back Stairs *180*
paranoia *130*
Parkin, Anthony *114*
parole *167*
pathology *105, 149, 154*
peace petitions *43*
Pearl Chambers *67*
Pedro the fisherman *208*
Pentre *15, 30*
Perry, David QC *213*
personality disorder *130*
Philips, Mr Justice *163*
Piccadilly *181*
piety *15*
pimps *107, 182*
Pindling, Lynden *194*
police *80, 88, 98, 119, 177*
  allegations of assault *141*
  Police and Criminal Evidence Act *79, 99, 151*
  police court *148*
  police fabrication *143*
  police protection *186*
  station sergeant *148*
  undercover officers *75*
politics *13, 30, 41, 72*
poll tax *186, 190*
Prague *46*
prejudice *164*
preparation *98*
Prescott, Mrs Justice Karen *201*
Preston *119, 122*
Price, Mike *136*
Prime Minister *212*
prison *68, 159*
prisoners *68*
  prisoner welfare *125*
Privy Council *205*
probate *154*
probation service *82*
procedure
  criminal procedure *147*
proof
  putting to proof *162*
prosecutors *148*
prostitution *107, 178*

protection *177*
  police protection *186*
protest *125*
psychiatry *128, 147, 154, 165*
psychology *165*
psychotic disorder *130*
Quarter Sessions *35*
Queen Elizabeth II *40*
Queen's Counsel *145, 181*
Queen's shilling *51*
radio *16, 18*
rag revue *63*
Randolph, John *70*
rape *28, 162, 185, 190, 205*
rationing *20*
recorder *186*
Regents Park *193*
regimental wit *57*
religion *197*
remand *141, 149*
  remand court *69*
remorse *162*
riots *190*
Rivlin, Geoffrey *97*
road traffic *183*
robbery *75, 163, 205*
Roberts, Bryan QC *175, 184*
Roda, Ricky QC *207*
Romania *42, 45, 58*
Roosevelt, Theodore *18*
Rose, Aunty *14*
Rother Valley *170*
Roundhay School *25, 50*
Royal Air Force *134*
Royal Army Service Corps *53*
Royal Courts of Justice *118*
rugby *26, 29, 50, 97*
Rumpole, Horace *28, 162*
Russia *57, 133*
Sanders, Roger *193*
school *25*
Schultz, Edith *134*
science *28*
  scientific evidence *143*
Scotland *119*
Second World War *133*

self-defence *136*, *151*, *156*
sheep *15*
Sheffield *145*
Shek, Chiang Kai *18*
sheriffs *184*
shooting *81*
  domestic shooting *147*
shoplifters *182*
Sikhs *146*
Silence of the Lambs, The *84*
Simmonds, Louis *30*
Slater, Det Insp *119*
Smith, Det Ch Insp *112*
Smith, John *120*
Smith, Robert *166*
smuggling *208*
Snaresbrook Crown Court *190*
Society Club *72*
Soho *181*
solicitors *49*, *63*, *146*, *151*, *182*, *207*
  duty solicitor *151*
South Kenton *14*
South Parade *173*
Southwark Crown Court *176*, *189*
Spandau Prison *134*
specialism *154*
speculation *118*
Spink, Kevin *100*
Spooner, Keith *109*
stabbing *151*, *165*
Stalin, Josef *18*, *45*
standard of proof *132*
standards *59*
statutorily senile *195*
Steer, Wilf QC *165*
St George, Edward *194*
St George, Henrietta *194*
stipendiary magistrates *175*
  flying stipe *184*
St Paul's *180*
Strand, The *179*, *181*, *190*
Strangeways Prison *129*
strangulation *105*
Straw, Jack *41*
striking similarity *164*
Supreme Court (Gibraltar) *198*

Swan Shopping Centre *91*
Swift, Elizabeth *132*
Swift, Ogden *28*, *33*
Switzerland *43*
synagogues *208*, *211*
tap on the shoulder *188*
tarts *182*
Taylor, Peter QC (Lord Chief Justice) *97*, *150*, *166*, *179*
Territorial Army *13*, *50*
test match *75*
theft *177*, *205*
Times, The *181*, *212*
Tonypandy *30*
Tory Party *26*, *210*
tour guide *72*, *187*
touts *182*
Trafalgar Square *76*, *190*
transvestites *182*
travel guide *176*
travellers *100*
treason *124*
Treaty of Utrecht *208*
trials *127*, *182*
Triay, Stagnetto & Neish *207*
Triay & Triay *207*
trust *10*, *70*
unions *64*
university *33*
USA *133*
ushers *174*
Valium *121*, *125*, *128*
Vaughan, Frankie *38*
vetting *57*
Viagra *191*
victims *94*, *163*
  murder victim a judge *119*
Vienna *42*
violence *84*, *102*, *141*, *151*, *190*
Wakefield *68*
  Wakefield Prison *160*
Walker, John *141*, *142*
Walker Morris & Coles *71*, *173*
War Office *57*
Warwick University *186*
Wasserzier, Ursula *134*

watchman *177*
wealth *177*
weapons *84*
West Midlands Police *141*
West Riding *10*, *34*, *67*, *172*
West Yorkshire *65*
Whitely, Richard *170*
White, Mike *55*
White, Rubalyn Agatha *117*
Whittle, Leslie *83*, *162*
Whittle, Ronald *91*
whole life sentence *95*
Widgery, Lord *142*
Wilde, Oscar *184*
William Bateson Coates & Co *175*
witnesses *82*
   expert witnesses *147*
World Federation of Democratic Youth *41*
wounding *75*, *135*, *205*
Yates, John *213*
York *72*, *145*
   York Minster *73*
Yorkshire *10*, *22*
   Yorkshire TV *83*
Yorkshire Evening Post *67*, *110*, *173*
Yorkshire Post *67*
youth courts *27*, *184*
Ziff, Arnold *71*

Sir William Garrow: His Life, Times and Fight for Justice
by John Hostettler and Richard Braby
Foreword by Geoffrey Robertson QC

A comprehensive account of lawyer William Garrow's life, career, family and connections. The book reflected in the TV series *Garrow's Law* in which legal John Hostettler and family story-teller Richard Braby—a descendant of Garrow—combine their skills and experience to produce a gem of a book.

'A law book yes, but boring no, a delight to read': *Internet Law Book Reviews*

Paperback & ebook | 2011
ISBN 978-1-904380-69-6 | 352 pages

Twenty Famous Lawyers
by John Hostettler

An entertaining diversion for lawyers and others, Twenty Famous Lawyers focuses on household names and high profile cases. Contains valuable insights into legal ways and means and looks at the challenges of advocacy, persuasion and the finest traditions of the law.

'A wealth of anecdote, not to mention entertainment for lawyers everywhere and indeed anyone interested in the inspiring and often startling and controversial history of the law': Phillip Taylor MBE and Elizabeth Taylor of Richmond Green Chambers.

Paperback & ebook | 2013
ISBN 978-1-904380-98-6 | 212 pages

www.WatersidePress.co.uk

Lightning Source UK Ltd.
Milton Keynes UK
UKOW05f1415010616

275393UK00001B/7/P

9 781909 976313